All of
Me

All of Me

My incredible story of how
I learned to live with the
many personalities
sharing my body

KIM NOBLE

with Jeff Hudson

piatkus

PIATKUS

First published in Great Britain in 2011 by Piatkus

A CIP catalogue record for this book
is available from the British Library.

Author's note
Much of the content of this book takes place in hospitals.
Where other patients are mentioned I have used pseudonyms to
protect their privacy. Some other individuals' names have
also been changed but their actions are all too true.

Cover artwork: 'Leave Me Alone' by Abi.
Title page and part title page artwork: 'Frieze People at Night' by Bonny.

ISBN 978-0-7499-5590-8

Typeset in Swift by M Rules
Printed and bound in Great Britain by
Clays Ltd, St Ives plc

Papers used by Piatkus are from well-managed forests
and other responsible sources.

MIX
Paper from
responsible sources
FSC® C104740

Piatkus
An imprint of
Little, Brown Book Group
100 Victoria Embankment
London EC4Y 0DY

An Hachette UK Company
www.hachette.co.uk

www.piatkus.co.uk

This book is dedicated to our much-loved daughter Aimee, the sunshine of my life, and our wonderful therapist for her footsteps in the sand.

Contents

Acknowledgements

Thanks to Jennifer Todd, Wendy Glaister, Lisa Dixon, Klare Stephens, Anna Tapsell, Campaign Against Pornography, Helena Kennedy QC, Michael Fisher, DCI Clive Driscoll, Lydia Sinclair, Dr Rob Hale, Pearl King, Valerie Sinason and the Clinic for Dissociative Studies, Professor Howard Steele, Saul Hillman, Nancy Dunlop, Ina Walker, Suzanne Haddad, Julia Harrop, Shirley Hickmott, Ami Woods, Debs McCoy, Andrew Simpson at Springfield Hospital, West Thornton Primary and Junior schools, Susan Booth, Fiona Tamplin and Riddlesdown Collegiate, Palma Black, Sharon Jendon-Rose, John Morton, Henry Boxer, Gillian Gordon, Beth Elliot at the Bethlem Gallery, Malcolm Wicks MP. Thanks are also due to Robert Smith for his continuous support, Jeff Hudson for taking on this difficult challenge, Anne Lawrance and Claudia Dyer for their sensitivity and understanding, the team at Piatkus/ Little, Brown Book Group, Anita and Derek, Saatchi Online for allowing separate personalities to have their own artist web pages and Outside In for accepting us as individual artists. A special thanks to Dr Laine and her husband, Andrew.

In memory of my Mum and to my Dad and his new wife, Jackie. To my sister, Lorraine, and her husband, Lol.

To my family and friends including those sadly lost along the way. To my next-door neighbour and friend, Jean, and in memory of her husband, Stan.

To my invisible friends inside, who at times are too visible!

To all those with or without DID who have emailed me about their hopes and fears.

Shattered

Kim Noble was born on 21 November 1960. She lived with her parents and sister and enjoyed an ordinary family upbringing. Her parents both worked and from a very early age Kim was left with a number of childminders – although they weren't called that in the 1960s. Sometimes it was family, sometimes neighbours, sometimes friends. Communities stepped in to help in those days. Most were kind and loving.

Some were different.

They didn't look after Kim Noble. They took advantage. They subjected baby Kim to painful, evil, sexual abuse. Regularly and consistently from the earliest age.

Kim Noble was helpless. She couldn't speak. She couldn't complain. She couldn't fight. She didn't even know that the abuse was wrong.

But she did know it scared her. She knew it hurt.

Yet she was so small, so weak, so dependent on her abusers for so much, what could she possibly do? And then her young, infant mind found a way. If it couldn't stop Kim's physical pain it could do the next best thing. It could hide.

At some point before her third birthday, Kim Noble's mind shattered, like a glass dropped onto a hard floor. Shards, splinters, fragments, some tiny, some larger. No two pieces the same, as individual as snowflakes. Ten, twenty, a hundred, two hundred pieces where before there had been just one. And each of them a new mind, a new life to take Kim's place in the world. To protect her. At last, Kim Noble was happy.

No one could find her now.

PART ONE

CHAPTER ONE

This is mad!

Chicago, September 2010. I never imagined the day I would find myself sitting in a television studio on the other side of the Atlantic. I certainly never expected to be invited by the most powerful woman in world media, Oprah Winfrey, to appear during the final season of the planet's leading chat show. But here I am and, as I take my seat facing Oprah's chair, I can barely contain my nerves. The most-watched programme in America is about to be filmed and I am that episode's star guest. And yet, as soon as Oprah sits down opposite, my inhibitions disappear.

Oprah's studio audience is here to see her. I don't kid myself that I'm the draw. The hundreds of people packing the auditorium reserved their tickets a year ago, months before I was even booked to appear. But the reason they love Oprah is she asks the questions that the normal American man and woman want to ask. I watch her lean in, gather her thoughts and build up to asking the Big One.

'Do you remember what happened to you as a child?'

Three hundred people fall suddenly silent. A few sharp intakes of breath. Then nothing, as they all crane forward expectantly for my reply.

'I remember parts of it,' I reply. 'Not any abuse.'

Murmurs buzz around that vast hangar of a room. Oprah looks momentarily thrown. If you watch carefully you can almost see her thinking, *I was told this woman had been abused! What's going on?* Backstage you can imagine a huddle of researchers thrown into panic.

Oprah maintains her composure. Then, ever the professional, she rephrases the question.

My answer is the same. 'No one did anything to me.' But I know what she means and decide to help her out.

'I have never been abused,' I clarify. 'But this body has.'

And then she understands.

Throughout our interview, Oprah referred to me as 'Kim'. I don't mind. I've grown up with people calling me that. It's all I ever heard as a child so it soon becomes normal. 'Kim, come here', 'Kim, do this'. It was just a nickname I responded to, not something to question. Why would I? I didn't feel different. I didn't look different. A child only notices they're out of the ordinary when adults tell them. No one ever told me I was special in any way.

I've grown up accepting lots of things that seemed normal at the time. Like finding myself in classrooms I didn't remember travelling to, or speaking to people I didn't recognise or employed doing jobs I hadn't applied for. Normal for me is driving to the shops and returning home with a boot full of groceries I didn't want. It's opening my wardrobe and discovering clothes I hadn't bought or taking delivery of pizzas I didn't order. It's finding the washing-up done a second after I'd finished using the pans. It's ending up at the door to a men's toilet and wondering why. It's so many, many other things on a daily basis.

Oprah found it unimaginable. I doubt she was alone. I imagine millions of viewing Americans were thinking, 'This is mad!'

After all, it's not every day you meet someone who shares their body with more than twenty other people – and who still manages to be a mum to a beautiful, well-balanced teenaged daughter, and an artist with many exhibitions to her name.

To me this is normal.

In 1995 I was diagnosed with Multiple Personality Disorder – now known as Dissociative Identity Disorder or DID – although it was many years until I accepted it. DID has been described as a creative way for a young child's mind to cope with unbearable pain, where the child's personality splinters into many parts, each as unique and independent as the original, and each capable of taking full control of the body they share. Usually there is a dominant personality – although which personality this is can change over time – and the various alter egos come and go. Some appear daily, some less regularly and some when provoked by certain physical or emotional 'triggers'. And usually, thanks to dissociative or amnesiac barriers that prevent them learning the source of the pain which caused the DID, they all have no idea that the other personalities exist.

This, I was told, is what had happened to Kim Noble. Unable to cope any longer with the trauma of being abused at such a young age, Kim had vacated her body, the doctors said, leaving numerous alter egos to take over. I am one of those alters.

To most of the outside world I am 'Kim Noble'. I'll answer to that name because I'm aware of the DID – and also because it's easier than explaining who I really am. Most of the other personalities are still in denial, as I was for the majority of my life. They don't believe they share a body and absolutely refuse to accept they are only 'out' for a fraction of the day, despite overwhelming evidence to the contrary. I know how they feel, because for forty years that was me.

I am currently the dominant personality. Simply put, I spend the longest time in control of the body. (On an average day two or three other personalities usually come out and do whatever they do, and in between I return.) I run the household and take primary care of our daughter, Aimee. I pay the bills (even though they're all in Kim Noble's name) and make sure we live a normal family life.

I wasn't always in control, however. As a child I probably only came out for a couple of hours at a time – and perhaps not even every day. As I grew older I seemed to spend more and more time in control of the body, until finally, with the encouragement of our therapists and doctors, I acknowledged the DID and took charge.

Why did I become the dominant one? I don't know for sure but I think the body needed me to. The woman known as Kim Noble turned fifty in 2010 and I suppose if you look at me I match that age in my knowledge, my experience and my behaviour (although I feel much younger). I'm told that the others who were dominant personalities before me are similar in that respect. But not all of Kim Noble's alters are like us. Even if they did accept the diagnosis of multiple personalities, many of them would not be capable of running a home. Many of them, sadly, struggle to cope with being alive.

Some of the alters are much younger – frozen at a particular point in time – and several aren't even female. This seems to surprise people the most. There are three-year-old girls, a little boy capable of communicating only in Latin or French, and even a gay man. Some know their parents; others feel lost. Some are well balanced; others struggle with the scars of their past. One is happy with a lover, some have friends; others are mute, reclusive. Some exist to live life to the full; others have tried to take their own lives.

Our own lives.

Like a lot of people trying to understand DID, Oprah wondered if our multiple personalities were the different facets of Kim coming to life. In other words, one of us is Angry Kim, one of us is Sad Kim or Happy Kim or Worried Kim, and so on, and we come out when the body is in those moods. That's not how it works. We're not moods. We're not *Mr Men* – we can't (in most cases) be defined by a single characteristic. We're rounded human beings, with happy sides to our personalities, frivolous sides, angry sides, reflective sides.

Oprah couldn't hide her surprise.

'Like a normal person?' she said.

'Yes,' I replied, 'because I consider myself to be normal.'

And I am. When I'm in control of the body my life is no different to anyone's reading this book. I have the same thoughts, the same feelings, hopes and dreams as the next woman. The only difference is I'm just not here to live those dreams as often as I would like. None of us are.

The different personalities come and go from the body

like hotel guests through a revolving door. There are no signals, no signs, no warnings. I'm here one minute and then somewhere else. In between it's as though I've been asleep – and who knows what has happened during that time? I don't see anything, I don't hear anything, I don't feel anything. I have no understanding of what happens when I'm not there. I may as well be in a different country. It's the same for all of us. We are either in control of the body or completely absent. We're not witnesses to each other's actions. As I've said, the majority of us don't even know – or accept – the others exist.

Coming back after a personality switch is like waking up from a nap. It takes a few seconds of blinking and looking around to get your bearings, to work out who you're with, where you are and what you're in the middle of doing. The only difference is with a normal nap you soon realise you're in exactly the same place you went to sleep, whereas I could disappear from my sofa and wake up again at a pub or a supermarket or even driving a car and not have a clue where I'm heading.

It's not only me who has to come to terms with it, of course. The other personalities find themselves in exactly the same positions and respond as best they can. Shortly before flying over to Chicago I drove into my local petrol station. When I pulled the trigger to turn the pump on nothing happened. Everyone else seemed to be getting fuel so I went into the shop to ask what was wrong.

The lad behind the counter was staring at me in disbelief.

'I can't believe you've got the nerve to come back.'

'What are you talking about?'

'I'm talking about you driving off last week without

paying.' As he spoke he showed me a picture of the car and me – so he thought – behind the wheel.

A few years ago I would have argued and shouted and told him to get some new glasses so he didn't accuse innocent people. But I knew what had happened. I'd driven there, filled up – and then there'd been a switch. I don't know who it was but they obviously realised they were in the car, they had no recollection of putting petrol in, so naturally they drove off.

Simple, really – but I could see it looked bad.

Luckily, because I was a regular customer, the guy believed my 'silly me' act when I told him I'd just forgotten. Standing there while he went through his little lecture about calling the police next time was utterly humiliating, especially in front of a growing queue of people. But it was less painful than trying to explain DID. I'm not ashamed, embarrassed or shy about it, but sometimes you have to pick your battles.

If that episode had happened before I accepted I had DID, the outcome would have been very different. In fact, I'd probably still be arguing with the cashier now. It wouldn't matter that it was all captured on film. I would have known I was innocent and fought and fought – just like I always did when people accused me of things I hadn't done. Sometimes it seemed like my whole life was spent defending myself against crimes I hadn't committed. I seemed to lurch from one argument to another, at school, at home, at work or with friends, and all the time I'd be saying the same thing: 'It wasn't me.'

You can imagine how confusing life must have been – and how it must still be for the personalities who refuse to accept the truth. Yet somehow I coped. These days it's the innocent parties who have to deal with us that I feel sorry for. For example, a few years ago I called the police about something and a couple of officers arrived at the house. I went into the kitchen to make them a coffee but by the time I'd returned, they'd vanished. Then I realised the time. It was an hour later. There must have been a switch. Only when I spoke to the police-man later did I learn the truth: another personality had arrived and literally screamed at them to get out of her house! That took some explaining . . .

I have a thousand stories like this. All the personalities must have. Life is a constant struggle, even when you know about the DID. Sometimes, though, the only thing you can do is laugh. A while ago there was a problem with the computer so the dominant personality at the time drove over to our ther-apist's house. Our therapist's husband is very good at fixing things like that. Unfortunately, when they went to fetch the machine from the back seat of the car, it wasn't there. Obviously one of the other personalities – not me! – had come out and discovered a computer in the car and had done something with it. Whether they took it to a repair shop or sold it or lost it or just gave it away, we never discovered.

At least I can drive, however. Not all the personalities are so fortunate because many of them are children. A fifteen-year-old called Judy occasionally appears once I've parked. From what she's revealed to our therapist, the first few times were quite scary until she realised the car wasn't going anywhere. I don't think the body would allow itself to be endangered by having a non-driver in control of a moving vehicle. Now the worst thing that happens is Judy just hops out and catches the bus home – leaving me to work out where our car has got to. Every minute of every day throws up new adventures.

Speaking of driving, sharing a body, I think, is a bit like being the driver of a bus. Regardless of how many passengers are on board, there's only one person in control. The only difference with us is that any one of those passengers can take over the steering at any point.

Oprah wasn't alone in assuming that our mind must be a crowded place with all those voices arguing with each other about which way to go like some kind of Pushmi-Pullyu. That, after all, is what it's like for many people with DID whose fractures aren't as extreme as Kim Noble's. Yes they have multiple personalities but these personalities can hear what the others are saying, they can see what they're doing and they can sometimes even talk to each other. You can't imagine them losing a computer or throwing policemen out of their house or not realising they need to pay for things. Even if a particular alter didn't do something naughty at school, at least it would realise why it was being told off.

Life must be so much simpler for them – but thank God I'm not like that!

My thoughts are my own. When I'm in control of the body, that's it – there's no one else. It would drive you crazy having all those voices in your head. Imagine being able to see what other people are doing when they're in charge of your body? It makes me feel sick even thinking about it. It must seem like having a gun to your head and being forced to do things against your will. No matter what you see or what you hear or what you remember, there would be absolutely nothing you could do.

As for having personalities watching me go about *my* business, that's no way to live, is it? I can't think of anything worse than being spied on all the time. Picture it: you'd always know that whatever you did, whatever you thought, wherever you went, you'd never be able to escape.

I've spent enough of my life locked up under twenty-four-hour guard in mental hospitals to know how much I would hate that.

So, who are the other personalities who influenced my life without my ever realising they existed? Thanks to Dr Laine, the therapist who has treated me and all the other alters of Kim Noble, as well as observations from our daughter who tells me what the others are like, I've learnt quite a lot.

Bonny was the dominant personality before me. She was 'out' and in control of the body for the majority of the time, just as I am now. When she was in charge, I was just another one of the other personalities coming and going. It's impossible to imagine now and it certainly didn't feel like it at the time. Even when, years later, I was told again and again that I only 'existed' for an hour or two a day, I rejected the very idea. How would *you* react if someone told you that?

Were they saying I was a role that this Kim Noble woman likes to play? Or that she'd made me up like a character in a film? Or that she changed into me? Were they suggesting I was Frankenstein's monster?

That wasn't what they were saying at all, I know that now. But I wouldn't listen. I didn't want to understand. I was just like all the other personalities who are still refusing to listen today.

One day, perhaps, they'll accept the truth as I did and then their lives will make a bit more sense. As much as I hated discovering I was just another personality, the relief of not being so confused all the time was incredible. Whether I liked it or not, at least everything began to make sense. Even that feeling of always being in a rush, needing to get things done, of time running out, suddenly became clear. Without realising why, I'd somehow always known I only ever had a few minutes to achieve things.

Bonny took charge shortly after our daughter Aimee was born. She is the one who fought the council for access after Aimee was snatched at birth by social services. Unfortunately the stress of that struggle took its toll. If it hadn't, if Bonny hadn't cracked up under the pressure, if she were still the dominant personality, then I wouldn't be writing this book and we would never have become artists.

And I would still be in denial about DID.

When Bonny retreated to the background, Aimee was devastated. Bonny is the one she called 'Mum'. It took a while for me to earn that honour.

Before Bonny there was Hayley. I only discovered her when I found lots of old bills lying around addressed to her in Richmond, Surrey. That's where Hayley lived during the 1980s – while Bonny lived in Croydon and I had my own flat in Fulham. Three addresses for three different personalities – I don't know how we afforded it. Just one example of how complicated our lives have been.

Hayley was a force of nature – she had to be, considering some of the things she endured. During her six or seven years as the dominant personality we got our first – and only – long-term job. Unfortunately, that was around the time that she was exposed to the activities of a paedophile ring. When Hayley reported the ring to the police, she received anonymous warnings to be quiet. Threats of physical retaliation escalated until one day a man threw acid in her face and someone tried to set light to her bed with her in it. Fire is the most harrowing experience for any human and it has continued to affect us all. The good news is Hayley was a strong person – at least for a while – and she continued her fight against the attackers. The bad news is the effort caused her to burn up. Like Bonny, after years of fighting for our rights she faded into the background, cowed and exhausted.

And then there are the others, the ones who come out sometimes every day or every week or every month. They all have their own patterns, their own triggers. For one it's water – one of the personalities, Spirit of the Water, can't resist coming out whenever there's a toe to be dipped or a shower to be had. For another it's food. Judy takes over for most of my mealtimes. Salome, a highly religious Catholic woman, always emerges when we go near a church.

And then there are the children.

Katie, at three, is the youngest alter to regularly come out. She used to be around a lot more when Aimee was younger because they loved playing with each other. Sadly, the older Aimee gets, the less Katie wants to play with her. She just wishes Aimee would stop ageing – like her.

At least Aimee had some fun times with Katie. I don't think the little boy called Diabalus has had much laughter in his life but I don't know because he doesn't speak English. When he first came out he only wrote in Latin. After that he spoke to our therapist in French. If Oprah thought my life was mad before, what would trying to fathom how this personality is fluent in two languages when I can't speak a single word of either have done to her? It tips most people over the edge.

Another child with communication problems is Missy, an elective mute. She and Aimee have wild times together, especially when they're painting. But something in Missy's life has made her too terrified to speak.

Which brings me on to Ria. That's the name I've given the frightened twelve-year-old who seems – apart from Kim – to have suffered the worst of the sexual abuse. Ria thinks her name is 'Pratt' because that's what her abusers called her. It was actually on *Oprah* that Ria revealed for the first time the extent of her memories. It was so harrowing I could barely watch it – literally. Every time Ria came onto the screen there was a switch and it was Ria herself watching TV. It took four or five attempts before I stayed in control long enough to learn her secrets.

Ria remembers being abused. I don't know how many of the others do but their various ways of suffering suggest previous trauma. Judy, for instance, is bulimic. She's convinced we're fat even though we don't have a spare inch anywhere on us. Then there's anorexic Sonia, who, far from throwing up, refuses to eat anything. I can tell when she's been at mealtimes because I'm usually starving afterwards. Abi used online dating sites to combat her loneliness, while Ken, a twenty-something gay man, is depressed by the homophobia he experiences on a daily basis.

They all have their issues. Dawn's suffering, however, has nothing to do with the child abuse. Perhaps that's why it's the one problem I identify with most. Dawn was the personality who gave birth to Aimee. She was also the one who witnessed our daughter being taken by social services. The trauma sent Dawn into hiding. By the time she returned too much time had passed and she refused to believe Aimee was her little girl. To this day she's still searching for her baby. To Dawn it's as real as the search for Madeleine McCann, even though Dawn knew Skye was alive.

Then there's Julie, whose erratic behaviour – squirting fly spray on bus travellers and trying to drive with her eyes closed, for example – contributed to our being diagnosed as schizophrenic. Together with Rebecca, they nearly got us sectioned for the rest of our lives.

Rebecca started it all. Whatever her memories, she is the alter who is struggling most to deal with her past. Rebecca is the one who took the overdoses time after time. She's the one who got us locked up in mental institution after mental institution. She's the one who nearly ended it once and for all in a hotel room in Lewes.

In hindsight, being diagnosed with DID and knowing about the other personalities earlier would have explained to me why I got into so much trouble at school, why my parents and teachers were always calling me a liar, and why I was kidnapped, as I saw it, by one asylum or therapy centre after another. Perhaps then I wouldn't have thought I was being experimented on by doctors who accused me of having anorexia, bulimia and schizophrenia. And maybe I would have believed them when they said they were doing it all for my own good – to stop me trying to kill myself again.

If I'd known the body really was doing these things, then forty years of my life would have made so much more sense.

But, as impossible as my life seemed being hurled from one crazy situation to another, like a pinball pinged around by unknown players, it was still preferable to knowing the truth. Because to accept that my body really was doing these things would mean accepting something else.

That it had been abused as a child.

And obviously our brain didn't want us to know that.

The whole point of DID, as far as I can tell, is to protect a person from trauma. It's a defence mechanism that kicks in to stop something unpleasant from ruining your life. As Oprah pointed out, it's no different from anyone pushing a dark memory to the back of their mind in order to get on with their day, whether it's being told off by a teacher at school yesterday or splitting up with your partner. If you don't deal with the pain or anxiety – if you can't resolve it or stop it or forget it somehow – you'll spend every day thinking about nothing else. Your life will be as good as over.

Some memories are too big to bury in one mind, though, and that's why Kim's fractured into so many others. If she saw an abuser locally or someone who reminded her of them, or if their names were even mentioned or their memory flitted into her head, she could just vanish.

The tragic downside, of course, is that the abuse still happened. Kim's body was still subjected to unspeakable tortures – except other personalities were now the victims. Kim had no way of knowing, but her disappearances opened the door to the ordeals suffered by so many others. We – our therapist, Bonny, Hayley and me – know Rebecca was abused, and Ria and Diabalus and so many others. We don't know how many times they suffered before they too found a way to hide, leaving another poor soul in control of the body. But we do know that their lives would never be the same again.

I was lucky. I was never abused. That's how I was allowed to grow, unlike the child personalities stuck forever at such a young age. Not only was I never a victim, I had no idea it was going on. If Kim Noble's alters were co-conscious, like most DID sufferers, then I would know everything. We'd all know everything and we all would have seen it happen, whether we felt it or not. How would that help Kim then?

That's why the body makes it so hard for the personalities to ever accept we have DID. Because in order to accept it you have to come to terms with the fact that men or women have abused your body – and thought they were abusing you. It's very plausible that I have met my body's abusers. I don't know who they are. I don't want to know. But many of the other personalities do. They will never forget and they will never recover.

From the moment I became the dominant personality I promised I would discover as much about the life – or lives – of Kim Noble as possible. After a lifetime of confusion, I needed to have the facts – however unpalatable I found them. However, trying to tell this story when, for a lot of my life, I was only around for a fraction of a day at a time has been hard.

Fortunately I've had wonderful help from the one person who knows more about Kim Noble than anyone – our therapist, Dr Laine. Just as I often used to come out during sessions that Bonny or Hayley had travelled to, so the other personalities have all had numerous sessions themselves over the years. Sometimes one of them will have a genuine need to see her, or perhaps she will want to see them on the dominant personality's behalf. (For example, if there is a concern about how a personality is behaving.) It is through therapy sessions with Dr

Laine that we have learnt so much about the abuse each personality has suffered and their other trials. So she knows my story, she knows Hayley's story, and Bonny's, and Katie's and Judy's and Diabalus's and so on and so on. You'll see scenes from some of their lives at the start of each chapter.

Of course, I'm well aware that if Bonny were still the dominant personality then this book could read very differently. The same is true of Hayley – and I hate to think what would be written by Judy, Ken, Rebecca or any of the others. We all have such different memories; we've all experienced so many different things.

For my own part, I admit, for a long while the tempting thing to do would have been to give up when the whole world seemed to be conspiring against me with lies, brutality and incarceration. I wouldn't have been the first personality to fade away and I wouldn't have been the last. But I didn't. I struggled on to lead the life you're about to read and I came out the other side. A life as a proud mum and a successful artist.

My name is Patricia – and this is my story.

CHAPTER TWO

It wasn't me

The room looked as it always looked and smelled as it always smelled. The girl didn't like it. She didn't know why she was there. Where was Mummy? Where was Daddy?

The sound of the door closing made her freeze. The footsteps drowned out the sound of her tiny, terrified breaths.

At least she had her bear. Teddy was her favourite. The one she always slept with. The one she always cuddled when they hurt her.

'Well done, Pratt,' one of the grown-ups said afterwards. That's what they always called her. 'Now get out of here.'

'Kim Noble stand up!'

The entire class fell silent. I'd never seen Mrs Baldwin so angry. She was a lovely teacher, normally, very tall and thin like a witch, but friendly. And she could do magic. She would rub a sixpence in her elbow and make it disappear before our eyes. You never knew where it was going to pop up next.

Right now, marching across the room, she looked like she wanted to make me disappear.

But why?

'What did you do that for?'

'I haven't done anything,' I mumbled, shocked at her fury.

She grabbed my arm exasperatedly and pointed at the sleeve.

'Then what is that?'

I stared at my wrist, then the other one. I could feel the eyes of thirty classmates burning into me. My entire blouse was covered in thick splodges of black paint. My skirt too.

'I didn't do it.' It was all I could think to say.

'Oh really?' Mrs Baldwin was calming now. 'Then who did?'

I stared at her blankly. I had no answers. Again.

'It wasn't me,' I said. 'I swear.'

Standing outside the headmaster's room a few minutes later, wet and cold from the paint touching my skin, I just wanted to cry. If another girl hadn't arrived I would have been in floods.

'What are you here for?' she asked sullenly.

I pointed to the paint.

'Oh, right,' she said, already bored. 'Nice.'

'What about you?' I asked.

The girl smirked. 'I hit someone.'

'Really?'

'Course I did. He deserved it. But I'm not telling him that!'

She gestured towards the head's closed door.

I felt like crying even more.

'But I didn't do this,' I insisted.

'No, of course you didn't,' she laughed. 'I didn't hit anyone either!'

Headmasters must hear that every day. But I really hadn't done it. I knew I hadn't.

Had I?

*

That paint episode is probably my earliest memory. I was five years old, at West Thornton junior school. In fact most of my early memories were spent outside that office. I was always in trouble. Always saying, 'It wasn't me,' and always being called a liar. Hardly a day went by without me thinking, *It's not fair.*

Forty-odd years later I can see it from the teachers' point of view. Mrs Baldwin had seen me pick up that paint. Watched me cover my hands in the stuff then smear it down my sleeves and lap. Witnessed it all with her own eyes – then heard me deny it.

What else was she supposed to do?

Anyone would think it's an open and shut case. Guilty as charged.

Except it wasn't me.

But if it wasn't me, then who was it?

You could say my problems with identity started the day I was born.

My parents wanted a 'Gary'. Based on no medical evidence whatsoever, James and Dorothy Noble were convinced they were expecting a son to go with their daughter Lorraine. A short list of boys' names had been duly drawn up, with Gary the winner.

And then I popped out.

Bureaucracy didn't give you much breathing space back then and a maternity nurse was soon hassling Mum and Dad for a name to put on the birth forms. When they couldn't think of anything the nurse said, 'Well, I've got to write down something. I'll put "Elaine".'

'Oh no,' Mum said. 'We've already got a Lorraine. Elaine and Lorraine? That won't work.'

'Fine,' the nurse snapped. 'Then we'll call her Kim.'

And that was that.

I still struggle to grasp how that episode was allowed to have happened. Whoever heard of a nurse naming your child? I was a little girl when I found that out. I remember saying to Mum, with all the impudence of youth, 'Well, no one else is going to choose the name of my little baby!'

Little did I know …

I was born on 21 November 1960 at the Mayday Hospital in Croydon, south London – a place I would come to know all too well later on. Because my sister had been delivered via caesarean section, the doctors thought it best to bring me out the same way. Two weeks later I was diagnosed with double pneumonia, rushed back into hospital and pumped full of antibiotics. The outlook was so bleak a priest was summoned to perform an emergency christening and the Last Rites. In the end, the pneumonia would have less of a lasting impact than the drugs.

Although nowhere near as dangerous, I also suffered from jaundice for a while. No one looks good with yellow skin, but when your hair is as red as mine it's quite a clash of colours. If ever the family wanted a laugh at my expense, they always brought that up.

But, as I learnt just a few years ago, a touch of jaundice was the least of my worries. I was actually lucky to be born at all.

When Mum discovered she was pregnant again, she didn't exactly jump for joy. In fact, she couldn't think of anything worse. You didn't have the options that women have today. David Steele's Abortion Bill didn't come in until 1967. So Mum did what a lot of scared women were doing at the time. She bought some tablets on the black market and washed them down with a bottle of spirits.

I found this out a few years after Mum died in 1994. One of my godmothers, bless her, decided the time was right for me to know the truth. I wish she'd kept her mouth shut. There are absolutely no positives to take from the news that your mother risked her own life to try to end yours. I cried for days.

You blame yourself, which is stupid, because I hadn't even been born. But you can't stop thinking, *Why didn't she want me? What had I done wrong?*

Did she ever love me?

And of course by then it was too late to ask.

Sometimes ignorance is bliss. That could be the story of my life ...

If you're a superstitious sort of person – and I'm absolutely not – you would have me down as born under a bad sign right from the start. Think about it: unwanted, abortion-survivor, wrong gender, named by a stranger, and born the colour of a Swan Vesta.

It never augured well, did it?

When I was born we lived in Shirley, on the new Shrublands council estate. Then when my grandfather died, Mum and Dad bought his house and we all moved in to live with my grandmother about a mile away. It was only a three-bedroom house so I shared the main room with my grandmother, which I really loved. I probably saw more of Nan in those early years than anyone. She was always around the house, cleaning or cooking or standing on the step smoking her Embassy cigarettes, watching us play. As a rule, Mum would do Sunday lunch but Nan would cook dinner the other days because Mum was working. Afterwards she'd usually pop round to her brother's house – two doors down – but always be back for hot chocolate and a book in bed by about ten.

Lorraine had the box room and my parents took the middle one. Nearly half a century later I'm still living in the same house.

Families stuck together more in those days. Over the road was an uncle, two doors down was another one, and various other relatives were dotted around the vicinity. We were very close-knit. It was a nice neighbourhood, actually. Very community-spirited.

Like half the local population, Mum and Dad worked at the ICL factory on the A23. That's where they met, both dressed in their company-issue white coats, like doctors. Dad actually worked on some of the first computers. He used to come home with these punch cards for us to play with. We had loads of them around the house. When the factory shut down the whole area took a bit of a kicking.

I think we must have come across as being such a perfect family. My mum and dad seemed very happy. And then they had us two. It must have seemed a very rosy picture.

But behind closed doors . . .

We weren't an open family. When I was seven my dad had an affair and left us to set up home with his other woman. Nobody told me, even though they knew the woman's son was

in my class at West Thornton Primary. I could tell that Mum
was upset about something and there had been a lot of arguments recently. The first real clue I got was this lad coming up
to me one day with, 'Your dad taught me how to spell your
name.'

'Oh,' I replied. What else did he want me to say?

Then it was 'Your dad bought me a football' or 'Your dad
took me to the beach'. Random sentences, really, which I just
ignored. When he began having a go at my mum I cut him off
completely. I didn't know what his problem was but I couldn't
be bothered giving him the time of day. I thought, *If he's trying
to bully me he's not very good at it.* It just made no sense.

Gradually, though, I began to put two and two together.
I didn't exactly get four straight off. I got as far as realising
Dad wasn't around any more and that was it. It didn't occur
to me to think he'd found another family. It was as though
he'd just ceased to exist. Vanished off the face of the Earth.
But I don't remember being worried. No one mentioned him
at home. Not Lorraine, not Nan and not even Mum. I guess
from that I knew he hadn't died. That was good. I was sure of
that. But any more information wasn't forthcoming and I
didn't push it. It just didn't seem important. I had my own life
to get on with.

All was revealed a couple of months later. Not by Mum or
Dad, of course. We were at home. I was watching TV while
Lorraine was on the phone in the hall. Then she came in and
spoke to Mum and Nan in the kitchen. I heard their voices getting louder but I tried to blank them out. As long as I wasn't
involved I didn't care.

But I was involved. We all were.

'Dad's coming home,' Lorraine announced. 'He's just asked me. And I said yes.'

You said yes?

'Why didn't he ask Mum?'

Lorraine shrugged.

I don't know why Dad had asked her or what gave her the right to make a decision for Mum. But it had to be for the best, didn't it? Families need fathers. We needed ours, anyway.

Judging from the pans being crashed in the kitchen, though, I don't think Mum agreed.

It was arranged that Dad would come round the next day. That was the plan anyway. But about an hour after the phone call, when I was getting ready for bed, I heard a key in the front door. I tiptoed out onto the landing and saw the familiar figure of my dad stepping in. He had a big old battered army suitcase which he put down in the hall. It was dark but even from my vantage point he didn't look great. His right eye appeared bruised and there was a cut on his cheek.

I ran back to my room before he saw me. A few minutes later Nan and Lorraine joined me.

'Your dad's back,' Nan said.

I nodded.

'I think it's best they have some space to themselves. I've spoken to your Aunty Peg. You can stay there tonight.'

Aunty Peg was Mum's sister. She only lived around the corner so it didn't take us long to walk there. On the way Lorraine filled me in on a few more details. My mouth fell open at some of it. That was the first I'd heard of Dad's affair. Lorraine seemed amazed I hadn't known. Why should I have? It wasn't on my radar. I was seven. People didn't have other

families in my world. I didn't know where Dad had gone but I
hadn't let it worry me. Half the time I had enough trouble
working out where I was.

I might not have cared what he was up to but Mum's reaction had been suitably explosive. In hindsight, I didn't know
how I'd missed it.

Dad, Lorraine explained, had been carrying on with
another woman for a while. When Mum found out she'd
exploded – as had Dad's sister, Ivy. Apparently they'd both gone
round to see this 'other woman' but they'd done more than see
her. I don't know who did what but Dad's girlfriend got one
hell of a beating. Ivy, apparently, had to be stopped from stran-
gling her. Dad had apologised, said it was over, but Mum
wouldn't let it lie so eventually he and the woman had run off
together.

I listened to Lorraine, stunned. It all seemed a bit unreal.
Then I remembered the kid in my class and it brought the situation home. That's why he'd started saying those things about
my mother. He wasn't a bully. He was just really upset. If anything he'd been looking for a friend who could sympathise
with the mess his home life was in.

And I didn't have a clue anything was even wrong. Again,
my ignorance was actually protecting me.

I guess the boy's family equalled the score. I still don't
know what drove Dad back home initially but Lorraine filled
me in on why he was a day earlier than he'd promised.

'The woman's husband tracked them down. He gave Dad
a right going over.'

So it *was* a black eye.

Poor Dad.

Physical wounds heal of course and, within a couple of days, Dad's eye was right as rain. Mum's injuries were of the mental kind – she was mortified that the world suddenly knew our family's business – and I don't think she ever recovered. I remember her often telling me not to say 'I hate' about anyone. 'You can dislike someone but you can never hate them,' she used to say.

But Mum hated that 'other' woman for ruining the façade of her happy marriage.

Dad's problems didn't stay with me long. Nothing did, really. I always seemed to be rushing from one thought to another. A large proportion of my days were spent on things like just trying to keep up with a conversation. So often it seemed as though I'd walked in on something halfway when, judging from what was being said, I must have been there since the beginning. Lorraine knowing so much more about Mum and Dad's set-up didn't surprise me. Only knowing half the story was par for the course for me, whether it was at home, with friends – or at school.

Schooldays passed in a blur. There were fun times, of course, and I had plenty of friends. They're not what really stick in my memory, though. More often than not I just recall being punished for something I hadn't done. The paint episode with Mrs Baldwin certainly wasn't a one-off. She was always chasing me for something. And I lost count of the times I heard the head say, 'I don't know what we're going to do with you, Kim.'

'Kim'. Always Kim.

I didn't understand and I didn't question. That's just how it was.

There were plenty of things I didn't understand or query. Like why Mrs Baldwin never called my name from the register. Everyone else in the class heard their name and said, 'Here, Miss.' She never called mine. I used to worry she was marking me down as absent. *Mum won't believe me when I say I was here*, I thought. I was in trouble so often why should she?

But I never asked why.

Tests were a problem for me as well. I never did very well. But who could blame me? Half the questions seemed to be about things I'd never been taught. I don't know how the other kids managed to answer some of those things. *They must be getting extra tuition at home,* I thought. *Or they're cheating.*

There was no other explanation. I hadn't missed a day at school all year. My attendance record was exemplary. But I swear I hadn't heard of half the things they put in the exams. Or if I had, I certainly couldn't remember them. My memory was bad, I was beginning to realise that. But not that bad, surely?

Then there was the trouble. I couldn't avoid it. Sometimes it just seemed like I was being set up. As if the whole class was in on a joke and I'd just walked in at the last second. Even my various form teachers during my time at West Thornton seemed to be in on it. On another occasion, after I'd left Mrs Baldwin's class, I was staring at the blackboard, trying to work out what was on it. I could see words although a second ago there had been numbers. Before I could ponder further, I heard the teacher's raised voice.

'Right, you've had enough warnings.'

I was concentrating so hard on the blackboard it barely registered. *Who's for it this time?* I wondered without looking up.

The teacher grabbed a wooden ruler from his desk and

stormed across the room. He stopped between me and another girl, Irene. She looked terrified.

'Hand out,' he snapped.

Wonder what she's done?

Then the teacher glared at me.

'Both of you!'

What?

'But ...'

'Hand!' As he spoke he grabbed my wrist and delivered a stinging crack across the knuckles with the ruler.

Instinctively I put my knuckles in my mouth to try to soothe them. It had the opposite effect. It felt like my hand was on fire.

'Don't suck them, Irene,' I said to my friend as her knuckles got the same treatment. 'It makes it worse.'

That was wrong as well.

The teacher spun back round. 'Still talking?' Then he took my other hand and whacked me again.

'Anyone else got something to say?' he demanded, scanning the room. Not a peep. The only noise you could hear was Irene sobbing quietly. My hands felt like they might burst but I wasn't going to give him the satisfaction of making me cry. But, God, I thought I was going to be sick from the throbbing pain that jolted through me, like waves, every few seconds.

With two hands out of action I couldn't pick up a pen, so that was the rest of the lesson wasted. I just sat there stewing, sore and humiliated. And, as usual, utterly, utterly mystified. What was his problem? I hadn't said a word to Irene. In fact, I couldn't remember speaking to anyone at all that day.

It's hard to appreciate while your joints are pulsing like

Belisha beacons, but knowing you're being punished for nothing is almost worse than the punishment itself. Physical pain
heals eventually but mental torture stays with you. You can't
relax. You can't afford to let yourself believe for one moment
that everything is all right. Not when a teacher can haul you
out of your seat with zero provocation.

I remember occasionally looking at other kids misbehav-
ing and thinking, *They'll be lucky to get away with that.* Usually the
teacher was on the same wavelength and it would end in the
familiar way – *whack!* The teachers always seemed to have a
reason for dishing out the clips round the ear on the others. I
couldn't get my head around it. They didn't lash out randomly
with anyone else. Just me.

Like the punishment itself, if something occurs regularly
enough it becomes the norm. My default position, if you like,
was to be told off. Even to myself I sounded like a stuck record
sometimes. 'It's not fair, it wasn't me. It's not fair, it wasn't me.'
I went for days when that's all I remembered saying. But I truly
believed it. I was innocent. I hadn't done anything.

Even when I wasn't being punished, I always seemed to be
being made to do things I didn't want to. On the day I'd got
covered in black paint, I'd been sent to the head and shouted
at. Then I was despatched to the staff office to get some fresh
clothes from the 'lost and found' basket. Usually it was only
kids who'd wet themselves who were sent there.

I trotted along to the office and knocked on the door. A
teacher took one look at me and knew why I was there.

'Come on then, get those things off,' she said kindly, and
began rooting through the supplies.

I didn't move.

When she turned round holding a new blouse and skirt she was surprised to see me standing in the same place.

'Quick sticks,' she chivvied. 'You need to get back to class.' Still I didn't budge.

'Okay,' she sighed, 'I'll help,' and she leant forward to undo my button. Still not moving, I folded my arms tightly so her fingers couldn't get in. In a flash, her good mood vanished.

'Stop messing around!' she barked and tore my arms away.

I tried desperately to knock her hand away, screaming, 'Get off!'

I honestly don't know what came over me. All I knew is I could not let that woman undress me. I couldn't explain it. She was a stranger. It was wrong. I couldn't let her do it.

Then things got worse. Another grown-up came over and she literally grabbed my arms from behind to restrain me, then forced me to the floor. Now I couldn't even kick out. The other woman scrabbled around at my buttons, then stripped off my skirt as well. Both of them were shouting at me to behave but I couldn't stop myself. The urge to fight them off was too strong.

'Leave me alone! Don't touch me!'

'Nearly there,' one of them said through gritted teeth. Then with an oversized but clean skirt fastened around my wriggling waist she said, 'Right, done – now get back to your classroom!'

I scrambled up and flew out the door, heart racing with every stride. Mrs Baldwin glared as I entered the classroom but all thoughts of the black paint had disappeared. Even the telling off from the headmaster was forgotten. There was only one thought in my head: *They mustn't touch me. I don't want them to touch me.*

*

Discipline-wise, life at home was much more straightforward. If anything, my sister bore the thick end of the attention there. I remember Lorraine doing her 11+ but when she decided not to go on to A-Levels Dad went apoplectic. Really, absolutely ballistic. It didn't bother me in the slightest. Maybe it should have, but I was an outsider. That's exactly how I felt, anyway.

Lorraine rarely did anything wrong. I remember a few occasions when she got into trouble for mischief we'd both got up to, or sometimes she'd even get a telling off for something I'd cooked up on my own, but she never complained. Maybe that's the advantage of an older sister. That just made me think she looked guilty because I always blabbed, 'It wasn't me!' when I hadn't done something. Not that it ever did me any good.

It was horrible being around Mum and Dad when they argued but sometimes you couldn't avoid it. Occasionally it was so bad that I'd burst into tears. I just felt so scared that they were being mean to each other and I was so young I didn't know what to do. That normally quietened them down and then they'd both call out, 'Come here, come to me' and I'd be frozen with worry, not knowing which of them to go to. I remember Lorraine saw that once and rushed over and cuddled me herself. Then she turned to Mum and Dad and let them have both barrels for upsetting me.

Every so often I would get found out for some mischief or other. Whereas at school I'd have received the ruler or perhaps even the slipper on the backside, Dad preferred to turn a blind eye whenever possible. Mum too. With her it was an all-or-nothing response. Sometimes she'd barely acknowledge my naughtiness. On other occasions she would fly at me with a rolling pin or rolled-up newspaper so I'd dart upstairs. She'd begin following, then stop, with me skulking inside my room safe in the knowledge Mum would already be turned around and wandering back down. She never made it to the top. You knew you were safe up there.

Mum was happy enough pulling us into line but she refused to get involved in any outside quarrels. You know what kids are like. One minute you're best friends with someone, then they've said something or borrowed something and you've fallen out like it's World War Three and you're on different sides. I remember being hit by a little girl on our street and went flying in to tell Mum – who couldn't have been less interested.

'You'll have to sort it out yourselves,' she said, barely looking up from her newspaper.

'But she hit me!'

Mum sighed. 'What do you want me to do about it?'

'Tell her off!' It was all I could think of. That's what she'd do if it were me or Lorraine.

'I'm not telling anyone off,' she said flatly. 'There's no point. You'll have made up in two minutes.'

She was always like that. Never wanted to get involved with kids' business. Nan, on the other hand, was my champion. She must have been out this day, otherwise I would have gone straight to her. Nan didn't think twice about tearing up the path and grabbing the first child she met by the scruff of their neck. It didn't matter if it was the right one or not, they were getting a piece of her mind. No one messed with Nan's little girls.

There was only one occasion I can think of where Mum

really got herself involved in something I'd done. It was cold weather so we were allowed to wear tights at school and somehow I must have snagged the top of them on the underside of my desk. The head of a nail was sticking out from the woodwork and that must have done it. I was lucky it only ripped my tights and not my skin. Mum didn't see it that way.

'You can't be trusted with anything!'

She looked particularly threatening at the time. A few days earlier Lorraine had been too ill to finish her newspaper delivery round so Mum had gone out instead. I don't know the last time Mum had ever ridden a bike but she only managed a few houses before falling off and spraining her wrist. So now, as she gesticulated angrily at me, all I could think was how much it would hurt if her wrist plaster cast connected with me.

I explained what had happened and waited for her to say she didn't believe me, as usual. Weirdly, she just listened, then said, 'Right, get our coats.'

Half an hour later we were back at the school and Mum was shouting at my teacher for endangering her daughter's health by leaving sharp nails sticking out of the furniture. I was so embarrassed. I thought, *Nothing good will come of this. I'll have to pay somehow.*

That's how it seemed to work with teachers. They didn't let you get away with anything.

It wasn't the only time Mum's behaviour had consequences. As a result of all the antibiotics pumped into me to combat the double pneumonia when I was born, my teeth had become seriously discoloured. At first Mum told me not to worry because as soon as my baby teeth dropped out, my adult ones would be as white as new. Then she spoke to a dentist and suddenly there was a change of plan. Without immediate action, she was told, there was a good chance that my baby teeth could actually infect the new teeth as they formed. In the 1960s this could be treated in one of two ways. Generally, the dentist would paint the affected teeth with a protective black coating to stop the rot spreading. To me that sounded vile. Who wants to have black teeth?

I had no idea that the other option available was even worse – but Mum did.

'That's the coward's way out,' she explained. 'But we're brave, aren't we?'

I nodded, not realising the consequences.

The alternative to having your teeth blacked out was having them extracted. One by one. That was Mum's plan. She was going to get to the root of the problem – and have them all out.

I was fine about it up to the point that my name was called. Then I stepped into the dentist's room and saw his assistant preparing the tray of gleaming, silver tools. That's when it dawned on me what was about to happen.

'Mum, I don't want to do it,' I said quietly.

But she wasn't interested in what I wanted. And she certainly didn't want to be questioned in front of someone as important as a dentist. That's not how people behaved then.

'Don't be such a baby,' she hissed firmly and gave me a shove towards the chair.

Five minutes later I was absolutely sick with panic, screaming to escape.

'Don't let them! Mum, help!'

But she didn't help. She smiled apologetically at the dentist as he held me firmly in place, then she left the room.

I despised her that day. While I suffered unspeakable operations, she just sat in the waiting room like she was expecting a bus. When I emerged, shaken and in tears, she said proudly, 'You've no idea how hard it was to make that decision.'

Mouth distorted by empty, swollen gums, I thought, *No, I really haven't.*

Nan's sister, Kate, had followed her GI boyfriend back to America after the war and every so often Nan would disappear for a few weeks to visit her. That meant I got the full run of our large room. That was never as much fun as I hoped. I hated sleeping alone. I was convinced people were snoring under the bed or hiding in the wardrobe or behind the curtains. I always got nightmares when I was on my own, which Mum blamed on watching too much of Ken Dodd and his Diddy Men. I knew it wasn't that, though.

Sometimes Nan's sister would visit us instead, which was always fun – for me, anyway. She always brought such brilliant gifts and took me and Lorraine out to eat at nice places. But twenty years in the USA had taken its toll. She spoke so loudly in public that Mum hated going out with her.

'Honey, how much is this?' she'd bellow across a crowded shop while Mum died with embarrassment.

I always looked forward to my great-aunt's visits but other relatives and guests failed to make so much of an impression. My mum grew up on our road so we always had people popping in and out, from any of her dozens of friends to the numerous extended family members who also lived locally. She

was extremely popular, well liked and welcoming, and everyone knew the key was always left in the door for you to stroll
in. So it was no surprise when Mum announced one day that
my dad's brothers were coming over.

'Who are they?' I asked.

'You know very well who they are,' she snapped. 'You've
seen them plenty of times.'

I thought, *I haven't. I've never even heard of them.*

Maybe I'd just forgotten their names, I decided, and everything would fall into place when they arrived. My memory
wasn't the greatest, after all. When I heard a car pull up outside
I rushed to the window expectantly – and watched as two complete strangers climbed out.

False alarm, I thought. *They must be visiting someone else.*

Then our front door bell rang and they came in.

Dad's brothers must be coming later, I decided.

Even as Lorraine and I were ushered into the lounge for
Mum's traditional formal welcome I was still adamant Dad's
brothers must be arriving later. I didn't know this pair from
Adam.

But they seemed to know me.

'Hello, Kim,' one of the men said. 'How's school?'

'Fine, thank you,' I replied, searching for any sign of famil-
iarity in his face. But there was nothing. No clues at all. *Who are
you?*

My sister was gabbing away with the other one. Either
Lorraine knew them or else she was bluffing well. I didn't
understand. But it wasn't the first time I'd met strangers who
seemed to know me. I never let on that I couldn't remember
them. That would be terrible manners. So I always went along

with it until I could work out who people were. When your
memory's as bad as mine you learn to do these things.

When Nan was off in America or just out and about, and with
Mum and Dad both working, they had to look elsewhere for
help with us. Childcare options in south London in the 1960s
weren't as formal as they are today. You used whoever offered.
To my young eyes some babysitters on our street seemed barely
a year older than the little ones they were minding, although
they must have been.

Before I started school I was passed around all sorts of sitters. With Mum and Dad so busy, I kept going to them on and
off for years, in holidays, after school or at weekends. Sometimes it was other families. One more to look after didn't make
a difference. Other times it was just neighbours. I remember
one. There was a bloke who lived near us who used to sit on his
front step dipping bread in milk and whisky. Looking back,
nothing about him makes you think 'perfect childminder
material'. Even then I remember being disappointed whenever
I was dragged round there. People without their own kids don't
have any toys for you to play with. Most likely you're just going
to mess up their place. 'Don't touch that', 'Put that down' –
that's all I ever heard. You wonder what's in it for them. My
only real memory of being at this bloke's is waking up in his
bed in the afternoons. I don't recall being put down for a nap
or any of the build-up. I don't recall anything apart from his
cups of bread and whisky and then waking up in his smelly bed
every time I stayed.

I never went to America but Nan and I did go down to
Bognor to stay for a week during the holidays. This was when

Mum and Dad were working. Then once a year, in summer, we'd all go down to the Butlin's holiday camp nearby as well. Dad, Mum, Lorraine and me. I always had fun but the days used to whizz by. A week felt like a day. I loved the amusement arcade but Lorraine preferred the swimming pool. I often used to go along with her but never made it in. I'd pack my costume, grab my towel and go along to the baths but never get in. Not once. I remember wandering back to the chalet the first time and Mum asking if we'd enjoyed it.

I said, 'I didn't go in in the end.'

'Don't listen to her,' Lorraine piped up. 'She was in there longer than me.'

'You liar! I wasn't.'

'Were so.'

And so it went on. I thought, *Why on earth would my sister make up something like that?*

It wasn't the first time and it wouldn't be the last. My life was full of stupid arguments like that. For me it was normal.

Like so many things.

CHAPTER THREE

Where am I now?

Katie skipped into the room, her head full of possibilities for adventure. With so many people around, the potential for games was endless. Any three-year-old knew that. She bashed around the adults' legs for a while, ignoring the random hands tousling her hair absent-mindedly as they carried on their conversations above her head. On the other side of the room she saw her older sister, Lorraine. Lorraine was usually nice to her. Apart from the times she told her to go away. Katie decided to run over and say, 'Hi.'

'And where do you think you're going?' a voice said.

Katie felt herself being scooped up and lifted aloft. Like a trophy on display.

All eyes in the room were on her. People were cooing, family, friends and neighbours equally impressed by her pretty dress and neat hair. She didn't know the occasion but everyone seemed so happy. Just as she had been until a few seconds ago.

A camera flash went off. She felt like she was flying. Any other time she would be whooping for joy. What toddler didn't enjoy that sensation?

The flying stopped. She was being brought closer for a hug.

Don't touch me, *she thought.* Don't touch me.

But what could she do? She was a child. She was three. And she always did what she was asked. Those were the rules. Obey, obey, obey. However much it hurt.

The strong arms holding Katie aloft wrapped around her and various 'oohs' and 'ahs' peppered the friendly hubbub of the room. Katie didn't care. Her hands remained rigidly at her side until she was able to fold her arms. That would put a barrier between them. Her face stayed turned away. There was no way she was hugging back. Too many memories of that other person. She wouldn't kiss. Not again. Not after last time.

Life was getting more confusing by the day. Did I tell anyone? Of course not. You assume everyone else is going through the same things as you. No one thinks they're different from the rest, do they? I'm as normal as you. I still believe that. But I couldn't deny that odd things were happening more and more often.

Schoolwork wasn't breaking any records but I had friends there and Mum let me enrol at Brownies and Girls Brigade. I was even allowed to go on a camping trip. The tents were already in place when we arrived but we still had to cook, wash up and generally get by in the great outdoors. I only remember staying two nights but it was probably longer. It seemed too far to go if not.

Christian Endeavour was another group I was allowed to join although this one didn't have the happiest ending. Maybe it was because their standards were higher, but we were in the church hall one night and there was a noise from the window. Twenty pairs of eyes swung over to look. A group of boys were jumping up to see in, all calling, 'Give us a wave!'

We all started giggling at the sight.

'Friends of yours?' the CE leader asked.

'Me?' I was shocked. 'No, I've never seen them before.'

It was the truth. They were wearing our school uniform so I suppose I'd seen them around, but I certainly wouldn't say I 'knew' them.

'Well they seem to know you,' she said.

The group leader went outside and chased the lads away. The giggling in the hall took longer to quell. Afterwards she pulled me aside.

'We don't encourage that sort of behaviour with boys,' she said. 'And we don't welcome liars either. Perhaps it would be better for everyone if you spent your Friday nights elsewhere.'

'But ...'

'I think it would be best for everyone.'

Thrown out – by Christians! And I had no idea what for.

Our road and the surrounding area were comfortable places in the 1970s for kids to play. No one worried about strangers or traffic. The only rule was being back for mealtimes. You went out after school and came in for your tea. At weekends you'd disappear after breakfast and pop back for lunch and dinner.

Knock-down ginger was a popular game, although it was rarely risked on your own street. The last thing we needed was some old bag complaining to Mum and Dad. Sometimes men would come haring out of their front doors and try to get you with a bucket of water or lads would chase you round the block waving a belt. One day a woman flung the door open before I'd even left her porch. She must have been waiting for us. I turned on my heels as quick as lightning and I was in such a panic I convinced myself she yelled, 'I'll be telling your mother! I know where you live, Kim Noble!'

I must have misheard. I'd never seen her before in my life. People were always bluffing like that.

Bad eggs was another favourite, or there was hopscotch, or just sitting on walls eating sweets and talking. Boys had one area and girls another. We were very segregated at that age.

Being a kid on the streets, especially in summer, was a bit like working shifts in a factory. As the smells of cooking began to waft from each house, we all knew playtime was nearly over. When the first mum stood on the front step and summoned her little one that was the cue for the rest of us to traipse home. That was our whistle telling us to clock out and clear off for another day.

The streets emptied as quickly as they filled and as usual it was just me, last girl standing again. Home since Dad had returned was not the haven it had once been. Individually my parents were exactly the same towards me and Lorraine. No change in their behaviour there at all. Towards each other, though, they could be evil.

Mum's heart had been broken when Dad walked out. That was his fault. That was damage he caused. She had been over the moon when he'd come back, beaten and bruised, tail between his legs, begging for one more chance.

'I don't know what I was thinking, Doll,' he said. 'She led me on and I was weak.'

It was the wrong decision for everyone. They were forever at each other's throat. Arguments replaced all conversation. Mum loved Dad but I don't think she ever got over his betrayal. Despite Dad's best efforts, she couldn't find it in herself to wipe the slate clean. He couldn't leave the house without being accused of having another affair.

'I know where you're going, Jim Noble!'

Of course he always denied it. 'Look, I won't go out if that's how you feel.' But by then it was too late. The seed was sown, a row was brewing, and ten minutes later he'd be storming out again. We'd hear his car start up, heavy on the accelerator, then screech off up the road. And, in his defence, the more Mum accused him of everything under the sun, the more Dad started to go out to escape her nagging, which of course just gave her more ammunition.

It was a poisonous atmosphere really.

Mum really struggled to hold it together sometimes. I remember arguing with Lorraine in the lounge – business as usual as far as we were concerned – when there was this crash from the kitchen. Next, Mum flew past us and stomped up the stairs. When I looked in the kitchen I saw she'd been halfway through preparing dinner. Everything was strewn over the worktop. A few minutes later she appeared downstairs again clutching an overnight bag.

'Satisfied?' she said coldly.

'What's going on?' I asked.

'I've had enough. I'm going.'

'Mum, don't leave us!' we both chorused together. But she wasn't listening. She opened the front door and without even looking back, stepped out. I dived onto her coat to drag her back but she just smacked me away. Then the front door slammed shut behind her.

'Where's she going?' I asked Lorraine.

'Dunno,' she said. 'But it looks like she's running away.'

She came back a few hours later and refused to discuss it. But it happened quite a few times over the years. Usually, we discovered, she was just hiding next door. Who knows what our neighbour thought when Mum pitched up with a suitcase?

Small things seemed to set Mum's temper off. She wasn't a passionate person and didn't like to get involved in conversations on 'big' subjects. Every so often, though, she'd just explode. Once during a row with Dad she put her fist through a glass window. She literally just punched it, then stared at the blood pouring from her wrist. We rushed around getting bandages and sweeping glass and trying not to scream but it was terrifying.

I suppose it all stemmed from her problems with Dad but Lorraine and I didn't know that. It wasn't in their nature to keep us informed of things. They'd never even officially told us that Dad had left. He was often out after I went to bed. Not seeing him in the evenings wasn't out of the ordinary. In the end we pieced together bits and pieces. All we knew for sure was that the less time they spent in each other's company, the better.

There were other impacts on our lives. Mum announced one day we were going on holiday to Jersey. It became clear that Dad wouldn't be going. I could look forward to a week without them tearing strips off each other. *That will be nice.*

But it didn't work out that way.

We all got in the car for the short journey to the station. Dad got the luggage out of the boot and we all said goodbye. Then Dad climbed back into the driver's seat and said, 'Well, it's just us two now.'

I wasn't going.

I had no idea why I wasn't invited. I think it was the school holidays so that wasn't an issue. I just know I had to watch while Mum and Lorraine packed their bags, all excited like they were the sisters, and not me. The things they were going to do, the places they were going to see, the fun they were going to have.

Without me.

It got worse. Dad obviously had to work so to give Nan a break I was farmed out for the odd day to the usual babysitters. Some I liked, some I didn't. I think these days families think twice about letting certain people look after their young ones. That wasn't such a consideration back then. On the positive side I didn't seem to be anywhere long. Sometimes I wouldn't even remember going, just waking up and then being collected by Dad or Nan. Still, that was normal.

Strangers though they were around the house, Mum and Dad did manage to put their differences aside when they needed to. When I was ten, we all went on a family holiday to Yugoslavia. I think this was quite unusual in 1971. Cheap foreign flights hadn't really come in then but it must have been a package deal. I really can't imagine why else we would have done it.

For some reason Lorraine's boyfriend, Bob, was allowed to come as well. He was quite young, with a skinhead haircut, but that actually helped him because the rest of us caught nits. All I remember of that holiday is scratching my head. But then so much of my childhood left me scratching my head . . .

A five-year gap between sisters is fun when you're young and great when you're older. But for a few years in the middle it can be hellish. No fifteen-year-old wants her kid sister sniffing around. Lorraine preferred to spend her time with her boyfriend so the last thing she wanted was being shackled with me. Mum sometimes asked her to babysit me, especially on a Saturday when she liked to go out with friends for a drink. That always caused a fight.

Sometimes Mum and Dad would go out for the night together or more usually they went out separately at the same time. Once or twice they even stayed away overnight. When Nan was around it didn't matter. Everything changed when she was away. I remember Lorraine getting a finger pointed at her and made to promise not to have any parties.

'Of course I won't. I swear.'

No sooner was the sound of Dad's car out of range than there was a knock at the door – the first of many for the evening. Some of the faces I recognised, some I didn't. They were all at least five years older than me, a lot of them skinheads like Bob. Most were a bit shocked at a kid like me being there.

Lorraine tried to get me to go to my room but I refused.

'I'm telling Mum and Dad if you make me.'

'You wouldn't dare!'

'Want to find out?'

I spent the rest of the night being given piggy-back rides up and down the garden by Lorraine's boy friends. Anything to buy my silence.

My sister must have thought she'd been so clever, even if she did have to give in to my blackmail. The next morning the house was spick and span and by the time Mum and Dad returned you'd never have guessed what had gone on.

That was, until our next-door neighbour came round for a cup of tea and mentioned it to Mum. All hell broke loose then. Lorraine was grounded for a week and for once I got away scot-free – even though I'd spent the night at the party as well!

All Lorraine wanted was to get married and move out. That finally happened when she was eighteen. She looked beautiful but I don't remember the ceremony, just the dancing afterwards. My brother-in-law had started his police training at Hendon but didn't finish it and had become a fireman. Lorraine always had a thing for men in uniform. I was happy for her, of course, but even more so because once she moved out I got her room. It didn't matter if it was the smallest room in the house. It was my own space.

With Lorraine gone, there was one person fewer to argue with. And now at least when Dad and Mum started their bickering I had a refuge. I remember leaving the table when they'd started shouting at each other.

'Where do you think you're going?' Mum demanded.

'To my room.'

Not Nan's room. Not my shared room. *My room.* You've no idea how good it felt to say that.

Speaking of the table, I don't remember many mealtimes. I didn't have much of an interest in food, really. Or so I thought. Yet when I saw some pictures of me as a ten-year-old recently I couldn't believe my size. From the age of seven I'd just seemed to get steadily bigger and bigger. One minute I was a cute-as-a-button skinny kid. The next I was getting a round face, chubby cheeks and thick arms and legs.

I couldn't believe these were really pictures of me.

It made no sense. That's not my recollection of being ten, eleven, twelve at all. I wasn't a fat child. I wasn't skinny like I am now, but definitely not overweight. How could I have been so large? I never even ate anything. Usually I'd just sit down and pick.

But it explains why people sometimes called out 'Fatty' when I walked by. I just never thought they were talking to me.

The ICL factory closed when I was twelve. All my friends' dads worked there so a dark cloud hung over the whole area for a while as people scrabbled for new jobs. We had it worse than most because Mum worked there as well. That was two incomes lost. Luckily Mum found another factory role and then took an office position working for the government. Dad went into social services as assistant manager at a day centre for the physically handicapped. As far as I could tell, they both worked hard. I assume that was true. They were certainly away from home a lot.

I liked Dad's new job. One of his duties was taking the patients out on day trips. Sometimes they went to the beach, sometimes to a zoo or just to a park. Whenever there was space he invited me to tag along. I had lovely days swimming, going on trips to Hastings or watching Crystal Palace play football. Dad had his work cut out with the rest of them so I was mostly left on my own. But that was nothing new. I enjoyed my own company, anyway.

I think my parents' work ethic in those early years must have rubbed off on me – although I didn't have a clue how it came about.

I often found myself in odd situations I couldn't explain. I assumed everyone did. That's life. You deal with it, don't you?

So when I realised I was in a huge kitchen, surrounded by strangers, and with my elbows deep in dirty washing-up water I just thought, *Okay ... where am I now?*

I honestly had no idea how I'd got there. Or where 'there' was. But my friend Clare was standing at the sink next to me. She was chatting about something. Boys, I think.

I nodded. I did a lot of nodding, I remember. Agreeing with people saves you saying anything. I learnt that at a very young age.

It didn't take a genius to realise I was supposed to be washing the plates. That's what Clare was doing, between telling me about this lad or that one, and I guess that's why I had my hands in the water too. But why?

And where am I?

I pretty much followed Clare's lead for the next few hours as I pieced my predicament together. We appeared to be in a restaurant or café kitchen because of the waiters bustling in and out, and our job consisted of nothing more complex than scrubbing every single plate and cup and knife and fork and bowl and tray and – you name it, they used it. And we washed it.

A guy who must have been in charge kept coming over to make sure we weren't slacking. He picked up a spoon and held it to the light.

'Very good,' he said. 'Now you just need to go a bit faster.'

God, it was tiring. The worst thing was not knowing when it would end. I thought it must be lunchtime judging by the food being ordered but I had no idea when I'd be allowed to leave.

And if I ask Clare she'll think I'm thick.

So I kept quiet.

When we finally got the cue to dry our hands and pack up for the night I thought, *I'm glad that's over.* Then just as we were about to step out, the boss man said, 'Thanks, girls. Same time tomorrow.'

Oh no. What the hell have I got myself into here?

As soon as we got outside I recognised the place as being in Shirley. Not only that, but there was Dad waiting in his car.

What's he doing here?

How he knew to pick me up when I honestly had no idea how I'd got the job or even found my way into work was beyond me. But Clare seemed to know and as we both climbed into Dad's car I thought I'd better show willing.

'What time shall I see you tomorrow, Clare?'

'Same time as today should be all right.'

That doesn't exactly help me . . .

'So, about ten then?' I suggested.

'Only if you want to be an hour late,' Dad said.

'Yes, let's do half eight again, shall we?' Clare added.

Why is everything such hard work? I wondered. As I made my way home I stared at my poor, puckered hands and realised, *I don't even know if I'm being paid for this.*

Just another one of my typical scrapes.

School was equally confusing, more so in fact now that I was at Tavistock Secondary. Some of my friends spent a lot of time covering exercise books with their names. Signature after signature. I think they were practising autographs for when they were famous, like the Bay City Rollers, David Bowie or David

Cassidy. That never appealed to me. Having 'Patricia' scrawled all over my English book seemed ridiculous. I don't actually think I had my name on the front at all. It didn't matter. I knew whose book it was.

More importantly, trouble and accusations still seemed to follow me around just as they had at West Thornton. Mostly I was punished for talking when I hadn't been, missing lessons or being in the wrong place at the wrong time. Then there were other things along the lines of the black paint incident. The worst was being held back after school for trying to climb out of a window. They said my skirt had snagged and I got trapped, and that I was still swinging, head first, when I was found. *Rubbish. Just rubbish.* Someone had it in for me. That was the only explanation.

Meanwhile, it didn't matter how long they made me sit there, I would never admit to something I just hadn't done. I was prepared to wait all night. Unfortunately, so was the teacher by the look of the stack of books he had next to him ready to mark. For more than an hour he just ignored me, head down until he reached the end of the pile. Then he leant back in his chair and tutted.

'Still denying it?'

'Denying what?'

'You were caught red-handed.'

'I wasn't.'

'You had to be cut down from the window.'

'I didn't.'

'Look at your dress. It's still got the hole where the window snared it.'

There *was* a rip. I had no idea how it had got there. Must

have been a thorn playing on the field at lunchtime. Maybe my coat zip had got stuck. It didn't matter. All I knew is it hadn't been caused by a window.

Unsurprisingly, when it came to reports I feared the worst. If staff were prepared to lie to my face, who knew what they would come up with when they had a little time to prepare. I thought about hiding them from my parents but chickened out. In the end Mum and Dad weren't annoyed by what they read – just mystified.

'I don't understand,' Mum said after her second read. 'How can they all have such different opinions?'

I shrugged.

She read some bits out to Nan.

'"Lovely, good-natured", this one says.'

'That's good.' Nan smiled at me.

'But then you've got "disruptive" from this one, "attentive" from another one and your maths teacher says "needs to control her temper". What are you doing there? It's like they're talking about different people.'

I couldn't help. I was at as much of a loss to explain it as anyone. I'd never lost my temper during maths, what was he on about? Mum was right. They must have got me muddled up with someone else. Or they had another agenda altogether.

At West Thornton Primary the worst that happened was a visit to the head or an occasional rap across the knuckles. At Tavistock they had a complicated disciplinary system – first you were put on report by your form tutor, then your year head, then the headmaster – but all of it entirely non-violent. Even if you'd exhausted all those steps, the final punishment

was equally pacifistic compared to a clip round the ear –
although the effects were so much worse.

I don't know if there was a move in the 1970s to get away
from corporal punishment or whether someone at the school
had watched too many war films, but their approach to discipline was sensory deprivation.

I remember being in a school corridor. I couldn't remember getting there but that was fine. Situation normal. There
was no one around except a teacher walking a couple of yards
ahead of me. I racked my brain to work out why I was there
and where I was going. With no other kids around I didn't
have a clue. Then the teacher spun round.

'Keep up!' she snapped.

That was good. I knew I was meant to be following her.
But why?

I realised we were near the head's office. My immediate
thought was, *What have I done now?* Then I realised we were
walking *away* from his room. That was a good sign. Maybe I
wasn't in trouble at all.

From the way the teacher was hustling me along that
didn't seem likely. But I hadn't done anything. Of that I had no
doubt. There had to be another explanation.

Was I ill, then? Was she taking me to sick bay? I looked
down and checked both hands and legs. There was no outward
sign of injury. My stomach felt okay – a few butterflies, that
was all. And my head was more confused than aching. *No*, I
concluded, *I'm fine.*

Was everything all right at home? Sometimes kids were
summoned to the office to take a phone call. Only in emergencies, but it happened.

My head was still spinning with possibilities when the teacher stopped by a door I'd never noticed before. That wasn't uncommon. There were plenty of unexplored parts of that large building. Most classrooms had glass in the door so other teachers could peer in. This one, I noticed, was entirely made of wood. It looked more like a cupboard entrance.

'In here,' she said, and flung the door open.

It wasn't a cupboard but then it wasn't much of a room, either. And it definitely wasn't a sickbay. If anything it looked more like a gaol cell. There was a solitary chair and table in the middle and that was it. No shelves, no bookcases, no cupboards. Absolutely nothing apart from those two pieces of furniture looming ever more ominously in the centre.

The teacher flicked on the light. Without it there was just a small, frosted window to allow any illumination. The reason I hadn't noticed initially how dark the room was then became obvious. All four walls were painted bright orange. Hideous, Day-Glo tangerine, like a traffic light stuck on amber.

For the first time I had an uneasy feeling about it.

'Sit down and make yourself comfortable,' the teacher instructed and I duly obeyed. What choice did I have?

'I'll be back to check on you later. I suggest you use this time wisely to reflect on what you've done.'

And with that passing shot she closed the door. The room seemed suddenly darker, and smaller and colder. The tiny frosted glass window peered down eerily now as I took in my surroundings. Apart from the desk and chair there was literally nothing else there. Not even any work. No pen, no paper, nothing. What was the point of having a desk if they didn't give me anything to do on it?

Suits me, I thought. *I don't want to do any work anyway.*

So I sat there. At first I thought the teacher would appear any minute so I stayed in the chair. After what seemed like hours I dared to get up. There was nothing to see but at least I got to stretch my legs. I stared at the window. The frosted glass meant I couldn't even see out. There was literally nothing to do in there. Nothing at all.

I learnt later I'd been subjected to a day in the 'reflection room'. You were despatched there to sit and mull over your transgressions with no outside distractions. That was fine in principle. In practice, what if you hadn't committed the crime you were being punished for? What if you had no clue why you were being dragged there? It just meant I spent six hours fuming over the injustice of it all. By the time I emerged I was angrier than when I'd gone in.

That's the problem with sensory deprivation, I've read. It's meant to promote some meditative behaviour. In small doses I believe this is possible. Anyone exposed to these conditions regularly over a long period of time might suffer different effects. Paranoia, hallucinations, depression and anxiety are natural consequences. By the time I was released I was convinced I was suffering all four.

And of course it happened to me again and again.

And again.

I didn't know how I'd got that weekend job in Shirley but I do know it didn't last long. At least it didn't appear to. After being driven like slaves we were too tired to walk home. Dad had to come and pick us up instead. I hated it but I don't recall being fired or resigning. In fact, I went to bed one

Friday night expecting to turn up at work the following day as normal.

That didn't happen.

The first thing I noticed was that I wasn't in the kitchen. *Okay, that's fine. It can't be far away.*

But where was Clare? For those eight or nine hours each day we barely left each other's side. We worked together, took our breaks together and left together.

She must be in the loo.

I waited for a few minutes, then decided to look for her. The room I was in was dark and filled with coats on hooks. I didn't remember coming in but there was my jacket. The door was ajar so I went out.

Straight into a shop.

Panicking, I dived back into the room and slammed the door.

Okay, that's weird. It's not the kitchen. It's not even the restaurant. It's a department store full of people.

When I heard footsteps approaching I thought I'd die. *If I'm found in here they'll think I'm shoplifting.* I considered hiding behind the coats but decided against it. If they discovered me there it would look even more suspicious. No, better to front it out. I took a deep breath and felt my heart almost bursting through my top. I wished I was invisible.

The door suddenly flung open and a neatly coiffed woman bowled in.

'There you are!' she called cheerily. 'All ready to get started?'

'Er, yeah,' I heard myself say. 'I'm ready.'

I followed her back out and a girl called Kelly showed me

how to fold clothes, tidy shelves and generally make our section of the huge shop look presentable. Of course, you only
have to look like you vaguely know what you're doing and customers are soon queuing up with questions. I did my best but
by the tenth one I just felt like screaming, 'How should I know?
I don't even know which shop I'm in!'

As I said, just another one of my typical scrapes.

CHAPTER FOUR

My pilot light is going out

Judy cringed as she pulled on the skirt. She hated squeezing into these stupid tight clothes. What was the point of PE anyway? It only made her sweat. Sport was for thin girls who looked good in their kit. Not people like her, people with legs as fat as hers, people who just looked so hideous stomping around the netball court. It was embarrassing. It made her want to curl up and die. She wished she had a chocolate bar.

She knew the boys would see her as she made her way out to the court. She knew they'd call her 'fatty' like they always did. She knew they'd be making their lists and giving all the girls marks out of ten for this and that. And she knew she'd be getting zero for her figure. A big, fat zero.

For a big fat girl.

It didn't matter if she scored ten for prettiness or cleverness or funniness. Nothing mattered apart from that nought.

Judy looked around. The last stragglers had gone, dragging themselves out to their weekly humiliation. The changing room was empty. If she didn't hurry she'd be told off again. But if she did hurry, she'd have to endure the vicious taunts as usual.

Judy picked up her bag and headed to the toilets, went into a cubicle and slid the bolt.

I'm better off here, *she thought.* No one will find me here.

When you do a jigsaw puzzle you start with the corners, then hunt out the edges, then try to pull them into order. Finally you can think about looking for some sense in the middle section. Without knowing it, that's how my early years felt. And without understanding why, the older I got I was happy if I could just get the borders lined up. Much more than that was a real bonus.

School wasn't the problem. There you are compartmentalised and everyone knows where they should be and roughly what they should be doing. It was the journeys to and from Tavistock that threw up the problems. I'd suddenly be aware of walking and not remember where I was going. If I had my school uniform on then it was a good guess that it was a school day. If there were others around I could work out whether they were heading for lessons or escaping home.

Once I found myself alone near the gates. I didn't know how I'd got there or where I'd come from. Nothing unusual about that.

I did the standard checks: I was carrying my school bag and wearing my uniform. It was a weekday.

But the path was deserted. Either everyone was already in and I was running late, or they'd left hours ago and I was still here. Or was I ridiculously early for some reason? I studied the building. There were a few lights on. That didn't help.

Is it morning or evening?

Should I go in or walk home?

Either could get me in real trouble if it was the wrong choice.

Where are my friends? Where's Clare? Where's Irene?

I must have stood there for a quarter of an hour,

anguishing over which way to head. Then I noticed something familiar.

Cooking! One of the nearby houses had the oven on.

That was all the information I needed. It was dinner time.

I have to get home.

Getting home after an episode like that would usually follow the same pattern.

Mum: 'Where have you been?'

Me: 'I don't know.'

Mum: 'Fine. Be like that. Dinner's ready.'

She never probed any further. I suppose she thought I was keeping secrets. What would I have said? 'I sometimes appear in places or with people I don't know.' I wasn't even sure that was what was happening. How could I put it into words?

In itself, the fact that Mum, or Nan for that matter, never questioned my behaviour reassured me that everything was normal. If people act weird around you, then you ask them if they're all right. That's the natural response, isn't it? That's how I am with my daughter. Get everything out in the open. If no one pulls you up for acting oddly, you infer from that that they know what you're going through. That it's how they live as well, even if you can't necessarily see evidence of it. And so you just carry on as normal. Carry on in the only way you know how.

Mum had her own problems, of course. The whole family did. I was only a child but I could see that things with Dad were at best tolerable and at worst downright unpleasant. At the same time as never telling us anything, neither made any attempt to hide anything either. I just wasn't considered important enough to be informed. If they wanted to fight, they did it right in front of me. I heard all sorts of accusations flung in Dad's direction. Then he'd take off as usual. It didn't matter if I was in front of them or safely upstairs. Even from the sanctity of my room I'd feel the shudder of the front door slamming.

I don't remember discussing anything with Nan. Maybe she didn't know what was going on either. In the evenings we would sit together and she would stroke my hair. But we never spoke. Not really. We all just concentrated on our own lives.

I noticed Lorraine start to pop round more and more often. She'd begun to moan about her husband, which was a shame. They'd only been married five minutes but I suppose they'd been together since they were young. You're not the same person at nineteen that you were at fourteen. Hearing her suspicions of his behaviour made me sick. It was Mum and Dad all over again.

Speaking of Dad, he wasn't quite himself. Every time I saw him, which wasn't that often, he seemed to be complaining about a bad back. I don't remember him being particularly active but suddenly he was coming straight in from work and collapsing onto the sofa. Even that seemed to cause discomfort after a while. One day I came downstairs and he'd moved onto the floor. It wasn't the biggest front room in the world and he took up most of the space. I didn't know anything about bad backs but I thought he should see a doctor.

'It's just a bad back,' he insisted. 'A bit of rest and I'll be right as rain.'

Day after day, week after week, this went on. Whenever I was in the house he'd be stretched out on the floor, writhing around.

'I'll be all right when I get comfortable.'

He didn't look all right, though. And he didn't sound it.

Then things started getting weird.

I got home one day as Nan was cooking dinner. Dad was already on the floor in the front room. He hadn't been to work for weeks. I stuck my head around the door to say hello but all he could say was, 'Shut the door, for God's sake! I can't stand the smell.'

What smell? The only aroma in the house was food – onions and mince at a guess. But I didn't question. I pulled the door closed and went upstairs.

Dad didn't join us to eat.

'He's not up to it,' Mum said.

I could work out that for myself. The sounds through the thin partition wall were awful. One moment Dad was shouting at himself because he couldn't get comfortable. Then he was swearing at the foul smells seeping into the lounge. Poor Nan, having to listen to her food compared to everything from rotting veg to blocked drains to dog mess.

'Well, I like the smell, Nan,' I said, although I didn't seem to eat anything as usual before finding myself in bed.

The next night was the same. By the end of the week Dad was shouting from the moment I got up until the time I went to bed. Always about the food. Always about the vile stench. If anyone dared open the front room door while there was any vegetable preparation going on, you soon closed it again. Any conversation at breakfast was drowned out by his ranting.

Same with dinner. At the weekend it was easier to just stay out for most of the day.

But still he just said it was a bad back.

'Leave me alone. I know my body. I just need a rest!'

Eventually he gave in and a doctor was allowed in to see him. Dad told him the same story. It was just his back. He just needed some peace and quiet – 'although chance would be a fine thing in this house.'

'I'll be the judge of that,' the doctor said.

I don't know what went on in that room but after ten minutes the doctor was on the phone ordering an ambulance.

'What's the problem?' Mum asked him.

'Your husband's got extremely low blood pressure. He needs hospital treatment. Urgently.'

I don't remember Dad being carried into the ambulance or whether Mum went with him. But I do recall sitting down for mealtimes was enjoyable again without the soundtrack of his abuse.

Mum went to the hospital at some point and Dad revealed he had a stomach ulcer. That was why his back was hurting. It also explained why eating was a complete no-no, and how even the smell of food set him off.

'They're going to operate and then I'll be fine.'

Mum was quite matter-of-fact when she relayed the details to us that night. I don't remember visiting Dad. Weirdly, a school friend was admitted to the same hospital for appendicitis and I did go to take her a bunch of grapes. Half the class was there whenever I went. I recall seeing her and later standing outside Dad's ward. But I don't remember going in. Just standing there, wondering where I was, then going home again.

Mum went in after the operation. Dad was asleep in his bed so she went to speak to the consultant.

'Is everything all right?' she asked.

'Yes, perfectly straightforward procedure. We were lucky to catch it in time.'

'Will it return?'

'Will what return?'

'The ulcer.'

The consultant stared at Mum like she was mad. She wondered if they were speaking about the same patient.

'Jim Noble,' she said. 'You just operated on him. You took out a stomach ulcer.'

The consultant stared at Mum and said, 'My dear woman, your husband didn't have an ulcer. He has cancer. We've just removed three-quarters of his stomach.'

Cancer? Dad hadn't told anyone. God knows what the consultant thought but Mum felt such an idiot. *Typical of him, though,* she must have thought. *Always keeping secrets.*

Dad was put onto a ward with the other people who'd had similar operations. He was only forty-two and the youngest one there by several decades. Mum hated going to visit him. One day she came back and said one of the old boys who'd had the same op as Dad had died in the night. The next day she said another one had gone. Then a third.

'I think we're going to have to prepare for the worst,' she said. She burst out crying, joined soon after by Lorraine. Later Mum told me, 'You never cried. You were always so hard.'

But Dad was a fighter. They might have been dropping like flies around him but he plugged away. After a few weeks the doctors said he could come home. The next thing I knew,

he was back in the lounge, because he was too weak to climb
the stairs every day. But at least he wasn't angry any more. We
could cook without listening to him screaming about the
smells wafting in.

For a while things were back to normal. Then one day Lorraine
arrived and announced she'd left her husband. He'd cheated on
her. They were over. There was no way back. I didn't want to
give up my room but she refused to go in with Nan. Everyone
else agreed.

'It's not right for a married woman.'

I wasn't too happy about that but generally Lorraine and
I had never been closer. Five years is a huge gap when one of
you is interested in boys and the other is still playing with dolls.
By the time Lorraine had moved back in we were both old
enough to get along. The older we got, the less important the
gap seemed.

Friday nights were important times for Lorraine and
Mum. That was Mum's night out with the girls and once
Lorraine was back, she started going out with her as well. At
fourteen, I was too young so I stayed in with Nan. Sometimes
we played games, sometimes we listened to the radio or
watched television if Dad didn't mind our being in the front
room with him.

One Saturday Dad had felt strong enough to leave the
house, although his bed was still set up in the front room.
Mum and Lorraine were out for a good time as usual. Nan and
I were talking when the phone went.

'Who's ringing at this time?' she said as I went to answer.
'Give them a piece of my mind.'

I picked up and said, 'Hello?'

For the next minute I just listened as an hysterical Lorraine screamed down the phone. I managed to pick out bits and pieces.

'Mum's been run over! You've got to come down. Don't tell Nan. Whatever you do, don't let her worry.'

So many instructions I barely had time to respond. Then the line went dead.

I went back to Nan.

'Who was that?' she asked.

'Oh, it was Lorraine,' I said. That was the easy part.

'What does she want at this time?'

'Mum's fallen over. She's drunk. Lorraine wants me to go and help her back.'

'That girl,' Nan tutted. 'I'm not waiting up to see this.'

I grabbed my coat and ran out the door. It was a five-minute run from our house. Mum, Lorraine and a man friend had been crossing the road at the roundabout joining the A23. A car had come bombing around the corner while they were all mid-crossing. Lorraine had been last in the line so she was just scraped. The man was knocked clean over and Mum, who'd been furthest into the road, was slammed onto the bonnet. Lorraine said that was the only reason the driver stopped, because he couldn't see anything with Mum filling the wind-screen.

I didn't know any of this as I tore along the pavement. All I knew from Lorraine's message was that things were bad. Terrible even. But nothing prepared me for the sight of dozens of flashing blue lights dominating the night sky. Police cars and ambulances were completely blocking the road. Vehicles stacked back in both directions as constables tried to keep the traffic flowing. A small crowd of people had gathered around the scene. As I fought my way through, I saw Lorraine sitting with a blanket round her. A policeman was talking to her. But where was Mum?

Then I saw her and my heart sank.

She was lying in the road, exactly as she'd landed. Two medics were checking her. They were talking anxiously. But worst of all, I could see a policeman crouching down, shuffling around her like a crab. He was marking her outline on the road.

I thought they only did that for dead bodies.

Then the penny dropped.

Oh God!

Lorraine saw me, then we forced our way over to Mum. She was out of it, completely unconscious.

She's not going to make it.

We shoved past the medics and I sighed with relief when I saw Mum's eyes flicker open. When she saw us she said, 'My pilot light is going out.'

What a time to be thinking about the cooker, I thought. But at least she was alive.

She said it again. 'My pilot light is going out.'

'Don't worry, Mum,' Lorraine assured her. 'I'll light it when I get home.'

But Mum wouldn't stop. That's all she could manage to say in her weak, pathetic little voice. 'My pilot light is going out. My pilot light is going out.'

Then she passed out again and I thought we'd lost her for good.

I stared at Lorraine. *What do we do now?*

Suddenly, there was a twitch and Mum came back. And what did she say?

'My pilot light is going out.'

As petrified as I was, I struggled to keep a straight face. It was so bizarre. Mum was flitting in and out of consciousness and all she could think about was that.

It was only afterwards we worked out what she meant. Mum was dying. She could see that. Death was claiming her and in her mind she could see her life force being snuffed out. She wasn't worried about the cooker at all. She was talking about herself, about her own pilot light.

It seemed to take an age to move Mum into the ambulance. Seeing that police outline made me feel sick. They obviously thought her pilot light was going out for good. Lorraine went to the hospital but I went back home. The next thing I remember is Lorraine coming home the next morning, ashen.

'Mum's serious but stable,' she explained, tears flowing. 'They don't know if she'll make it.'

It was a horrible time. We had to tell Nan of course and she was devastated. You feel so helpless when someone is in hospital.

Life had to go on as much as possible. Dad made me go to school. Afterwards I set off to visit Mum in hospital. On the way I saw our neighbour. Her face fell when she spotted me.

'Oh, I'm so sorry to hear about your mum.'

I nodded. 'Thanks.' What else was there to say?

'You must let me know when the funeral is.'

Funeral?

'Mum's not dead.'

The neighbour was shocked.

'But . . .'

'What have you heard?' I demanded. But the woman clammed up.

I ran off, distraught. Had something happened to Mum while I was at school? Or had she died and I'd just not remembered? That could happen. That would be normal for me. Why hadn't they told me?

By the time I reached the hospital I was a wreck. I felt the nurses' eyes burning into me as I ran up the corridor and braced myself for the worst. Any minute now one of them would take me aside.

But there was Mum. There'd been no change. The neighbour had been wrong.

I've never been so relieved.

It turned out the whole neighbourhood was buzzing with the news that Dorothy Noble had been killed that night. I suppose enough people had seen the accident scene. You know how rumours build in small communities. When the police have drawn an outline around your body, that's never a good sign. But I wish people had done some research rather than leaping to conclusions. I lost count of the times I was commiserated with because of my mother. Even though I knew the truth, every time it happened I couldn't help worrying that this time they might be right – and I'd just forgotten.

I did my best to visit Mum most days. At first I couldn't believe it was her in that bed. She had more bandages than an Egyptian mummy. When they started to come off I saw her skin was black and blue. She was in a really bad way.

I went in one day and got as far as the ward double-doors. I remember pushing them open and that's it. I didn't think about it again until later that night. We were having dinner when Nan asked, 'Did you see your mother today?'

I can't remember!

'I think so,' I said.

'Well, did you or didn't you?'

I literally don't know.

'Yes, of course I did.'

But really I had no idea. I'd opened the ward doors but did I go in?

A couple of days later it was Mum's turn to confuse me. As usual I'd gone directly to the hospital from school. As I skipped into the ward Mum smiled weakly.

'Did you forget something?'

'No, why?'

'Well, what have you come back for? I only said goodbye to you five minutes ago.'

What on Earth's she talking about?

'I've just got here,' I insisted indignantly.

'If you say so,' Mum said with the weariness of someone used to her daughter's tall stories. I knew that tone. She used it on me all the time.

'Only kidding,' I bluffed. 'I just wondered if you wanted me to bring anything tomorrow.'

And that was how I got away with it.

A few days later it was even weirder. Mum greeted me this time with, 'Hello, stranger.'

'Hello,' I said, oblivious to the sarcasm.

'Did you have something better to do yesterday?'

Mum claimed she hadn't seen me for two days, whereas I knew full well I hadn't missed an afternoon visit that week. Monday, Tuesday and now Wednesday – I'd been in every day. *Mum must just be tired,* I thought.

And then, on my way out, I noticed the nurses' board in the corridor. Thursday was written at the top of the board. I wondered whether I should point out their mistake. For some reason I didn't bother.

No wonder Mum's confused, though.

The doctors were happy with Mum's recovery. For her, though, it wasn't happening quickly enough. Against medical advice she discharged herself and got a taxi home. It caught everyone out. With Mum on crutches there was no way she could make the stairs. But Dad was still sleeping in the front room. After some argument he transferred all his stuff upstairs and Mum took up camp in his place.

It wasn't perfect but she was home and she was alive.

It had been the worst year of my life. Probably the worst for any of us – and it was about to get worse. First Lorraine's marriage had broken up, Dad had got cancer and Mum had been in intensive care for a fortnight after being run over on a night out. And then there was Nan. We'd barely got over the other events when I came home from school to see an ambulance pulling away from near our house. My first thought was Mum. Had she had a setback? Inside I found a note. Nan had had a stroke. She was going to the hospital for a check-up. She should be all right.

Should?

I wasn't even sure what a stroke was. I certainly couldn't

face anything happening to Nan. I hadn't really thought of it before but she was my bedrock.

Before I knew it Nan was home and apparently with no side effects. She'd had a 'funny turn' as she called it but she was on the mend now.

'Don't worry yourself about me.'

It was hard not to. In fact, when I went over the year's events I realised I'd actually been the lucky one. Sure, I'd had to endure a hideous run of events but what family doesn't go through a period like that every so often? Each instance was unpleasant, yes, but not really out of the ordinary. And, on the bright side, at least I seemed to be all right.

So why did I wake up one morning to find my stomach had just been pumped?

CHAPTER FIVE

There's no helping you

'Hello, Samaritans. Who am I speaking to?'

The voice was calm, reassuring and friendly.

'Hello?' it repeated. 'I'm Sam. You don't have to tell me your name. How are you feeling today?'

Rebecca shook as she clutched the handset tightly. Her knuckles were white with effort, as though if she let go of the phone she would drown. In a way she would.

The man called Sam spoke again, trying to cajole a response from his silent caller. 'I'm not doing anything if you just want to talk.'

Nothing.

'Hello? Hello? It's all right, whatever you want to say won't go any further.'

Rebecca listened, smiled, then replaced the receiver in its cradle. She was glad she'd called. It was comforting to hear the stranger's voice.

Then she picked up the bottle of white tablets and tipped them into her mouth.

'What are you playing at?'

Mum was leaning over me. I was in bed.

'Do you have any idea what you've put us through?'

She was angry. Jabbing her finger when she spoke. Crutches leaning against her chair. And she'd been crying as well.

What have I done now?

Right: deep breath, collect the evidence. Harder than usual. My eyesight was fuzzy, like a TV with a weak signal. I blinked – *nothing* – then scrunched my face trying to tune the picture in. Then I shook my head. Big mistake. It was pounding, as though my brain were trying to fight its way out.

Focus, Patricia. What do you see?

It wasn't my room. I knew that. Too big and the wrong colour. And too bright as well. No wonder I couldn't keep my eyes open. And who were the other people? They were in white and blue.

Memories of visiting Mum at Mayday came flooding back.

Nurses. Doctors.

I was in hospital. But why? I arched my head left. There was machinery as far as I could see. It was like being in an episode of *The Six Million Dollar Man*. Mum was staring at me, waiting for an answer. I didn't know anything. Normally I would have worked it out by now. This time I was stuck. I knew I was in a hospital bed and I knew I was hooked up to some scary-looking equipment. Something was wrong. But that was as far as it went. Whatever Mum was mad about I'd have to work out later. At the moment she knew more than me.

I needed to tell her something – even if it was just my usual 'I don't know' – so I cleared my throat.

Ouch!

It was as though someone had set light to my chest. Searing, hot pain coursed from my lungs up into my mouth. I had to cough to clear it but that just made the fiery pain worse.

What the hell are these machines doing to me? I wondered angrily. Instinctively I pulled my head away. I needed to escape. *They're burning me inside.*

A woman appeared next to me. She didn't look angry like Mum but she wasn't smiling either.

'Relax, Kim, just take it easy.'

As she spoke she reached over to check a cable running from the machines – into my arm. I was plugged in! I hadn't noticed. There was a clear tube coming out of my left hand. I panicked for the first time and tried to scratch it off.

'Stop that, Kim!' the woman said. Her voice had changed now, from calming to firm. She grabbed my hands and separated them.

'Listen to the nurse,' Mum's voice reasoned. 'You've done enough damage.'

I looked up at the woman and finally she smiled.

'You need to rest,' she explained, her voice warm again. 'Don't speak if you can help it. You've been through a lot.'

I nodded but with my head flat on my pillow the movement was almost imperceptible. It was enough for the nurse. She checked something else on the machines, dabbed a cloth on my forehead and stood back.

'She'll be in pain for a while,' she said, obviously addressing my mother. 'Don't rush her. She'll speak when she's ready.'

Thank you, nurse, I thought. She had bought me some time.

But still I was none the wiser. Why was I here? What had happened to me?

And why did Mum look like she wanted to kill me?

I began to search for the jigsaw pieces, starting as usual with the edges. What was the last thing I remembered? Being at home. Before that it had been school. What had happened to me in the interim? Maybe I'd fallen, tripped down the stairs, or become sick. I flexed my foot and felt my toes respond. As far as I could make out, there was nothing physically wrong with me. It was just my throbbing head, sore eyes and burning throat.

No good, I thought. *I haven't got a clue what's going on.*

Before I'd just panicked. Now I felt scared. Piecing things together was part of my life. It was just routine, something I did naturally. Something I thought we all did daily. Normally it gave me answers. This time I was scratching my head. The few things I could deduce didn't bode well. I was in hospital, in pain. After the year our family had endured, that was the last place I felt safe. When Dad had gone in they'd removed half his stomach. Mum had been in agony for ages while she was stitched up after her accident. And most recently, of course, Nan had been taken there.

I needed to get out but that couldn't happen until I knew what was wrong – or what they thought was wrong – with me.

I don't know how much time passed. When I looked again Mum wasn't there. The nurse – or was it a different one? – was clearing away some equipment. I studied it for clues. It was all pretty nondescript apart from one thing: a long, black tube. It reminded me of an old torture device I'd seen during history at school. I couldn't imagine what place it had being in a hospital.

The nurse noticed me watching her.

'Oh, you're awake?' she said cheerily.

I think I grunted something like 'yes' and nodded again. The pain in my neck was still there but I had more mobility this time. But after that I was silent, desperately fishing for information. I'd learnt that the less you said, the more others filled the gaps. Most people can't stand silence.

'I hope you won't be so silly again,' she went on. 'You might not be so lucky next time.'

Silly? Next time? Lucky? What was she talking about?

'What's that thing for?' I pointed at the tube.

'This is the thing that saved your life, that's what it is.'

Still none the wiser. 'What does it do?'

Without breaking her stride the nurse explained, 'It's what we use to pump the stomachs of naughty girls who have eaten things they shouldn't have.'

'Oh,' I said. Then I realised she was talking about me.

'Is that why my throat is on fire?'

She laughed. Gallows humour, I think they call it. 'Your throat and plenty else I imagine. I really hope you never have to have it done again.'

She left the room and I watched her go. She'd seemed nice enough and I guess she'd wanted me to get better. But the only word in my head was, 'Liar!' I'd never heard so many lies in my life. The more I thought about it the angrier I got.

How dare they do this to me! I should call the police. Doctors can't go around shoving pipes down kids' throats for no reason. Why didn't Dad and Mum stop it?

What was it the nurse had said? 'Naughty girls who have eaten things they shouldn't have'. That was it. What did she mean by that?

What had I eaten? If anything, I was hungry; starving in fact. I felt like I hadn't touched a crumb for days.

I determined to have it out with her next time she came in but I must have fallen asleep first. The next thing I remember is Mum being back again. She was wearing different clothes. She must have gone home to change.

'Why did you do it?' she asked again.

'Do what?' I replied.

She rolled her eyes and sighed.

'No one can help you if you don't tell the truth.'

God, it was worse than being sent to the headmaster's office. Why were people always accusing me of things I hadn't done? It was so unfair.

'I am telling the truth,' I insisted. 'What did I do?'

'There's no helping you, is there?'

And that was her last word on the matter. She spoke about other stuff, like school friends who'd asked about me, messages from family, gossip from the street. That kind of thing. But she refused to be drawn on the reason for my being there. That was a mystery I would have to unravel without her.

Where do I start?

Suddenly I was at home. I closed my eyes in the hospital and woke up in my own bed. I didn't question it. I often found myself waking up when I couldn't remember going to sleep. There was nothing out of the ordinary about that. The only question on my mind was why I had been attacked by the doctors like that. It still hurt to swallow and the idea of eating anything made my stomach turn.

Nan wasn't happy to see me home. She kept saying I'd betrayed her. I couldn't work out why. That was horrible enough. Then I saw her have a row with Dad. Nan was shouting, 'They were mine, she had no right taking them!' and Dad was yelling, 'You should be more careful where you leave these things!' It was worse than watching him argue with Mum.

Speaking of Mum, she pretty much ignored me for a while. It was as if our hospital chats had never happened.

The worst thing about being home was the nightmares. Bedtimes were bad enough generally but each night I'd wake, sitting bolt upright, thinking of some hideous half memory. I had no idea what was triggering the response but the result was the same each night. Sometimes Dad called out to me to shut up. Other times Lorraine came rushing in or Mum's voice drifted up from the front room. Was I all right? What was going on?

I was fine, but as for what was happening to me, I had no idea.

After a few days' recuperation at home Mum decided I was well enough to go back to school. I was actually grateful. The atmosphere at home between Mum and Dad wasn't great. Mum was still sleeping downstairs even though her leg was a lot better. Maybe she wasn't in a hurry to get back up with Dad.

Breathing too heavily still felt like sandpaper on my lungs so I took it easy that first day back at school. As soon as my friends saw me I was bombarded by attention – and questions.

'Are you all right?'

'What were you in for?'

'Did you have an operation?'

'I heard it was your heart.'

I batted them all away as best I could.

'I'm fine. It was nothing. Just a check-up.'

Nobody swallowed that. I'd been away too long. The majority of people quickly lost interest, though. Those that didn't were just annoyed by the obvious lie.

'We're your friends. You can tell us.'

Still I kept my own counsel. What was I meant to do? I didn't have a clue what had happened. All I could say for sure was that the doctors had kidnapped me and performed some sort of illegal operation. I couldn't understand why my parents weren't kicking up more of a fuss. Look how Mum had exploded when I tore my tights at school.

Then the mood started to turn. My friends didn't believe my story. Whispers started doing the rounds. I was a liar. I had secrets. No one would be my friend.

Then they pulled out the big guns.

'I heard she tried to kill herself.'

'At one point she was technically dead.'

'School drove her to it.'

'She's just an attention seeker.'

It seemed that everyone had an opinion. Some of the rumours were obviously flights of fancy. Some of them were just plain vicious – complete strangers were passing the gossip on to me by accident and it was getting worse with every telling. The consensus, however, was that I was a liar. And completely mental.

Just what I need.

One by one my friends began to drift away, even though

I swore nothing had gone on. I don't remember many conversations with anyone after that. Everywhere I went, though, there was the sight of people turning away from me, accompanied by that unmistakeable sound of a conversation halted as soon as you enter the room. It was incredibly unsettling. When I needed my friends more than ever to help me through the weird hospital experience, this was what I was faced with.

What's their problem? How would they like it?

Facts didn't come into it. Yes, I'd seen the black tube used, so the nurse claimed, to pump my stomach. Yes, my nan had told me to steer clear of her medication. And, yes, everyone was speaking as though I'd popped handfuls of pills. But I knew I hadn't. It didn't matter what anyone said. I knew it was all lies.

And then a fortnight later it started all over again ...

'I thought we'd seen the last of you.'

The voice was familiar. I opened my eyes. No, I must have been mistaken. I'd never seen this elegant-looking woman before in my life.

Her eyes were fixed on mine, waiting for them to open and focus on her. I couldn't place her mood. She just looked sad.

'You can't go on like this,' she said softly. 'We've got to sort you out.'

I went to say something but there was an explosion of pain in my chest.

Oh, God, I'm back here again.

Panicking, I flashed a look around me. The machines were there. The plug was in my hand. It was a different room – similar but subtly different in ways you notice when you've got nothing to do but stare at the walls for days – but it was in the same place. I'd been dragged back to Mayday Hospital. I was on Ward 1. They'd hurt me again.

And they were blaming me.

I thought, *I've got to get out. These people are going to kill me.*

I scrambled around the bed. Where were my clothes?

'Come on, Kim, you know you can't get up yet.'

The woman's tone wasn't that of a stranger. I stared at her for what seemed like ages, waiting for a jigsaw piece to drop into place. Nothing came. I didn't know her.

But she seemed to know me.

'Are you ready to talk this time?' she asked.

'Talk about what?' I spluttered, chest sore as hell.

'Well, for a start, about why you did it this time? You know I can't help you if you don't tell me what's wrong.'

I shrugged. Whoever this woman was, she was acting as though we knew each other. Usually I'd go along with it but as far as I was concerned, being treated like a medical experiment changed the rules.

'Do I know you?' I asked quietly.

'Oh, Kim,' she sighed. 'What are we going to do with you?'

I didn't reply. The woman came closer. She looked like she was considering her next words. Eventually she said, 'Okay, have it your way. I'm Dr Picton-Jones, your psychiatrist, as you well know.'

Psychiatrist?

'I'm the person charged with finding out what's driving your behaviour,' she continued, 'and trying to keep you out of the asylum.'

Asylum?

'What – like nuthouse?'

I completely forgot the pain in my chest. Panic over-whelmed me and I felt myself actually break out in sweat. I swear I could hear my heart pounding double-time. Asylum? This was all getting out of hand.

'Look, I don't know why you're keeping me here. I need to go home.'

'Of course you do,' the doctor smiled, 'and believe me, there's nothing more I would like to see than you go home – and stay there. But you seem to enjoy coming back here, don't you? So, do you want to tell me why?'

Glaring at her, I shook my head. This doctor's nice words didn't count for anything. She was still telling the same lies as the rest of them.

They must have drugged me in hospital. I don't remember Dr Picton-Jones leaving. The next thing I recall is Mum being there.

'Look,' she said firmly, 'the doctors here want to have you sectioned. Do you know what that means?'

'No.'

'It means they lock you up in the loony bin and throw away the key.'

'Why would they do that to me?'

Mum didn't know whether to laugh or shout. In the end she did a bit of both. 'Why do you think? To stop you trying any more of this nonsense again!'

'What nonsense?' I yelled. 'Why won't anyone tell me?'

Mum's smile faded. Suddenly she looked like she was going to cry. I really didn't want to see that.

'I just want to come home,' I said quietly.

Mum nodded but she still seemed sad. She explained that Dr Picton-Jones was fighting for my rights in the hospital. Standard procedure was to have me packed off to somewhere like Warlingham Park, a scary-sounding Victorian mental institution. The doctor was doing everything she could to keep me out of there. 'It's no place for a child,' she said.

There were two ways of keeping me out of there, Mum went on. One was to not try to hurt myself again.

'Do you think you can manage that?'

I felt like screaming again. 'Of course I can! Who would want to hurt themselves? The only people hurting me are the doctors in this place!'

Mum sighed as she pulled on her coat to leave. She seemed resigned to events, I could tell that, even if I didn't know what those events were.

What I did know for sure is that she was swallowing the lies the hospital was telling about me.

According to the nurses' chart at the foot of my bed I was in for almost a week. I remember being there for about two days. Possibly three. Even then I was only conscious for a couple of hours at a time. They must have been keeping me on some pretty fierce pills.

Speaking of pills, when discharge day came again, this time they packed me off with a prescription of little blue tablets.

'These are for your nightmares.'

'What nightmares?' I couldn't help asking. Yes, I suffered bad dreams – but how did she know that? I'd never told a soul.

The nurse exhaled heavily, her patience already

exhausted. That was unfair, I thought. I'd never even seen her before. *She could at least talk to me civilly.*

Seriously though, what nightmares? I'd never discussed any dreams with a living soul. Certainly no one who had access to black pipes.

'Take one a day,' she continued professionally. 'They'll aid your sleeping.'

'Fine.'

Back home that night, with Nan standing over me, I tentatively opened the packet and popped a little blue oval into my mouth. I don't know what I was expecting but that was pretty much the last thing I remembered. The next night it was the same pattern. Tablet, water, knock-out. I still didn't know what all the talk of nightmares was but, I thought, *If these things can stop the hospital dragging me back in I'll keep taking them.*

If that's what it took to keep them happy, then okay, I could play that game.

It didn't work out like that. A week or two drifted by and then once again I found myself staring up at the same pastel ceiling, my throat feeling like a flood of lava had passed recently along it.

Back to square one.

The doctors this time exuded a wearied air like they'd seen it all before. I didn't recognise most of them but once again they seemed to know me – or know of me. There were plenty of heated discussions at the foot of my bed. One would argue this, another would suggest that. I just lay with my eyes closed, pretending to be asleep, but straining to hear every word. It wasn't easy listening. They couldn't have been more impersonal if they'd been talking about some insect on a medical student's dissecting table. And they really didn't seem to like me. Why else would they conjure up these lies?

'It's just attention-seeking,' one said.

'Picton-Jones says there must be a problem at home.'

'The only problem is her. She enjoys causing a fuss.'

'Well, the girl says she'll do it again if we discharge her.'

'She's manipulative. I for one suggest we don't give in to her blackmail.'

'So we're sending her home.'

'Of course. Agreed?'

'Agreed.'

And that was it. I couldn't tell if they shook hands but it sounded like they were agreeing on a price for a head of cattle. Not deciding on a terrified girl's future.

At least they helped me on one matter. Dr Picton-Jones had disagreed with them, it seemed. Perhaps she really was on my side. *Maybe she's not like the others,* I thought. *I'll make more effort next time.*

That next time came quicker than I hoped. Or so it seemed. Keeping track of time was never my strongest suit. I was beginning to see that. In any case, the way the hospital kept me brimmed full of drugs everything was so hazy. Then Dr Picton-Jones appeared at my bedside on discharge day. She was with another woman, a smart-looking blonde who gave a little wave when I looked at her. I smiled back.

'This is Miss Kerfoot,' the doctor said, after introducing me to the stranger. 'She's a social worker. You might also say she's the last throw of the dice as far as this hospital is concerned.'

More gobbledegook that meant nothing to me. I tried to

look impressed. If this woman was a friend of my only ally in Mayday then she deserved the benefit of the doubt.

'Miss Kerfoot will be assessing your home environment,' Dr Picton-Jones went on.

'What for?' I blurted out. Ally or not, I couldn't help it. 'There's nothing wrong with my home.'

'Then it shouldn't take very long to sort out, should it?'

Miss Kerfoot just stood there, still smiling. She seemed genuine enough. She explained she'd be popping round in the next few days to see how I was. It was her job to look for symptoms that weren't necessarily medical. Once again, more jargon I couldn't interpret. So I nodded, and I smiled. Anything to speed the process up and get me home.

The next time I saw Miss Kerfoot was at home. I came downstairs at about five o'clock and she was just there, sitting at the dining table surrounded by files and paperwork. I had no idea how long she'd been around. She must have spoken to Mum and Dad but by the time I entered the room Dad had scarpered and Mum was in a silent fury. Whatever had been discussed hadn't pleased her one bit. I didn't think much about it.

'It's you I've really come to talk to,' Miss Kerfoot said, unfazed by my sudden arrival. I sat down opposite her and she asked me how I was, how I felt about my sister's break-up, my dad's illness, Mum's accident and Nan's stroke. I answered as best I could. They all made me sad.

'Have you cried about them?'

I shook my head.

She nodded and made a note in one of the files spread across the table.

I was vaguely aware, while we were talking, that the noises from the kitchen were getting increasingly louder. Pots were being crashed, pans thumped down onto the worktop and plates thrown around. That was unlike Mum. She was careful and considerate. Normally. But not today.

Then the penny dropped.

As far as Mum was concerned, strangers had no business poking their noses where they weren't wanted. She must have hated this social worker being there. As a family we preferred to keep things to ourselves. That was our strength, in Mum's eyes. After all, these were the people who hadn't even told me when Dad had walked out.

I found myself raising my voice just to be heard by Miss Kerfoot. I wasn't particularly thrilled by her being there either but at least she said she wanted to help me.

'All I want is to stop you going back into that hospital,' she assured me.

Hallelujah for that.

'But what can you do about it?'

Before she could answer, Mum came bustling out to set the table for dinner. Before Miss Kerfoot had a chance to move any of her things Mum flicked the tablecloth and threw it down over the whole table – covering box files, note pads, pens, everything – then slammed cutlery down in front of the pair of us. Miss Kerfoot's face was a picture. She had a knife balancing on top of a folder and a fork mounted on what looked like a book but it could have been her glasses case.

'Well, I . . .' she began, but there were no words. What could anyone say?

Both of us stunned into silence, our guest carefully folded

back the cover and retrieved her things. While Mum carried on bustling around the kitchen as though nothing had happened, Miss Kerfoot didn't take her eyes off her. Only when she was ready to leave did she take me to one side.

'I should warn you, I'm going to recommend getting you out of here,' she said.

'Why? This is my home.'

She smiled. *That's her 'nice' smile,* I thought. *Her sympathetic one is probably the same.*

'I don't know what the reasons are, but this is not a healthy atmosphere to be living in. I think you need time away.'

'What atmosphere? What are you talking about?'

'Your parents don't have a civil word for each other. They make no attempt to hide it when you or Lorraine are in the house. Everyone's obviously struggling to cope with your father's illness, your mother's accident and now your grandmother. And then there's your sister's marriage problems.'

I shrugged. It didn't sound good when she put it like that. But they were still my parents. The only ones I knew. Their behaviour was what I was used to. I wished they'd get on better but it didn't bother me. I was like this, they were like that. That's the way it was. The only thing I cared about was learning why the hospital kept kidnapping me and subjecting me to God knows what.

According to the medical reports and various hearsay assessments from my friends, the reason I kept being admitted into hospital was for treatment for pill overdoses. Dad had stacks of distalgesic tucked away and, he'd told the doctors, I was downing them by the handful.

Utter rubbish.

I didn't know why he would make up something like that or why the hospital would believe him. I didn't dare question him about it. He obviously had his reasons.

Later that night I wondered whether the social worker was right. Maybe I should get out. But where would a fourteen-year-old go? It was completely impractical. I suppose if Lorraine was still with her husband I could have moved in with them. As it was, I had no options. I was stuck at home. Stuck with all the lies. I wasn't going anywhere.

I just have to make the best of it.

Soon I discovered the decision wasn't mine to make.

CHAPTER SIX

You're in the system now

Ken opened his eyes and automatically blinked in the sunshine. The warm breath of the wind in his hair felt good. He felt like staying there all day.

But where was 'there'?

Didn't matter. It felt good.

He was sitting on something hard, possibly concrete, probably a wall or something similar. He could feel that without even looking. His hands, planted beside him for support, pressed against the rough painted brick surface. His legs swung free over the side of the bench or block, or whatever he was sitting on. That's all he could tell. After that he was lost, fresh out of ideas, but in no hurry to find out. The breeze on his face felt so good.

One more moment, he promised himself. Then I'll get up.

Ken had things to do. He always had things to do and so little time to do them in. Where did the time go?, he found himself wondering.

He enjoyed the quiet warmth of his solitude for another few seconds, then, prepared for the glare this time, opened his eyes into a careful squint.

And then he nearly fainted.

Directly opposite him was the middle section of a block of flats. He *was level with floor six or seven. Between him and it there was nothing but air. No road, no path, no walls, no glass.*

Ken looked down, then left and right. His mind was spinning. Why hadn't he worked it out? He was perched precariously over a ledge at the top of a multi-storey car park. The ledge was no deeper than two bricks. It was designed to keep people in. At shoulder height, it should have done the trick. What the hell was he doing balanced dangerously on top of it, legs dangling sixty or so feet above the ground? Gasping for air, he guided his fingertips until they found the back of the wall, then he dug his nails in for dear life. It wouldn't stop him falling but he felt better. He had to do something. After all, one sudden movement and the rest of him could follow his feet over the side.

Ken suddenly remembered luxuriating in the spring breeze on his face a few seconds earlier.

What if I'd leant forwards and not back?

It didn't bear thinking about. His stomach was churning fast enough as it was.

Ken attempted to edge himself backwards. The obvious thing to do was swing his legs back up but the ledge was so narrow he was afraid the momentum would topple him in the other direction. But he couldn't just sit there. A big gust of wind and he could be blown over. And in any case, who knew how strong this wall was? After a few nail-biting seconds he leant back as far as he dared over the car park floor and let himself fall. No sooner had he begun moving than his legs were able to swing upwards. He grabbed the top of the wall with both hands and lowered himself to safety.

For a minute or so he couldn't move. He just stayed there, hands and face pressed against the wall, covered in sweat and his heart threatening to burst through his shirt.

Why had he been there? What on Earth had he been thinking of?
One false move and that would have been the end of Ken.

He shook his head. It wasn't the oddest thing that had happened
to him but it was the most dangerous.

Ah well, he thought, it's over now, no harm done, and slowly
he walked away, past the parked cars and unsuspecting shoppers. He
couldn't waste his time in a multi-storey car park.

Ken had things to do.

Nobody told me anything. That was the story of my life. Friends didn't tell me where they were going. Teachers didn't tell me what homework had been assigned. Mum didn't always call me for dinner. And no one told me when, why or how I kept ending up in Mayday Hospital surrounded by medics talking about stomach pump procedures. Completely out of the blue, it felt like I was trapped in a nightmare. I couldn't help thinking, *In a moment I will wake up and everything will be all right.*

But every time I woke up things were just as bad. If anything, they were getting worse.

Mum had made perfectly clear her feelings on the whole involvement of social workers in our family business. In her eyes I'd brought shame on the family. She was more interested in what the neighbours thought than solving any problem. Dad did what she said or nothing at all. The less time they spent in each other's company the better. I didn't mind. Anything for a quiet life. That was our family motto.

Neither of them spoke to me about the hospital visits. It was as if they were pretending nothing had happened – even though it kept happening. Dad did what he could but his main contribution was accusing me of taking his pills. Day after day it was the same stuck record.

'What were you thinking, taking my distalgesics? They're dangerous, Kim. When will you learn?'

'I haven't touched your distalgesics.'

That was normally enough to shut him up. He hated confrontation, even with me. Unfortunately that also meant there was no way he would take the hospital to task, I knew that, not even when they were kidnapping me every other week for God knows what reason. Neither he nor Mum seemed to have any interest in helping me cope or trying to stop the stomach pumps happening. Why not? Why wouldn't they step in? It was as if they were blaming me.

I realised I had never felt so alone in my life.

School was going from bad to worse as well. In class I struggled to keep up. I would stare at the blackboard, then at my textbook, then at my friends, then back at the board, all the while absolutely nothing sinking in. What did the chalk words mean? Why was I on a different page to my friends? How come everyone knew what to write and not me?

It was as though I'd missed the lesson where we were taught how to do it. It wasn't just the time I missed being in hospital. Some lessons I had every day . . .

There was always the option of raising my hand. Experience told me that never went well. This time I went for it.

'I don't understand, Miss,' I ventured bravely.

'Well, perhaps if you weren't talking all through my lesson you'd follow it a little better.'

'I wasn't talking, Miss,' I claimed. Immediately, though, I

knew that was a mistake. I could see the hackles rise on the back of her neck.

The worst thing about school was the time I spent in the orange room. I seemed to spend half my time in there for no reason. I was always finding myself incarcerated from morning till home time. And always for the same reason: absolutely nothing at all.

Every time I discovered myself there it felt like another punch in the stomach. Another twist of the knife.

Why were they doing this to me? What had I done wrong? They were as bad as the doctors. How were they allowed to get away with it?

I knew kids who bullied other pupils – even when they were grassed up they didn't get punished like me. I'd seen students do unspeakable things in class and not get half the orange room time that was always being dished out to me. How were teachers allowed to lock me up so indiscriminately? What had I ever done to them? Surely there was a law against it?

I don't know if they were related but after my first hospital sentence I seemed to spend more time in the orange room than ever. That was all I needed. Subjected against my will to unfathomable experiments at the hands of NHS psychos, then no sooner had I recovered enough to go back to school, thrown in this tangerine prison.

I know it happened a lot because Mum mentioned it once at home. She must have been sent a letter. I tried to tell her I was victimised but she wasn't interested.

'You're lucky they don't throw you out,' she said. 'And then what will you do?'

If I'm honest, other kids seemed to hate it more than me.

My friends said it drove them mad staring at those four satsuma-coloured walls all day. I never experienced that. For me it felt like I was in and out in no time. I certainly didn't spend the day reflecting on my misdemeanours, if that's what they were hoping for. Not only did I have nothing to apologise for, I didn't even remember leaving half the time, although obviously I did.

I could have coped if I'd deserved to be there. If I park on a double yellow line today, I don't like it when I get a ticket but I accept it was my fault. It would be a different story if I hadn't parked illegally and I still got the fine. Any punishment is exacerbated when you don't deserve it. An eye for an eye didn't come into it when I was growing up. As far as I was concerned I had been the victim of bullying all my school life. Not by pupils. By teachers, by the head, by the system.

That sense of injustice continued outside school. All adults seemed to have it in for me, whether I was at work, in class or shopping with friends. Worst of all, though, was the treatment I was subjected to in hospital. If it happened outside Mayday you'd call it torture. How else would you describe being drugged then invaded by coarse hosepipes? Being flushed out by water and saline? That's what they told me they were doing and I believed them – I had the scars every time to prove it. How else would you account for the days of pain, the enforced imprisonment and – most unpleasant – those sneering faces of doctors accusing me of scheming for my own reward?

What reward was that? What could I possibly gain from putting myself through that hell?

Not all of the faces were so bad, I have to admit. Some of the nurses said nice things to me, I suppose, although I knew they were the ones who'd dragged me there in the first place so that didn't count. It didn't matter what they said. Dr Picton-Jones and Miss Kerfoot, the social worker, were the only ones who seemed to be on my side consistently even if I didn't enjoy hearing some of the things they said. That didn't matter. I would work everything out for myself. Then I would show them.

Before I could do anything, however, I found myself face to face with the doctor once more.

It's happened again!

That was the first thing I thought when I looked up and saw her face. She looked like she'd been talking to me. I must have been asleep. Couldn't she tell? But I was here now. I looked around. I was on Ward 1 at Mayday. That much was obvious. That's why the doctor was here – Ward 1's other name was the 'psychiatric ward'. I didn't think there was a bed on the dormitory I hadn't been in.

I tuned into what the doctor was saying. It was the same old guff about trying to understand why I do things.

Here we go again.

'What things?' I asked.

'You know very well. Why do you keep overdosing on your grandmother's pills, and now your father's medication as well?'

Overdose?

I desperately wanted to shout out: 'I don't! It's a lie.' I really needed to tell her, 'They keep bringing me here and torturing me with that pipe. They're experimenting on me for something. I don't know what but they'll say anything to keep me here. You've got to stop them!' I had it all planned.

'You're wrong, you know,' I announced defiantly. 'I haven't tried to kill myself.'

The doctor smiled and her whole face lit up.

'I know you haven't,' she said calmly.

'But you just said I had.'

'No, I said you took several drugs overdoses, each of which could have killed you. But I know that on each occasion you told someone what you'd done. If you'd really wanted to commit suicide you'd have kept it to yourself.'

I don't know how long I stared at her. I was having trouble trying to compute her words. Overdoses, suicide attempts and now non-suicide attempts. What the hell was she talking about? How was I the one on the psychiatric ward when she was coming out with stories like that? If anyone there needed help it was her.

I resolved to get out of Mayday as soon as the doctor's back was turned. I just needed to slip my shoes on and I could be out of there in seconds. *I don't know where I'll go but it's got to be better than here.*

It was as if Dr Picton-Jones read my mind.

'You'll be leaving here soon enough, Kim,' she said kindly.

That knocked a bit of wind out of my sails. *There goes the element of surprise . . .*

'But I'm afraid I've got some bad news.'

I shrugged. *Worse than being incarcerated here?* I couldn't see how.

I was wrong.

Before Dr Picton-Jones could reveal all, Miss Kerfoot the social worker came down to join us. We exchanged hellos and how are yous. Obviously I said, 'Fine, thank you,' despite feeling anything but. Then the doctor explained, 'I was just about to inform Kim where she'll be going from here.'

'What do you mean where?' I asked. 'I'm going straight home.'

'Not any more,' Miss Kerfoot said. 'That's not working for you, is it?'

'It's fine!'

'Well, we can't keep having you back in here every other week, can we? One of these days you're not going to be so lucky.'

I wasn't even listening properly by then. Not going home? What were they talking about?

Miss Kerfoot was giving me her best supportive face. I recognised it from her collection of sympathetic expressions. 'The doctor's done her best to keep you out for as long as possible,' she said, 'but you haven't been helping yourself. So I'm afraid you've left us with no choice. There's a bed for you at Warlingham Park.'

The doctor nodded. 'That's why Miss Kerfoot's here. She's going to help you pack your bags. I'm afraid you're in the system now.'

CHAPTER SEVEN

Lights out!

Hayley watched the woman's lips move. The words sounded English but they may as well have been a foreign language. She understood what they meant all too well. What Hayley didn't understand was why she was telling her.

'This is a secure unit,' the woman was saying. 'You'll be monitored twenty-four hours a day. You'll be escorted to the toilet where you'll go under supervised conditions and you'll not be allowed a bath until further notice.' She picked up a small pile of paper. 'And oh,' she added, 'you'll be wearing a paper gown for the first week or two. After that, if you're really good, we might let you have one with pockets.'

'Supervised', 'baths', 'pockets'? Hayley had had enough.

'What is this place?' she demanded.

The woman laughed, walked over to the door and closed it behind her. A second later a small metal panel in the door slid back and she stared through the gap.

'For the umpteenth time, it's Warlingham Park. But you can call it home.'

I magine being dropped onto a film set and the director has just called 'Action!' The scenery is in place, the props are

ready and everyone around you suddenly starts moving. The
spotlight hits you, you're the star.

But you've forgotten your lines.

I've lost count of how many times I felt like that. The last
thing I remembered was speaking to Miss Kerfoot and Dr
Picton-Jones. It seemed like a second later to me but they were
nowhere to be seen. In fact, Mayday Hospital had disappeared.
I wasn't in Kansas any more.

I didn't panic. I did what I always did: played detective.

What can I see?

*Nothing. Four dark walls. No windows. Worse than the orange
room. No furniture apart from a grey, metal bed fixed to the
floor.*

Am I in prison?

I rushed over to the closed door. Where was the handle?
How am I meant to open it without a handle? I pushed it –
nothing. Then again, harder. The door didn't budge. It was
made of metal and from the dull thuds I was making, pretty
thick.

I'm trapped.

Suddenly short of air. *Prison or not, I have to get out.*

I banged on the door with my fists, faster and harder until
I thought my knuckles would break.

'Come on! Open the door! Let me out!'

I was screaming now, aware that my voice had no echo
in this weird room, and genuinely terrified. There's nothing
worse than the claustrophobia of a locked door. I was desperate
now for some air. I was going to faint.

Suddenly a small rectangular window, about eye level,
appeared. A man's face was peering in.

'What's all the fuss, Noble?' he said. 'I've told you: it's solitary for you for another twenty-four hours.'

Now where was I? How did I get out of the cell? It didn't matter. I was just grateful to have escaped. But where had I escaped to?

Okay, I'm at a table, a large round one, shared with seven other people, all grown-ups. We're in a big room. Four or five identical tables. Fuddy-duddy décor in a really bad state.

There was a plate of grey food in front of me, half eaten.

Obviously a rundown canteen of some description, or a restaurant, but one I didn't recognise. I couldn't see any waiters so I couldn't check their uniforms. The windows weren't any help either. All I could see outside were trees and bushes.

What else?

The smell. There was something more pungent than the aroma from a kitchen. What was it? Then I realised. It was wee. The air reeked of old, rancid wee. I couldn't tell if it was coming from the carpet, from the chairs or from the diners themselves. Horrible. I pushed my plate away in disgust. There was no way I could eat now. Not in that room.

What is this place? Am I in an old people's home?

That couldn't be right. It just couldn't. The people on my table, though, were much older than me.

Anything else?

The noise! The more I concentrated on piecing my jigsaw together, the harder it became because of the raucous din. I hadn't noticed at first. It was the sound of fifty people talking at once – and nobody listening. I could make bits and pieces out. Some of it wasn't in English. Some of it didn't even sound like real words. One man was howling – not crying – literally howling as though he were trying to summon a wolf. Others sounded in distress. Angry, sad, upset, happy. Every emotion going was thrown in the mix. Every emotion, that is, except one.

The one that was slowly creeping up on me.

Fear.

I genuinely had no idea where I was. All I could think of was Dr Picton-Jones's chilling words: 'You're in the system now.'

I looked again around my table. For adults some of them had appalling manners. Some were dribbling, some were playing with their food, some were spraying it everywhere. I wasn't in McDonald's.

They've done it. They've put me in the nuthouse!

I felt my blood run cold.

I scanned the room. No one was walking around. I didn't dare stand up. But how did I get there? Had they drugged me? And how long had I been there? No one was taking a bit of notice of me. That's not how you treat a newcomer. Whether it's school, Brownies or a job, you normally get shown around on your first day. From what I could tell everyone was pretty comfortable with my being there. Which meant I'd been there some time.

How was that even possible?

What are they doing to my mind?

Actually, not everyone was comfortable with my being there. There must have been a cue to leave the table, which I missed, because suddenly half a dozen people leapt up and starting meandering around. They didn't exactly look like they had anywhere to go but they didn't want to be seated either. A few were shaking. One man's tongue lolled from his mouth like a chewing camel. Some shuffled. The only person who looked like she had a mission was a large, middle-aged woman. I couldn't help staring as she marched purposefully past my table. She must have noticed. She spun round and shouted in my face, 'My son! What have you done with my son?'

I nearly fell off my chair in fright. I honestly thought she was going to punch me.

I managed to splurt out, 'I haven't seen your son, sorry,' but she wouldn't take no for an answer.

'You've seen him, I know you've seen him. Where is he?'

I looked frantically around the room for help. No one came. I couldn't see anyone in a uniform among the scruffy throng. There was certainly no one looking like they were about to step in to save me.

'I haven't seen him, I promise.' My voice was barely audible now. It didn't matter. The woman wasn't listening anyway.

'You don't like black people, do you?' she said, leaning in towards me. Whether it was meant menacingly or not, that's how I interpreted it. That's how anyone would have responded.

The woman was so close I couldn't catch my breath to scream. I could barely think.

She's off her trolley.

That was obvious. But the problem was: how far off her trolley was she? Was she aggressive? Was it going to escalate? The woman was angry and twice my size – at least. I didn't stand a chance.

Just as I thought she was about to hit me, she took a step back and sneered, 'You've never seen a black arse before, have you?'

A black what?

Before I had even processed what she'd meant, the woman just pulled her pants down and shoved her backside in my face. I was literally pinned to the edge of the table by her big, fat bum. It sounds funny now. I'm smiling remembering it. But not back then. At that moment, at fourteen years of age, I'd never felt so threatened in my life. And never so dirty. It was absolutely terrifying. Absolutely humiliating. And, for all I knew, absolutely a sign of things to come.

Eventually a man in white appeared and escorted away the woman he called Sadie, still pulling her knickers back up, still shouting to the world that I'd stolen her son. No one asked me if I was all right. No one apologised. No one took any notice of me at all.

A sickening realisation hit me: if no one bats an eyelid then her behaviour must be par for the course. On the plus side, at least she'd confirmed something: I had been sent to a proper asylum.

Now I just need to get out.

'Five minutes to lights out!'

What?

A woman, dressed in the same pale staff uniform I'd just seen, was standing by the door. But it wasn't the canteen door. It was a different room entirely.

Where am I now?

I was standing next to a bed. I was in a room full of them, six going along one wall and another half dozen facing them. It looked like a hospital ward but the walls were pink, not sterile white. And there were no machines. I guessed it was a dormitory. My heart sank.

I'm still in the nuthouse.

Most of the other beds had people in them or next to them. They were all adults. Most were older than my mother, some of them older than Nan. The stench of wee was even worse than before. And the noise – it still didn't make any sense. There were only a few of them talking now but I couldn't make out a word they were saying.

That was the least of my worries, though. What was I meant to be doing? Was this my bed? Was I meant to be getting in? You can't always take these things for granted. Not with women like Sadie on the loose.

Sadie!

Just thinking of her made me sweat. Where was she?

No sign of her here.

For a moment I missed the security of the cell. At least I was safe there.

The beds were all set out exactly the same with a little wardrobe and a chest of drawers either side. Apart from the one next to me, they all seemed to be spoken for, which was a good sign. Gingerly I opened the wardrobe door, half expecting to be shouted at any second. Empty. I was expecting my clothes.

I stopped. That wasn't a good sign.

Then another thought flitted into my head. *How long have I been wearing this paper robe?*

Why had I just noticed? I was wearing underwear and this stupid gown made of some sort of thick, wrinkly paper. It was like a cut-price princess dressing-up costume. Now I'd noticed it, suddenly I couldn't get over how uncomfortable it was. Really scratchy, against my skin and my neck.

Most people were wearing normal clothes. A few had out-
fits just like mine except for one difference. They were made of
fabric. Exact replicas but obviously a lot more comfortable. It
didn't make sense.

Why me? Why am I the odd one out?

Again.

'Lights out!'

The woman was back. *Was that five minutes already?* I
realised everyone else was tucked up so I climbed into what I
hoped was my bed. The woman said, 'Goodnight, ladies' and
the room was plunged into darkness. As my eyes adjusted I
could make out her silhouette framed by the doorway, but that
was it. Then the door clicked shut and I heard the turn of a key.

Locked in!

But who with?

If I'd been scared before I was petrified now. It wasn't just
the darkness, although that didn't help. I just felt lost, abandoned. Why was I here? How long had I been here already? No
one was showing me the ropes. They were treating me like I'd
done it all before. But I hadn't. I swear I hadn't.

The questions kept coming. *Is this my life now? Is this where
I live? Am I in prison?* Each new thought brought me closer to
crying out.

I thought, *If I sleep, everything will be all right. Next time I wake
up, I'll be at home.*

But I couldn't sleep. The second my eyes closed the questions buzzed louder in my head. Where were my parents?
Where was Lorraine? Where was Nan? Did they know where I
was? Had they done this? Did they have me taken away?

The thought of being sent away by my own family was too horrible to contemplate. I didn't think I could become more miserable but that single thought did it. I didn't have time to dwell on it, though.

Because of the noises.

A low growl was coming from the furthest part of the room. I knew it was someone snoring. What else could it be? But everything sounds worse in the dark and the longer I listened the weirder the irregular guttural snorts seemed. After a while I had to remind myself they were coming from a human and when a similar noise started closer to me I jumped.

It's just snoring, I told myself. *You've heard that before.*

And then the muttering started. Little simpers came from one direction, a kind of rasp from another, followed by high-pitched tremors. In daylight they could have been giggles or something as harmless. At night-time, enveloped in blackness, it was the tell-tale sign of an unknown creature. It had to be.

When fear takes a grip you lose all reason. The louder the nocturnal chorus got, the more anxious I became, and the more anxious I became, the more horrific each noise seemed. I was no longer in a dormitory bed surrounded by women in various stages of sleep. I was in a tent, in a jungle, a sitting target for the vicious and unseen creatures snuffling outside my canvas shell. There were wild animals outside, monsters. I could hear them. They were so close I could almost feel their foul breath on my face.

Don't move, Patricia. Don't even breathe.

I was immobile with fright. What I needed to do, of

course, was close my eyes, cover my ears with a pillow and force myself to sleep. That was the only sensible thing. But you can't. No one could. Not with those sounds. The more scared I became, the angrier with myself I got.

Get a grip. There's nothing here to hurt me. Everyone's in bed.

Nearly everyone.

What the hell was that?

I held my breath. There it was again, a distinct scurrying sound. This wasn't my imagination. And it wasn't snoring, or even talking. Someone or something was definitely moving. It sounded exactly how I imagined a body being dragged along the linoleum floor would sound. I heard it again. *Don't be stupid.* If it wasn't a corpse, what was it? The sound was coming from the floor. A snake? A crocodile? Something low and coming my way.

My paranoia was running wild. I knew really it couldn't be any of those things but the uncertainty was driving me mad. Then I realised exactly what it was, which only made me more scared still.

The scuffling was feet in slippers, dragging along the floor rather than lifting off for each step. It wasn't a wild creature at all. It was a woman. And she was coming closer.

Where's she going?

I didn't dare look. If I couldn't see her, she couldn't see me. It's amazing the logic you cling to in hours of need. Eyes glued shut, I strained to hear where she was heading. Any trace of snoring completely tuned out. All I could hear was my own heartbeat – and that scraping getting closer and closer.

What if it was Sadie? What if she was coming to sit on me again? *No, calm down, she wasn't in the room.* Had she arrived late?

Had she got a key? Was she going to accuse me of hiding her son again?

I realised the footsteps had stopped – and with them my heart, or so it felt. Whoever it was, she was standing right next to my bed. I could hear her wheezing. Tiny, hoarse gasps punctuated by sharp intakes, rattling with spittle. And the smell! She smelt old, like some of Nan's friends. That nasty mix of lavender and urine. Really horrible.

Still, at that proximity, she could have had the aroma of a morning bakery and I'd still have been terrified. At least I knew it wasn't Sadie. She didn't have that stench of old age.

I didn't know if she was looking at me but suddenly the woman began to speak. Tiny, unintelligible words. Was she talking to me?

Should I answer her or not? What would she do if I ignored her?

I soon found out. There was a crash as the stranger took another step closer and walked into my cupboard. She was inches from my head now. I couldn't make out her words. Then there was the unmistakeable sound of a drawer being pulled back. She was going through my things.

I don't know how long I lay there, frozen still, too scared to move, too scared to breathe, as the old woman tore through my things. Each drawer slid open, invaded and slammed shut. Then she moved round to my empty wardrobe.

What's she looking for? Not her son as well?

I thought, *If she touches me I'm going to run.* But I wasn't convinced my legs would even work. I was so tense and yet I felt like jelly. I'd be lucky to stand up.

Suddenly I heard another voice.

'Come on, Mavis, back to bed.'

At last. My eyes flashed open. I saw a nurse planting a hand on the elbow of the old woman, who didn't resist. She just turned, still muttering, and let herself be led back to her own bed. As they left the nurse looked at me but I instinctively closed my eyes.

'It wasn't my fault!' I wanted to call out. 'It wasn't me.'

But no one ever believed that.

The horrors of the night passed without further incident. What happened in the morning was even worse. It began in the usual fashion: assembling the clues.

A couple of women are at sinks ... I'm in the bathroom.

I realised I needed the toilet. It was quite urgent. There was one free cubicle so I went over. Out of nowhere, an orderly called Cindy beat me to it.

Where did she come from?

'I was first,' I said indignantly.

She just laughed.

'Come on, I'm busting.'

'I'm not queuing,' Cindy said, 'I'm waiting.'

'What are you waiting for there?'

'You. For goodness' sake hurry up. I don't want to be standing here all day.'

I ran in and closed the door. Before I could slide the bolt a hand thrust the door back open.

'Hey, get off!' I yelled, trying to pull it back from whichever nutter was tormenting me now.

As I fell forwards I came face to face with Cindy the orderly.

'You know the rules, Kim,' she said. 'Doors open for you.'

'What are you talking about?'

'Doors, you know that. Twenty-four-hour observation, remember?'

Jesus, that can't be right. It crossed my mind whether she was even a real orderly. I reached for the door again but Cindy put a firm hand on it and shook her head.

'Are you going or not? I haven't got all day.'

'Are you going to watch?'

'I'm going to stand here, if that's what you mean.'

She means it. What a pervert!

I lifted my paper gown as carefully as I could and sat down. I was determined not to give this weirdo any satisfaction. But she wasn't looking. She was purposely facing the other way. *Seriously, what's the point of being there if she's not going to even watch?* I was more confused than ever.

As I washed my hands afterwards I could see the orderly in the mirror.

'Are you following me?' I called out angrily.

Cindy snorted. 'You know I am. We don't want you doing anything silly, do we?'

Silly? *What is this place? Who won't let you go to the toilet in peace?* Wherever I was, she wasn't joking.

'You've got half an hour in the telly room before your session with Dr P-J,' Cindy went on. 'Someone will call you.'

Dr Picton-Jones. I'd forgotten about her. I felt my heart lift for the first time in ages. She was the one who'd put me in here. She was the one who could get me out.

In the meantime I learnt my new home was called George Ward. The telly room was on the other side of the corridor to the dormitory. It was a big, square space, with chairs lined up

along each of its beigey-colour walls. There was a television in
the corner and a couple of tables. The door from our dormitory
was on one side; on the opposite was the entrance to the men's
quarters. Unlike the bedrooms this area was mixed. There were
groups of men reading, slumped asleep – at nine in the morning – or standing at the window talking – to themselves or so
it seemed. The women were in there as well. Everyone from
the canteen was, by the look of it. Not Sadie, though. I scanned
again. Definitely not there.

What had returned, however, was the noise – that constant cacophony of sounds that no one and everyone seemed
to be making. I tried to block it out and failed. It was like a wall
between me and reality. I couldn't get past it to enter the room
so I just stood in the doorway, watching, observing and thinking, *I don't belong here. Something is wrong.*

Dr Picton-Jones's office was stark, containing some medical posters, one large window, a desk, some books and a chair.
She smiled as she spoke. At first she did, anyway. Her façade
slipped to show her frustration soon after I opened my mouth.

'When can I go home?'

'We've been through this.'

'We haven't.'

'If you say so.'

'When can I go home?'

I didn't understand why she wouldn't tell me. *I've got rights.
You can't just keep me here.*

'As you well know, you're being detained here for your
own good.'

'Why do I have to wear this paper stuff?'

'So you don't try to do anything silly.'

'What can I do in this?'

'Nothing. That's exactly the point.'

She was getting me angry. I kept hearing this 'silly' word. The only thing I'd call silly was letting myself be locked up like a common criminal every other day.

At least I learned that I was at Warlingham Park, as I'd suspected, and I'd been there for three days. The first two I'd spent in one of the small observation cells coming off the communal area. That's the place you're put till you've acclimatised.

That's where Sadie was being housed right now, I learned. *Makes sense*, I thought. *That's why I only saw her at mealtimes.*

The doctor was still talking when I remembered another grievance. How could I have forgotten? Without waiting for her to finish I blurted, 'A sicko nurse wouldn't let me go to the loo on my own today. What are you going to do about that?'

'And what do you mean by that?' Dr Picton-Jones asked.

I told her and as I did she started shuffling paper.

'It's the same reason as last time. Until you can be trusted ...'

'... not to do anything *silly*? How did I guess? But what does that mean?'

'It means,' she said, 'that until we can trust you not to try to hurt yourself you're going to be watched like a hawk. We've been through this.'

Hurt myself? That same old chestnut again. Why didn't these people get some new lines? It wasn't myself I felt like hurting. It was Dr Picton-Jones and all the stupid people who were keeping me here.

'When can I get out?'

In a strange way, all this talk of escape seemed to please the doctor. I didn't know why. Perhaps she was relieved I wasn't giving up. It didn't really matter. She still insisted I was in there for at least a fortnight.

'Two weeks?'

'At least. Until we're satisfied you're no threat.'

A threat. To whom? That familiar feeling of boiling rage began to bubble inside me. As I left the doctor's room, my faithful orderly appeared at my side and I was suddenly filled with an intense desire to get out, whatever it took.

They can't watch me forever, I thought. *I'll just make a run for it through the door.*

So that's what I did. Or at least I tried to. There was a corridor leading from the common room out to a stairwell. That's where I needed to be. I waited until Cindy was distracted by some screaming, then strode over to the door. It looked pretty light. I twisted the handle and pulled. Nothing. I pushed. Nothing.

God, what is this?

Both hands on the handle now, I shook it. Not only did the door not open, it didn't budge, didn't even shake. It was obviously stronger and heavier than it looked. But why did they need anything like this here? I looked back at the common room. The rest of my fellow inmates were looking as distracted as ever. Marching between them was the orderly. I'd been rumbled. I wasn't going anywhere.

Not for a very long time.

Warlingham Park was an old Victorian mental institution. Its methods weren't much more modern than its architecture. Even Dr Picton-Jones admitted it was no place for a child. It wasn't fit for adults, either, Mum said. She'd only been visiting for five minutes when she gave a grand theatrical shudder and said, 'This place is horrible. These people give me the creeps. I can't stay here.'

And that was it, visit over, she just left, never to return. She'd abandoned me. Again.

CHAPTER EIGHT

What's it got to do with me?

'Take me back!'

The girl was out of control, screaming. Her face, flushed with rage, was threatening to turn the shade of her fiery red hair. The man and two women cowered, more in shock than fear. They were used to her episodes. The girl's erratic behaviour was nothing new. They thought they'd seen everything she could throw at them. This outburst, however, had arrived completely out of the blue.

'Why have you brought me here? I shouldn't be here. I don't want to be here!'

'Don't start.' The younger woman, the girl's mother, didn't have the patience to mollify her daughter. 'You asked to come back and that's the end of it.'

But it wasn't the end of it. Not for the girl. She'd been dragged from her sanctuary. Pulled back into the street where her nightmares had begun, the environment where she'd suffered so much.

The place she'd tried to escape through death.

Why had they done it? Why had they brought her there? She cried out again, 'Take me back. Please let me go back.'

The adults glanced at each other as the girl's rage turned to desperation and as one they thought the same thing they always did:

'It makes no sense.'

After the last horrific month, walking back into our house was the most comforting feeling in the world. At least I imagine it was. Unfortunately, that privilege was denied me. Yet again I had the feeling they must have drugged me with sleeping pills at Warlingham and carried me home. One minute I was there, in that stupid gown, looking forward to getting out. The next, I was in our front room with Mum and Nan.

As soon as I saw them I felt a stupid big smile break out on my face. I'd never been happier to see anyone.

I'm home. Back where I belong.

I never wanted to leave again.

It took a few seconds to sink in that Mum and Nan weren't smiling. In fact, they both looked like the cat had licked their cream.

'Is that it?' Mum was saying. 'All you can do is smile?'

Nan shook her head.

What's she talking about?

Then I wondered, *How long have I been here? Were they talking to me when I was unconscious and they just didn't notice? Is that the problem?*

'I'm back now,' I said cheerily. 'I'm not going away again.'

Mum and Nan looked at each other but said nothing.

Dad drove me the five or so miles. Yet again I did my time travel thing. Home – then not home. Front room – then a large place with lots of light and the sound of screaming kids.

Here we go again.

On the plus side I wasn't in Warlingham. I knew that immediately. That nasty stench of urine that permeated the very walls and carpets was absent. While my nose may have got a break my ears weren't so lucky and I was greeted by a noise level on a par with the old Victorian lock-up, if not louder. But this was good noise. This was the sound of kids shouting and laughing and just being kids. Even the ones crying sounded natural, not eerie like the haunting wails of some of the old fogeys I'd been stuck with.

Instinctively I felt more relaxed here than I'd been any-where recently. A woman – the only adult I could see – smiled at me when she came over.

'Would you like some lunch, Kim?'

I nodded. I couldn't remember the last time I'd eaten. She led me to where the noise was coming from, a large room that served as a dining hall. Chaos reigned absolutely. Babies, tod-dlers and kids of various ages were mucking around at their tables as the odd staff member tried to keep check. It was like being invited to a chimps' tea party. Food was going everywhere except in mouths. It was disgusting. Twice I nearly caught a face full of purée before I'd even sat down.

At least no one's shoving their fat bum in my face.

Even so, my appetite had disappeared as quickly as it had come. I couldn't wait to get down and . . .

. . . and do what?

The cloud descended slowly in my head but there was no shaking it once it had settled.

I'm stuck again, I realised. *Trapped God knows where.*

I remembered my last words to Mum and Nan and the way they'd just looked at each other. They'd known.

What the hell is going on?

I discovered later I was at a Croydon Council children's home just outside Purley called Reedham's. Once again, my psychiatrist and social worker had been responsible for sending me there. And once again they admitted it wasn't the ideal destination for me. At my ripe old age the inmates were usually being shipped out, not admitted. But the managers had made an exception for me. As one of the nurses explained, 'You're a bit old for us but Dr Picton-Jones said it's better than where you were. You'll only be here till she can get you in somewhere else.'

So, yet again I was being told it was in my best interests. That they were doing me a favour letting me stay there rather than be at home. That I was a lucky girl.

So why didn't I feel like it?

The thing about charity is it only helps if you think you need help. If you think you're fine, it's as unwelcome as anyone else interfering. Who cares about your intentions if you're stopping me doing what I want to do? Or living where I want to live?

After two nights at Reedham's I was shipped off again. This time to Crystal Palace in south London, and another institution for 'young people'. Apparently these young people would be closer to my own age.

'Oh,' I said, when informed of their plans for me. That's as much enthusiasm as I could muster. If they'd wanted me to get more excited they were out of luck.

I don't care who you stick me with. I just want to go home!

San Martino's, according to its brochure, was a big house in nice grounds that had been bequeathed to charity by an old lady when she died. Her stipulation was that it should be used to give better lives to girls with mental health problems.

That's nice, I thought. *But what have mental health problems got to do with me?*

After the massive scale of Mayday and Warlingham and then the big children's home, it was refreshing to discover I wasn't herded around with a pack of hundreds of other kids. In fact, when it was time to be introduced to the others living at San Martino's I couldn't believe it when only three girls came in. I continued staring at the door for a few seconds until I realised that was it. I thought, *That makes a change*. But a prison is still a prison however many inmates it has.

Whichever way you looked at it, I still hadn't asked to be there.

Everything about San Martino's was more intimate than I'd been used to although it took me a while to realise. I didn't exactly do cartwheels when I was shown my room. I assumed it was a holding bay where they assessed new arrivals, just as they had at Warlingham and Mayday. I couldn't even see the point of unpacking.

'Do you want a help with your things?' a smiley woman called Lillian asked.

'I'll wait till I get to my dorm.'

'Your dorm? There's no dorms here, dear. This is the only bed you'll be sleeping in.'

'Really?'

'Really. There are only three of you. We're not exactly pushed for space.'

My own room? Even though there were only a handful of us staying there, I still imagined we'd be sharing. I couldn't believe I was getting my own space. For most of my life I hadn't even had that privilege at home.

Lillian, I discovered, was the housemother at San Martino's. She cooked and cleaned and generally ran the place and looked after us. She lived in the building with her son, Jonathan. She was really lovely although, like everyone else, she assumed she'd told me things when she hadn't. Some days I didn't even see her but she'd refer later to something I'd allegedly done the day before. That was annoying. As I say, though, she wasn't the first to be like that. People normally treated me like I was stupid.

There were three other rooms near mine – again, one per girl – and then upstairs there was a little self-contained attic flat. The girl who lived up there had a little baby boy. I think she was seventeen or eighteen. I don't know what was wrong with her – or what they said was wrong with her – but she was lucky to be in an institution where they gave you so much freedom and privacy. I knew that from experience. No one was made to dress in cardboard here. Nobody spied on me when I went to the loo. You don't realise how much you take things for granted until they're taken away.

Nice as it was, though, I still didn't know why I was there. With the others you could see they had problems. They'd be all right most of the time, then something would trigger a rage or an argument or they'd run off or do something weird. One girl, Ailsa, was the worst. She was younger than me and quite bad. You never knew what to expect from her. Lillian had her work cut out with that one.

Ailsa was in San Martino's because she struggled to get through daily life on her own. Her carers – I think she grew up with foster parents – apparently were at their wits' end. Even I could see that she needed help. It was great that San Martino's would take her and sort her out.

Ailsa's problems were there for all to see. But what about

me? Why was I being cooped up there? It was Mayday and Warlingham all over again.

My first day at San Martino's passed in a blur. Before I knew it I was in bed, a table lamp illuminating the room. It felt strange, different. I held my breath. The silence was deafening. Even with a window overlooking the road there was hardly a sound. Such a contrast – and a relief – after the nightmare of Warlingham Park. My door had been locked after me, which I hated, but no one was screaming blue murder, no one was accusing me of stealing their child and no one was snuffling through my personal belongings. I didn't want to be there, admittedly, but I felt safe. It was an odd feeling. I'd never considered my safety before. No mistaking it now, though. Whatever San Martino's had to throw at me, I was ready.

I did some ruminating that night. That was unusual. So unusual, in fact, that I remember it. So many night-times, like the days, seemed to flash by. I could count on one hand the number of times I relaxed in bed with a book or had just a bit of time to gather my thoughts. I always seemed to be responding to something. Had I done this? Why had I done that? Who was doing something else to me and why?

For the first time in a long while, I was actually enjoying having nothing to do and just as much to worry about. Allowing for the fact I was incarcerated in a place I hadn't asked to visit, I still couldn't shake that sensation of being protected. Even though I didn't know Lillian from Adam, just having her downstairs was a source of great comfort.

I realised as well that one of my biggest memories was of always seeming in a rush. I may have been fourteen now but nothing had changed. So much of my day was spent working out where I was, why I was there and whom I was with. I never seemed to ease into days. So much of my trouble at school usually kicked off like that. More than once I suddenly realised a friend was sitting next to me and that was it.

Funny, hadn't noticed she was there.

So obviously I ask her how her holiday was.

She answers.

Then we're both told off for talking.

'That's your last chance.'

We take our punishment but – honestly – how was that my last chance? It was the first thing I'd said to my friend. It was the first thing I'd said to anyone at school all day. It was one rule for me. Another for everyone else.

I was told off for episodes like that again and again but I couldn't help it. I lived by that feeling of seeing someone and needing to get my thoughts out there and then. People crept up on me and disappeared so quickly. I had to speak to them when I had the chance. Who would begrudge me that?

The problem was, not taking into account my surroundings. Rarely did I stop to think, *Maureen's here, so is everyone else – I wonder why.* Life would have been much easier had I done so more often. The answer would have been: *because it's a school assembly, or an exam* or something similar. All the information I needed to discern whether it was a talking environment or not was in front of me, if I took the time to look. But time was the one thing I felt I never had. I was always in too much of a hurry to worry about paying attention to minutiae like that. Friends vanished as quickly as they materialised. Where and why I didn't know. I just needed to grab opportunities with both hands whenever they were presented, and damn the consequences.

That was how it seemed, anyway. Rarely did I think about it, if I'm honest. I went through life like a squash ball, smashed from one wall to another again and again. It didn't strike me as different or unusual or wrong. All I knew is I didn't like it. But how many millions of other kids had thought that? All of them, I supposed. I wasn't special. I was just unlucky.

The next day – I suppose it was the next day: it was the next thing I remember – Lillian served me breakfast and told me the bus would be along shortly.

'What bus?'

'To take you to school.'

'*My* school?'

'Yes, dear, your school. Tavistock.'

Lillian must have had the patience of a saint. At the time I didn't appreciate that. All I could think was: *my school? Why am I going there? I thought I was in this place for some sort of treatment.*

It's true I didn't think anything was wrong with me, but I assumed that's why I was there. The alternative was baffling.

If they don't think I need treatment then why do I have to stay here?

I thought about it for the entire bus journey. The conclusion, when it dawned, was obvious – but disturbing.

They just don't want me to go home. Am I so horrible they have to protect everyone from me?

I didn't notice arriving at school. Before I knew it I was back at San Martino's and it was time for dinner. We all ate together with Lillian. It was nice, like a family meal – but without the shouting and arguing. *Maybe I can get used to this ...*

I thought again about being quarantined from my family. Why would they do that? Why would anyone take that decision?

They were punishing me and I didn't know why.

Punishment takes different forms.

I wasn't sure if San Martino's was a detention centre or a hospital. It turned out to be a bit of both and nothing of either. We had our own rooms but the lounge, kitchen and front door were all locked at night. We were allowed to go to school but not outside the house unaccompanied. There was always someone looking over your shoulder, which I hated. Privacy is important to me.

Then there were the various organised activities in the evenings, which were supposedly optional but it was made clear we had to attend. On Monday nights it was informal art classes. I really didn't have any interest in painting or drawing but I was in the minority because the room was always full of adults from the surrounding area who were allowed to come as well. It felt odd being with outsiders who knew we were there against our will. The worst thing, though, was listening to the music. I think the guy who ran the classes, Jeff, only had one tape because the only thing he seemed to play was 'Consider Yourself' from *Oliver!* on repeat. I don't know if it was that song or the timing but I remember thinking, *I never want to see another paintbrush in my life.*

Little did I know ...

After a week one of the other girls asked me if I'd be going home soon.

'No, they want me here for a while.'

'What about visits?'

'My dad's come to see me.'

'No, what about visits to see your family?'

'Can you do that?'

'Easy.'

It might have been easy for her. Nothing in my life seemed to be that straightforward.

I broached the subject with Lillian. She showed me the phone and I called home. Mum said Dad would collect me on Friday, after work.

Great.

I went off to school with a spring in my step. Something to look forward to ...

Friday morning came and it was school again as usual. Then the bus took me back to Crystal Palace but instead of dinner and bed, I packed my bag. Dad was coming in a couple of hours. I was going home.

I don't remember being picked up but I do remember being at home. But only for about ten seconds. The next thing I recall is being back in Dad's car.

'Where are we going?' I asked.

'Don't start,' he hissed. I realised he was doing his angry driving. All noisy acceleration and late braking. Something had riled him.

I just thought, *At least it's not me,* and settled back to enjoy the journey.

We drove in silence after that and I relaxed, staring out the window at the familiar Croydon scenery as it whizzed past. I'd find out where we were going soon enough.

A few minutes later we screeched to a halt.

'Here we are – again!' Dad said.

His harsh tone snapped me out of my reverie. *Okay, if you won't tell me I'll work out where I am for myself.* The usual drill: look around for clues, see what I could learn.

It didn't take me long. I wish it had. I wish I hadn't taken one glance out of the front window and immediately recognised the old house in front of us.

I'm back at San Martino's.

I didn't know what had happened. Dad swore blind I'd kicked off the moment we'd got home. That wasn't true. I remember talking to Nan. She was in bed. She was recovering from another stroke. She told me off for taking Dad's tablets and I laughed. I presumed she was joking, especially when she called him names for leaving them out.

After that, Dad said, I'd changed. I started screaming, demanding to be taken back to Crystal Palace.

'Your father was worried about you,' Lillian told me after the howl of Dad's engine tearing away from the place had died down. 'They all were. You kept saying you didn't like it there.'

'No, there's been some mistake,' I said. 'You've got it wrong.'

'That's what he told me, dear. He seemed quite upset by it.'

No, no, no. That didn't happen!

'Lillian, why wouldn't I like it there? It's my home! I need to go back.'

The housekeeper shook her head. 'I don't think so, dear. Not tonight. It's too late and, in any case, I don't think your father will fancy coming back again so soon, do you? Not after what was said.'

'Nothing was said. Not by me.'

'Why don't you sleep on it and we will have a chat tomorrow?'

That was it. I was back here, just a couple of hours after I'd left. Why, though? I'd been looking forward to my freedom all week. I needed to get back to my family, to see my friends. Why would I insist on turning round again? I wouldn't. I hadn't done that, I knew it. What was the point of being in a place you could leave if people kept bringing you back?

It doesn't make sense.

It was a long weekend. Hard as I tried I couldn't fathom what had happened. What had possessed Dad to bring me back again? And why had he lied to Lillian?

Before I knew it, Monday was upon us and it was time again for school. I actually welcomed the short mini-bus journey to Tavistock, driven by a woman called Carol. It was good to have some order. Whatever happened during the day would be a welcome distraction. At least I wouldn't be trapped at San Martino's.

If I'd struggled at school when I lived at home, I thought that going to a comprehensive where most people knew I was being bussed in from a 'funny farm' was going to be a nightmare. There was no chance of keeping it secret. Carol's daughter was at Tavistock as well, and so was the sister of one of the other girls. They were nice enough but the idea of relying on them to keep their mouths shut was unattractive, to say the least. So I told my friends, who told their friends, who told their friends. I didn't care. What could anyone say to me that would make me feel worse than I already did?

In fact, it could have been a lot worse. I got the odd comment from some of the boys and one or two girls but generally people kept quiet about it. There was no doubt they all knew. Gossip passes around a school quicker than the common cold. If anything, I was a bit suspicious about how nice people seemed to be towards me. The majority weren't exactly supportive but they weren't mean either. I think a lot of people just wanted a laugh. I heard more 'fatty' comments than anything to do with being locked up. God knows why.

The majority of people kept themselves to themselves. With the way some of them responded when I walked by, you would have sworn they were scared of me. As if. I wouldn't say boo to a goose.

And yet, did that girl just flinch when I walked over? Must be my imagination.

I was at San Martino's for about four months. In that time I arranged to go home on weekend visits three times. Each one ended in exactly the same fashion. I would make the call, Dad would reluctantly agree to pick me up, the last episode all too fresh in his memory, and home I would go.

And then he would drive me back.

Sometimes it was the following morning, sometimes the same night. I can't explain it. It's not what I wanted. He hated it, he made that clear. In fact, I'm surprised he didn't hate me too. Anyone would, if they'd been messed around like that.

Except I hadn't messed anyone around. Yet everyone said I was changing my mind the minute I stepped into our house. I know that's impossible. But that's what they said. Mum, Nan, Lorraine, Dad and Lillian. I wondered what they were getting out of this big joke but nothing came. It was obviously their little game. I had to think that. The alternative was too harsh: if they weren't messing around for a laugh they were doing it to hurt me. No kid wants to imagine that of their family. I certainly didn't.

School, for a while, became a haven for me. The one place I could go and be normal. Yes, I still got into trouble, sometimes for unknown reasons as usual, but even that was normal for me. I lost track of the number of times I was put on report. My days spent in the orange room, however, made more of an impression – even if I couldn't always remember why I was sent there.

One particular visit stays with me. It was actually my last time there – although I didn't appreciate it then.

How I got into the room remains a blank. I don't know what I'd been accused of or how vociferously I'd denied it. I just remember being there. Staring at those walls, those hideous satsuma walls, then suddenly noticing a draught. I looked behind me and saw glass sprinkled all over the floor. A quick glance up and I knew the window had been smashed. It was the only explanation. Although it looked as though the pane had mostly come inside I knew realistically there was only a fraction of the detritus on the carpet. That meant the majority of the damage had fallen outside.

Which meant the problem had originated inside the room.

With me.

It couldn't have been. I would have remembered. I hadn't moved from the seat.

In which case, who had smashed the window?

My heart raced as I tried to work it out. It wasn't me, I knew it wasn't. Yet all the evidence pointed that way. As soon as the teacher came back, that's the conclusion they'd jump to. But I'd been framed. Again.

I don't know how long it took but eventually there was the unmistakeable sound of footsteps approaching and the door being swung open. The teacher didn't enter, just stayed in the doorway and called me out. I leapt out of my chair and ran towards the exit, towards freedom. I honestly thought I was going to make it. But just as I reached the door the teacher noticed my jumper.

'What on earth have you been doing?' she said.

I looked down. I was covered in tiny shards of sparkling glass.

It didn't take her long to glance up at the window, then trace the mess to the floor.

'Oh, I've seen everything now.' She stared at me, struggling to find the words. 'Trying to climb out of the window? Did you really think you would get away with it? Tell me you didn't. What on earth were you thinking?'

'I didn't do anything!' I bleated, but it fell on deaf ears. The teacher looked like she had gone into shock, shaking her head and muttering to herself. Her whole body was quivering, I noticed. She was shaking – with rage.

'That's it,' she snapped coldly. 'That was your last chance.'
The last chance for what?
I soon found out.

The letter was sent to my parents. I was not welcome at Tavistock School without a reference from a psychiatrist asserting that I was not a physical threat to myself or other pupils.

That's no problem, I thought. *Dr Picton-Jones can tell them I'm fine.*

I didn't see what possible purpose my doctor could have in not defending me to the school. But she found one. At least she had the good grace to explain her reasons to me personally. I hated her for it, but at least she wasn't hiding, like everyone else. She showed me her letter to the Tavistock. It said that, in her opinion, my mental health had improved impressively and that I had experienced no recent episodes of self-harming. However – and this was the crucial part – she could not in all conscience vouch for how I would behave in the future.

That last line was the final nail in my coffin. The Tavistock replied to say that until Dr Picton-Jones could make such assurances then I would not be welcome back.

'Is that it?' I asked her, stunned. 'Can't I go any more?'

'I'm afraid not. But we'll keep working on it, I promise.'

Those four familiar words came rushing back. *It doesn't make sense.* It was so unfair. How can you be excluded from school because of something you might do in the future – but haven't done yet? It was mind-blowing, staggering – and above all, victimisation of the highest order. Whoever was out to get me at the school had succeeded.

I'd never really got on at Tavistock, I admit that. But at least I'd attended. I always tried my best, whatever the subject. It wasn't my fault if results – and behaviour – didn't necessarily go my way. It wasn't for the want of trying.

So, I thought, I've been taken from my own home and now I've been kicked out of school. Someone was messing around with my life. That had to be it. What other explanation was there?

I didn't care about my education but I was surprised no one else did. I asked Lillian what I was meant to do about school from now on.

'You won't need that where you're going, dear.'

'What do you mean where I'm going? I'm not going anywhere.'

'Of course you're not, dear,' she said, clearly backtracking but not betraying even slight nerves.

But I was. I found out a few days later. I'd done my time at San Martino's. Now I'd been thrown out of school I needed to be somewhere that would try to do more than just house me. They'd help me as well. And so, bags packed yet again, I said goodbye to Lillian and the others and was driven across south London to Ham, near Richmond.

My next new life was just beginning.

CHAPTER NINE

The elves and the shoemaker

It was a Raleigh Chopper. Bright red, five gears controlled from a wicked T-bar gear lever on the central column, a long reclining seat and rear hoop backrest; dropped handlebars calling for outstretched-arm cruising. It was the closest thing to a Harley-Davidson a fourteen-year-old boy in the 1970s could get his hands on. Even the kickstand screamed 'motorbike'. And Ken had one.

Ken liked nothing more than bombing up and down the winding gravel paths, through the trees, over the grassy mounds. Nothing made him happier. It was every boy's dream.

Time up, he pedalled back to the four-storey building on Ham Common Road. He wasn't sure why he was there. If people couldn't cope with his being gay that was their problem. He wasn't going to apologise for it. What did they want him to do about it, anyway? But the nurses and doctors were nice. He always felt safe there.

L ife, it seemed to me, was like going to the station to catch a train. You buy a ticket, board your carriage, store your luggage. Your destination is an hour or so away.

Then the train pulls away and you realise it's actually a roller-coaster.

That's how it felt. I usually ended up where I was heading

but some of the routes I took to get there left me baffled – and often more than a little shaken as well. But, as I consoled myself every time: *it's the same for everyone.*

The Cassel Hospital was another lovely old mansion that had been handed over to medical causes. It was a lot bigger and originally a lot grander than San Martino's, and it was able to house more so-called 'troubled' teenagers as well as adults. It also had more live-in staff. The biggest difference between there and my previous home-from-home, however, was that we weren't just being given a roof over our heads and a bolt on the door. The Cassel was a therapeutic community, with sessions every day. Whether I liked it or not, the system had sucked me even further in. I was a 'patient' now.

It was a very busy place with a wide range of people. There was an adult unit, an adolescent unit and a separate family unit where whole families lived in. Usually there were about six families in situ at a time. Most often it was the mother who was the patient. So while her children attended the hospital school and the father would go·off to work as normal, the mum would spend her day having therapy at one session or another.

The adolescent unit was on the first storey of the main building, mixed in with the single adults. The family unit was an extension of the hospital, connected via a long corridor. The outpatient block would originally have housed the servants' quarters – that's how large the place was.

Of course, I wasn't told any of this before I arrived. My first experience of the Cassel was discovering myself at the foot of a magnificent sweeping staircase. Obviously I was no longer at San Martino's. I wasn't carrying anything or wearing a coat so I'd obviously been inside for a while. I looked again at the stairs: was I going up or coming down?

Suddenly a voice called out, 'Can't find your room?'

A tall, gangly chap was strolling down from one of the downstairs rooms.

'Come on,' he said, 'I'll show you.'

I smiled, as much at his really plummy voice as any-thing, and followed him up the staircase. I didn't know where I was but obviously I was there for a while if I had my own room.

'There you go,' he said, pointing to an open doorway. 'Took me a few nights to find my way around as well.' A few nights? How big was this place? Then I realised he might just be trying to make me feel better. 'My name's Carl, by the way. And you're Kim?'

I nodded. That was my title. That was what everyone seemed to call me. *Even though my name is Patricia.*

My room was warm and welcoming, although I decided to reserve my opinion until I met the occupant of the second bed. That turned out to be a girl called Barbara, who was very nice. She told me how hard it was to get into the Cassel. You had to be monitored and vetted for months usually, she reckoned.

I racked my brain. 'Cassel' sounded familiar but not overly so. At least I knew now where I was. I certainly didn't remem-ber being vetted, though. I'd have done anything to have failed that audition.

Another girl, Maureen, backed up Barbara's story. She had actually come over from America just to be treated there after trying to kill herself by jumping out of a high window.

I didn't find that out immediately. Apart from her depression she seemed as normal as me. Then there was Rosie, from Cambridgeshire, who had a real problem with obsessions and phobias. She wasn't the worst one, though. One of the women from the adult unit was convinced she was going to catch germs off everything. She hated it when her family came to visit and afterwards wiped down everything they'd touched. She got so paranoid about door handles that instead of using the door she'd climb out the window and jump across to the fire escape. If the staff had caught her that would have been the end of it and it was really dangerous. But she had to do it. I don't know why – and neither did she. She used to laugh about how weird it was as much as the rest of us.

Most people there were good fun, actually, and I spent a lot of time messing around with them. The only person who couldn't hide her frustration was Beth. I felt sorry for her because she was still a teenager so she was cooped up with us – even though in the outside world she'd had her own flat for two years.

There was a nice vibe to the place and because of the community nature of the set-up, we were all expected to pull our weight. For some reason my job more often than not tended to be cleaning the back stairs. This was really hard work but when I tried to get out of it one of the nurses said, 'Well, that's what you volunteered for.'

That wasn't right.

'No, I think there's been some mistake.'

'No, mistake, love. You told me yourself. You said you wanted to hide away.'

I bloody didn't. But if that's how she wanted to play it, at least I knew the score.

One of the other chores on the rota was laying the breakfast table. It was a woman called Cathy's job to come down in the morning before everyone else, and set the places and get the cereals, fruit, cutlery and crockery out. The families sorted themselves out separately but the rest of the adults, adolescents and staff would all eat together there. Just as I hated scrubbing the stairs, Cathy detested getting up early. Day after day we'd come down and nothing had been done. It wasn't the Cassel's way to lecture too heavily, although words were said at one of our group meetings. Then the next day we came and everything was set perfectly. The next day was the same and so it continued for weeks. Everyone was fed on time.

And then one day Cathy said, 'It's not me doing this.'

No one believed her, but she swore it was true.

'I haven't set the tables for ages. You know what I'm like at getting up.'

That bit rang true but as someone pointed out, 'Who's going to get up and do it if they don't have to?'

No one could answer that.

'What is this: "The Elves and the Shoemaker?"'

We all laughed at the idea of helpful little fellows popping out in the night to do nice things for people. It was a story I remembered from childhood. I think we had a little Ladybird book of it at home.

Weirdly, one of the staff said they'd seen me wandering around early in the morning, sometimes even heading back from the direction of the dining hall. That wasn't true. I liked my bed as much as Cathy. I never left my room before I had to. Why would I?

Although the Cassel was essentially a psychiatric hospital, its unique selling point, as far as I could work out, was that it eschewed any form of medication except for first aid or in emergencies. Its work was carried out entirely by various types of therapy – you name it, there was a therapy incorporating it somehow – and attendance was compulsory.

I was one of five or six adolescents. There was the same number of single adults plus half a dozen families. We single-tons had shared rooms, which was great, and a therapist and nurse between two. Basically there was always someone on the premises to talk things through with – although after the day's regular sessions, that was the last thing I ever felt like doing. Everything had been so thoughtfully set up. Nothing was left to chance. And yet the same thought still nagged:

This is all very nice – but I don't need therapy.

That wasn't what the staff thought, however. I was enrolled for therapy so that was what I was going to get.

At least they were looking for something wrong with me, I reasoned. They hadn't written me off. As much as I was confident there wasn't anything wrong, if they did happen to discover a 'problem' then they could 'cure' it and afterwards they might leave me alone.

With everyone being so welcoming I tried to fit in. It wasn't that hard. Just being around people my own age was a comfort. Like me, they all claimed they didn't know why they were there – that was incredibly bonding for us. As much as we liked the staff and doctors, from that moment we were united:

us against the outside world. For the first time in my life I felt like I belonged somewhere.

Like the rest of them I still had to attend school. In a way, I was fortunate having been expelled from Tavistock – I had no choice but to go to the Cassel unit school. A teacher would come into our building and take a wide variety of lessons. Some of the others were still enrolled 'outside' but that didn't stop them being uprooted and placed on the Cassel syllabus. In a way, then, the advantage was mine.

At least I could understand why I was sent to school. It was the law. It's what people do. A day of fifty-minute therapy sessions, on the other hand, just seemed like someone's punishment of me. There was so much variety, which should have been a good thing. In reality, it just gave me more to hate. What's more, it was really intensive stuff.

After my first session of therapy, and with my head still buzzing, I collapsed in bed.

I'm glad that's over.

But then I got up – the breakfast things had already been set – and realised there was more to come. Today it was the community meeting. Everybody attended. All patients from all groups, all staff, all therapists and all doctors attached to the unit – the whole 'community' in fact. I suppose some people respond better to crowds. I don't. On the other hand I didn't exactly respond brilliantly when it was one on one.

If I only knew what they're looking for. Maybe I'd be able to help ...

Therapy was the order of the day, all day and every day. One day was put aside for a one-on-one with the nurse, followed by your private therapist session. An entire day of talking about yourself like that is pretty hard going. Some people are born to do that. I found it suffocating. After thirty minutes I was sick of the sound of my own voice.

To bed, and then another day, another round of therapy – and this time the adolescent group's turn to share their pain and discuss their triumphs. That was all right. Barbara, Rosie, Stacy, Lucy, Maureen and I had got on well so far. It was a supportive atmosphere (although Beth refused to attend). We lived in the same quarters anyway so there wasn't much we wouldn't soon find out about each other if we didn't know already.

Thursday's evening therapy group was the tricky one – although less so for us adolescents than our other guests. As its name suggests, the Parent Adolescent Group was open not only to patients but their parents as well. After Mum's performance at Warlingham I was surprised when she turned up.

Amazingly, Dad was there too – thinking about it, Mum couldn't have got there without him. Our first group passed without him saying much more than his name but he'd made the effort to attend. I appreciated that, especially when he was still finding it so hard to travel far from the house. He'd started back at work but occasional days were written off to bouts of sickness. Too much exertion really took it out of him and there were times when he couldn't do much more than mop his own brow.

Everyone in the Thursday group could see how ill he was but he felt under pressure to attend. Whatever his own personal problems, he needed to park those and turn up for my sake. I knew how much it would have pained him to sit there, and not just physically. We didn't wash our linen in public. That was the Noble way.

The following week I wondered if Dad would bother

returning. No one likes to see their child undergoing even light therapy but watching him squirm in his seat while I was talking was more painful than the therapy itself. It doesn't matter what's said or whether blame is apportioned or not (and it isn't), there's always that implicit criticism of their parenting.

Anyway, week two arrived – and so did Dad. *Just about.*

He really looked rough as he scrambled up the tall old steps at the front. The nurse took one look at him and told him to sit down. Dad argued for a bit and then caved in. So it was that I did my second family adolescent session with my father sprawled in agony on one of the medical beds.

I think he made it the next week but the following Thursday didn't even get as far as Ham. He rang late in the evening to say he'd had to find a place to pull over on the journey and throw up. After that he would spend as much time at the session as possible but they normally ended with him moaning and groaning on a couch somewhere.

For all the good she was, Mum shouldn't have bothered either. But as normal visiting was discouraged, it was nice to see a friendly face even if it was in a session. I missed Lorraine and Nan. In fact, Nan's health was preventing her from going anywhere. I'd been in the Cassel about a month when I got a message to call home. Nan had suffered another stroke and died.

I don't remember crying. I should have done. The rock of my childhood had disappeared. Home would never be the same again.

Not that I'm allowed to live there anyway ...

My lack of visitors wasn't that bad, actually. The rest of us got on pretty well so I wasn't lonely. Rosie, who I shared my therapist with, was a lot of fun, and I was very close to Stacy as well, especially when we became room-mates.

After a month in the place I was told I was allowed home visits. Cassel policy didn't like visitors but trips back home were allowed Friday to Sunday. When Dad came for our Thursday session I asked him to take me back the following day.

'Are you sure?'

'Of course I am. I'm allowed home for the weekend.'

'You're not going to mess me about?'

'Why would I?'

He blew his cheeks out and sighed.

'Why indeed. All right, I'll come and get you.'

And he did. Straight after therapy I had a small bag packed and ready to go. I was waiting in the car park when he pulled up.

'Come on then,' he said, a nervous edge in his voice. 'Let's see how far we get.'

I didn't know why he was being so negative. I was really excited about going back. The only sadness was going home without Nan living there any more. That would take some getting used to.

The weekend passed without incident. That is to say, they let me stay without sending me back early. Then, on Sunday night, my now heavily pregnant sister drove me back again. I don't remember what we talked about but I do recall the sense of relief that I'd been allowed to complete the full visit. Dad hadn't thrown me back in the car the second we'd pulled into the road. He hadn't accused me of messing me around. Mum hadn't fabricated any stories about my wanting to go back to the hospital.

They must have got over that problem, I thought. *Maybe we can all get back to normal now?*

As far as I was concerned, everything was related. If Mum and Dad stopped saying I'd been causing trouble then perhaps I could leave this place and move back home for good. School would have to take me back then, surely?

It was worth dreaming about. In fact, I couldn't wait for the following weekend. I was determined to do it all again.

Bearing in mind I didn't want to be there, the Cassel has a lot of good memories for me. I made some very good friends.

And I remember being happy.

Before I knew it I had been there for two months, which became four, which turned quickly into six. I hated being away from home and I really didn't enjoy the constant therapy and every little thing being analysed. (At lunch once I was trying to cut into a bit of tough meat and it shot off my plate. Out of nowhere my therapist appeared, saying, 'Are you angry about something? It's okay to be angry.' Honestly, they'd look for meaning in the way you brushed your hair if you let them.)

But there were a lot of things to love about the place. It made me feel secure, I had good friends and most days there was a lot of fun to be had if you put your mind to it. I believe I was actually happy.

What made me happier still was knowing how highly the therapists regarded contentment. They were so sensitive to emotions and moods like anger, depression or envy that if you displayed something more positive they had to go to their note-books to look up what it meant. I'm exaggerating, but there was no denying that the patients who were adjudged to be happy with their lot were the ones allowed to leave. That, I realised, was my way out. That was my way of taking control of the rollercoaster.

I'm happy, I thought. *And if I'm happy they won't have any excuse to keep me in for much longer.*

Then a few weeks later they found one.

CHAPTER TEN

Can you fix it?

Sonia stared at her plate. It was obscene. A mountain of mash, huge chunks of meat and enough vegetables to feed an army. Disgusting. She looked at the others, tucking into their meals. Laughing and shovelling it in. Where were they putting it all? Didn't they know the harm it was doing?

No, she thought, they're lucky. Look at them. They don't put on weight like me.

She glared at her own sickening physique slumped in the chair. Why don't they? It's not fair!

As she sat there, the unmistakeable aroma of gravy wafted up from Sonia's plate.

Stop it! she thought, and shoved it away. But it was too late. There was so much of the smell already in the room. She tried to block it out. No good. It was like a cloud around her.

She had to admit, it really did smell good. And she was starving. It felt like she hadn't eaten for a week. Where was the harm in having a little taste?

'One bite,' Sonia told herself. 'That won't hurt, will it?'

Pulling her plate back, she cut a thin slice of lamb, then stabbed it onto her fork along with a tiny scoop of mash. A second later it was in her mouth and gone. It tasted amazing, like manna from heaven. Sonia allowed herself a moment to enjoy the sensation.

Then, utterly ashamed of her weakness, she shoved the plate into the middle of the table and folded her arms.

No wonder you're the size you are, *she thought angrily.* You pig. You greedy, fat pig.

There comes a point in most inpatients' lives when they accept their lot. I can't remember when mine arrived. There must have been a moment, though, when I finally appreciated, *This is where I live.*

I'd really fought to get away from Mayday Hospital. I didn't deserve to be there and I knew it. I'd railed against the lies and punishments thrown my way by various schools. As for the treatment meted out by Warlingham – that was just barbaric. No one should have to undergo that, especially a child. San Martino's, however, had been quite pleasant by contrast, despite the insufferable art classes. Even so, all I could think about was going home.

The Cassel was a bit different from a normal psychiatric unit. As I've said, they didn't force-feed anyone medication. Warlingham was packed with what looked like zombies staggering around, frothing at the mouth like rabid dogs. Forget the rules – that was the biggest incentive to behave there. You didn't want to end up like them. The Cassel, on the other hand, treated you all like adults, even if you weren't that old yet. That was a breath of fresh air. The doctors at Mayday had been so patronising, talking about me like I was a lump of meat. Here they were just caring. If I'm honest, a little too caring for my liking. All that incessant probing is not my thing. Other people can get off on talking about themselves to strangers but it really doesn't do it for me – even if I am being marked on my performance.

The best thing about the Cassel was the fact that they were actively seeking to understand. They wanted to discover a trigger for patients' behaviour, they wanted to cure it and then repatriate the patient back into the wider society. In other words there was an endgame: to get back into the real world.

Having weekends with our families was one method of kicking that programme off. If you could survive a few days then perhaps, further down the line, you could be trusted to have a week away from the hospital. Ultimately you might even be released into the community unmonitored – the ultimate ambition of the adults.

I'd had a couple of good weekends at home. Funnily enough, the longer I stayed in Ham the less often I felt the desire to go back home. One reason was I was having too much fun. Another is, with Nan's passing our house seemed less welcoming. Then, of course, there was the fact that I was seeing Mum and Dad fairly regularly, health permitting, at our family therapy sessions.

So I was surprised one Friday to get a tap on the shoulder during supper. It was the night orderly just coming on duty.

'Your father's here.'

That took me by surprise. Instinctively I looked behind her.

'No he's not.'

'He's in reception.'

I could see she wasn't joking so followed her out. Dad was reading a newspaper when I found him.

'There you are,' he said brusquely. 'I thought you might be ready at least.'

'Ready for what?'

'Ready to go home.'

'What – now?'

'Don't give me that. You're the one who rang me.'

What are you talking about?

I looked at the nurse, who nodded. I couldn't tell if she was agreeing with him or me.

'When did I ring?'

'This morning. "Come and pick me up tonight," you said. "I'll be ready, I promise." You know damn well you did.'

'No I never!'

Dad tried to say something but his words had vanished. I think he remembered the nurse watching and bit his tongue. 'Look,' he managed to spit out, 'are you coming home for the weekend or not?'

His eyes were burning into me as I thought about it.

'I'm going to give it a miss this time,' I said. 'I've got things on tomorrow. You should have said before you came. You can't go dropping in like that.'

Nurse or no nurse, I thought he was going to explode.

'I knew it was too good to be true! It didn't take you long to get back to your old tricks, did it?'

And with that he grabbed his coat and marched out the door.

I didn't know whether to chase after him or cry. Why had he come? I hadn't asked him to. Had someone else at the Cassel arranged it for me? Why would he come all that way if he didn't have to?

My day-to-day life in the Cassel was structured around the treatments. Evenings and weekends gave us a little more free-dom. In good weather we could wander around outside. There was actually a friendly atmosphere most of the time. There weren't many times in my life when I'd experienced that. At lunchtime, cooks would send food up by lift to the patients' servery and in the evenings the rota dictated which of us prepared dinner.

But it was the therapy we were really there for. We all hated attending the sessions. Everyone complained they dragged on and on. I couldn't always agree on that. Some certainly felt like they were going in slow motion, others whizzed by. I'd barely opened my mouth when the therapist would be announcing, 'It is time now', and thanking me for coming. Other patients said that was a sign I enjoyed it.

'I don't.'

'You must do. Time always flies by when you're having fun.'

I argued, of course I did, called them all sorts of names for good measure. But they had a point. What other explanation was there?

Adding weight to their argument was the fact that a year had gone by. Cathy and the rest said it felt like ten years. Not to me. I would have guessed a couple of months at the most. I'd hardly had time to do anything.

To mark my anniversary at the Cassel, or maybe that's just how I remember it, one of the consultant psychotherapists (doctors who were also therapists) took me and Dad into his office for an assessment. There was always more pressure on these meetings. Unlike the nurses and therapists, doctors never asked you how you felt.

They told you.

'Kim suffers from something called dissociation.'

Dad nodded. The word meant nothing to either of us.

People with dissociative disorder, he explained, can appear distant or disengaged with daily life patterns. It can appear, he said, as though they see different things from other people, or don't see them at all. Eating problems like anorexia and bulimia – both of which he felt I had – could be contributory factors. At an extreme stage it could also involve amnesia.

Dad leapt forward at that.

'Which would explain her memory?'

'Precisely,' the doctor agreed. 'If she suffers it to this level, and it's possible she does.'

What memory problem? Dad's the one who tries to pick me up when we haven't arranged it. You should have a look at his memory.

As for having anorexia and bulimia – that was just ridiculous. I wasn't even sure what the difference was but I knew I had no problem with food. And I definitely would never throw up if I could help it.

The longer the meeting went on, the happier Dad appeared. Even when he was told that dissociation is normally the result of some childhood trauma he just shrugged. 'I can't think of anything. She's always been like this.'

At least we agreed on that. There were no skeletons in my closet. Plenty of things to moan about. Traumatic, though? Nothing at all. Not that it mattered. The doctor didn't suggest Dad talk to me about it and he didn't think of it either. They could have been haggling over the price of a second-hand car.

Hello? I am here!

'This dissociation,' Dad said. 'Can you fix it?'

'We can certainly make it easier to live with.'

That was enough for Dad. When we left the doctor's room there was almost a spring in his step.

'Well, at least we know what's wrong with you.'

'There's nothing wrong with me.'

He wasn't listening. After all these years of being on the thick end of my behaviour, he finally had a label for it. I wasn't naughty – I was ill. Mum would like that. I could see that's what he was thinking. My behaviour wouldn't reflect so badly on her now.

'We did all we could. It's a medical problem . . . '

Being diagnosed with this condition I'd never heard of for something I didn't think I had may have appeased my parents but it made no difference to me. Therapy sessions were as tedious as ever. Mostly people treated me the same. Except at mealtimes. Something odd was happening then.

I sat down one afternoon with the others. Meals were prepared down in the kitchen and a cook came up to serve them. Today it was chicken. We were all talking so I didn't take any notice of the other plates arriving and people tucking in. She couldn't serve everyone at the same time. My meal would probably be next.

My plate was slid in front of me and I just stared at it.

The table fell quiet.

'What's this?' I called out to the cook.

'It's what you asked for.'

'I didn't ask for two eggs.'

'Yes, you did. Just like you did yesterday and the day before.'

I looked round the table at everyone else's fried meat and

chips. My friends would back me up. 'I didn't ask for this, did I?'

They all started eating. No one said a word.

Idiots.

I didn't know what their problem was. They probably just wanted to see me get into trouble. I would have done the same.

The cook wouldn't admit she was wrong. She refused to give me anything else, either.

'Well, I'm not eating these.'

'You are, or I'm calling the nurse.'

But I didn't.

A few weeks after that I went home for the weekend. It felt odd with Nan gone and Dad out as much as he could manage. Lorraine was around though. She was living close enough to pop round quite regularly. It was good to see her again, especially with the baby so close to being born.

Friday night passed without episode. Saturday flew by as well. On Sunday afternoon, however, I found myself back in strange yet familiar surroundings. It was a hospital, but not the Cassel and not Mayday either.

I closed my eyes as tight as I could.

It can't be happening again.

When I dared to look next I began to hyperventilate. I was right. I was in a hospital, wearing a gown. The label on it said 'Kingston Hospital'.

I hate to think how I got here, I thought. *But I know that I'm not staying.*

The ward was quiet as I got up and dragged my coat over the gown. I'd been brought in without shoes so barefoot it was.

As I stepped into the corridor I noticed a few visitors heading for the exit so I fell in behind them. Before I knew it I'd made it into the lift, down four floors and outside where a storm was just kicking off. As I hid from the pouring rain under the entrance's canopy, I thought, *What now?* I'd managed to escape before thinking of a plan. Kingston was too far from Croydon to walk home. That left me with one alternative. Pulling my collar up as high as it would go I set off. In bare feet. In the rain.

The Cassel here I come.

I was in the doctor's room again. Dad was sitting next to me. They were talking in hushed tones with lots of pauses, Dad picking his nails as he listened. I tried to pick up the gist. It sounded serious. It was about me, obviously. *They must be discussing the dissociation.*

'Obviously our treatment isn't working as well as we'd like ...'

The doctor sounded angry. No – disappointed.

'We thought we were making progress ...'

Dad was just nodding, resigned.

'If I thought there was any other way ...'

Normally with these conversations I should have worked out what was going on by now. None of this one, however, was making any sense.

'After the weekend's problem we can't take the risk of her being a danger to herself or others.'

What weekend problem?

I suddenly remembered Kingston. A shiver ran through me. They'd said I walked all the way back to Ham Common in the downpour, and looked shattered and confused when I arrived.

Why was I in hospital?

Instinctively I felt my chest. *Sore! No, it was just a dream. It must have been a dream. There and gone in the blink of an eye.*

Dad's voice snapped me out of my shock. 'Are you sure it's the only way?'

'At this stage I think we're left with no choice.'

'I understand.'

'Sectioning your own daughter is not something to be taken lightly. You have to consider the consequences,' the doctor explained. 'But in my opinion it is the best way forward. It's the only way to protect her.'

'Okay, I'll do it.'

I was still stunned at the realisation that Kingston hadn't been a nightmare. It *had* happened. My throat felt like I'd swallowed razor blades to prove it. Suddenly the realisation of what the two men were saying hit me.

Sectioning?

I'd heard about this.

Panicking, I said, 'There must be some mistake.' Dad and the doctor spun round to stare at me. I think they'd forgotten I was even there.

'You've brought it on yourself,' Dad said, although he couldn't look at me as he spoke.

'It's for your own good, Kim,' the doctor agreed.

'You can't do this!'

Dad still wouldn't look at me. Eyes fixed straight ahead, he said quietly, 'Where do I sign?'

*

I'm moving.

I looked around. Two nurses sat alongside me. I was lying down. They were wearing seatbelts. I tried to sit up. I was strapped in as well.

I'm in an ambulance.

'Where are we going?'

'You know where we're going.'

I recognised the nurse who spoke. She was one of the Cassel staff. The other one was a stranger. Probably part of the ambulance crew.

'Tell me where we're going!'

'You're going on a little holiday.'

'Where to?'

The other nurse spoke up.

'Warlingham Park.'

No!

'You can't! Take me back. Take me back to the Cassel! I want to go back!'

Funny how I was so conditioned by the system. It didn't even occur to me to ask to go home.

'You haven't fixed me. You need to fix me!'

That was the last thing I remembered.

CHAPTER ELEVEN

I'm not one of them

Rebecca tugged again on the sheet. It was taut.

That should be strong enough.

She looked again at the knot above her head and back down to the floor. She'd thought of everything. It would soon be over. She rolled her shoulders to relax, took a deep breath and stepped off the table.

Then everything went black.

'I'm sorry it came to this, I genuinely am.'

Dr Picton-Jones looked as sad as she sounded.

'I thought you'd been doing so well. What changed?'

I couldn't answer. The only thing that had changed was the way I was treated. That was the story of my life and she'd heard it all before. There was no point going over it again just so she could tell me I was wrong. So I kept quiet.

'Well, if that's how you want to be, so be it. Obviously you've been here before but you'll be under stricter supervision, until we're sure you're going to behave. And we need to start getting your weight back up as well, of course. I'm sorry about that but there it is.'

*

I'd known exactly where I was the second I opened my eyes and saw the four grey walls and that imposing, thick door with its menacing spy hole.

A room, with a bed, and nothing else.

It could only mean one thing.

Warlingham Park.

I don't know how long I was in that cell. Two or three days, probably. To be honest, it sailed by. It's horrible having no windows, nothing to do, but I made the best of it. I knew the drill. It didn't matter what they were accusing me of. It didn't matter what I denied doing. They wouldn't let me out until they were confident I'd calmed down, as they put it. So I climbed on my bed and waited.

Before I knew it I was back onto the main part of George Ward in one of the dormitory beds. The smell was unmistakeable. More wee, vomit and worse than any amount of cleaning agents could mask. If I never smell Dettol again it will be too soon. And the sounds. Those animalistic cries and chunters, the shouts of rage and delight and delusion. The whole foul cacophony that had followed me everywhere on my last stay. It was still here, as bad as ever.

I actually found myself wishing I was back in the cell. Although I couldn't get out, no one could get in. At least I was safe there.

What was the point in being good if you still got treated like this? I just wanted to shout at the top of my lungs, 'Let me out!'

But nobody would have come. The staff hear that all the time. That's what everyone at Warlingham says. Every day, every week, every year.

I spent so much energy trying not to be noticed by the other inmates that it was a day or two before I remembered Dad's role in my being there. It wasn't just doctors keeping me there. He'd signed something, I recalled. Dr Picton-Jones filled in the gaps. I was in Warlingham, she explained, because I'd been 'sectioned'. This was a legal order for a patient to be kept in hospital by the state – usually against their will – in order to protect them or others. A section was usually for seventy-two hours, initially. This was the emergency one, a bit like the police arresting you, then working out the case, before having to apply to hold you for longer.

I knew instinctively I'd already been there longer than seventy-two hours.

'Will I be let out soon?'

The doctor shrugged noncommittally.

'That's up to you.'

Apparently you can't do two emergency sections in a row so the next section block is for twenty-eight days. That's what they call the diagnosis period.

'That's how long you're here for, Kim.'

The doctors had four weeks to work out what's wrong with me, then, if they were successful, they could apply for a six-month period for treatment.

My blood froze at the thought.

'I can't spend six months here.'

'Let's hope it doesn't come to that,' the doctor agreed.

Then she explained that a six-month section wasn't the worst. As I understood it, after that comes the big one: six years. If you're hit with that you may as well kiss your old life good-bye. You're never coming out.

Never coming out alive, you mean, I thought as a shiver ran through me.

The prospect of anything more than a month terrified me. I'd just spent eighteen months at the Cassel but that had been like a holiday camp compared to my memories of Warlingham. I had to behave. Anything more than twenty-eight days would kill me. A bad choice of words as it transpired . . .

To action a section in those days, you needed the signatures of a psychiatrist and a social worker. In the absence of a social worker a member of the immediate family can authorise it.

That's what Dad had done.

Apparently they could have summoned a social worker to the Cassel. Dad knew that so he signed the forms while he was there for our meeting with the doctor. Knowing that I would have been sectioned anyway didn't alter how I felt.

As far as I was concerned, he'd betrayed me.

The dormitory. George Ward. Still here.

I tried to keep calm. A kind of sickness was welling in my stomach making me want to gag. But I wasn't ill.

I was scared.

It's all right, I told myself. *You got out of here before. You'll get out of here again.*

But when? What if they accused me of some new horror? What if they decided I required long-term treatment?

It was enough to drive anyone to tears but a sudden realisation gave me a glimmer of hope. One of the things I knew from my year and a half at the Cassel is how much they value closure. In day-to-day life that usually translates as being able to say goodbye to people when they or you leave. It makes the grieving process more bearable, they say. So the one piece of ammunition I had about Warlingham was that I hadn't had my perfect farewell. No therapist, I knew, was going to expect any improvement from me without that basic necessity. Which meant . . .

They're planning to send me back!

With the familiar nocturnal noises closing in, I just prayed I could survive that long.

I'd forgotten about the toilet thing. Every step I took, there was an orderly just behind, like an unwanted shadow. The worst part was, she didn't even try to hide it. She was like the worst secret agent ever. If I left my bed or the TV room – basically my only two options – she put down her magazine and sauntered after me. Not alongside me, not near enough to have a chat. But close enough to let me know she was there. Whatever I was going to do, she was going to see. And yes, that included going to the loo.

It was exactly the same set-up as before. Twenty-four-hour supervision. It was so tedious. I thought the orderlies would soon tire of trailing me around all day. There was nothing to do other than sit in the TV room. *If I'm bored doing it then they must be going out of their minds watching me do it.*

But they were clever about it. They would sit yapping to other patients nearby or do a bit of reading. They didn't have to be next to me to keep their beady eyes fixed in my direction. It didn't matter what they were doing: if I moved, they moved.

Even if I did manage to give them the slip and they did lose sight of me for a second, there was nowhere to hide from their ears. I was back in one of those paper gowns that rustled like dry leaves when I moved. The way the corridors echoed you could hear me coming a mile off. If you didn't hear me walking you'd still make out the sound of me scratching at my neck where the collar rubbed. It was horrible. My real clothes weren't in my wardrobe, either. I had no choice but to keep this stupid thing on.

Knowing the place didn't make it easier to live in. Some of the faces were familiar but there were new ones, too. Some looked open and friendly; others ready to rumble at the drop of a hat. Mostly, though, they just looked distant. Talking seemed to be an effort for the majority; talking clearly, anyway. You couldn't have a conversation. They slurred and they stuttered and many of their utterances came out in fits and bursts. It wasn't the patients' fault. I knew that. It was the drugs. Whatever medication was keeping them docile and unlikely to misbehave was also preventing them thinking and speaking properly. They were drugged up to the eyeballs. That just made some of them scarier.

Drugs, in fact, were all some of them cared about. The first words anyone spoke to me were, 'What are you on, then?' I realised he meant my medication. I told him, 'Nothing' and he scoffed and wandered off. I soon learnt that the level of your treatment is like a badge of honour. The more you're on, the more impressive you are.

Everyone who spoke to me asked the same questions:

'What are you on?'

'What hospitals have you been in?'

'What are you in for?'

'How long?'

All the talk, when it happened, was about discovering who was the worst patient there. I didn't care. I just wanted to be left alone.

The other question I was asked a lot was, 'Have you got any cigarettes?' Again, a negative answer would provoke an exodus. I didn't know then that nicotine was the currency in the hospital. The ones with anything about them traded cigarettes for favours or other items – just like they do in prison. But why did they think I'd have any? *I'm only sixteen.*

Scariest of all was the fear that I might be turned into one of them soon. The very idea terrified me. I had to cling on to my lack of closure at the Cassel.

They'll send me back soon. They have to.

I saw a lot of terrible cases at Warlingham. It was hard to tell with the medication, but plenty of people looked like they would struggle to live outside those four walls. Unlike at the Cassel, however, the staff's policy didn't seem to focus on getting anyone ready to leave. There was no drive towards repatriation or resurrection, which was another reason why I had to get out.

I saw a woman in a wheelchair one day. I thought it was odd she was there. *I didn't know Warlingham was a place for physical disabilities.*

What happened next scarred me forever.

An orderly was standing in front of the woman, who was slumped immobile, chin resting on her chest. The orderly knelt down and lifted the woman's head. Looking into her eyes, she said, 'You can walk. Come on, you can walk.'

Nothing happened. I didn't know what she expected her to do. *The woman's in a wheelchair. Obviously she can't walk!*

But the orderly wasn't having that. She fastened her arms around the woman and hoisted her forwards, to the edge of the chair.

'Come on, you can walk. You have to walk!' she said again, and with another tug, lifted the woman upright.

The woman was a bag of bones but still a really awkward shape to hold. I don't know if the orderly had planned it, but the disabled woman slipped straight through her hands and buckled onto the floor, like a doll crumpled over. She looked like she was dead.

I felt sick. I wanted to rush over. The orderly spying on me reached out.

'Leave her. It's what she wants.'

What she wants? How can she want that? How can anyone know what she wants?

I carried on watching. I wished I hadn't.

The other orderly manoeuvred the patient's limbs so they didn't look so contorted and then stood up. She made no attempt to lift her charge back into the wheelchair. I would have helped. Any number of people would have. But that wasn't the plan.

'You can walk,' she said again defiantly, then marched away without looking back.

I've got to get out of here. I must get out!

It turned out this poor woman's problems were indeed all in the mind. Her mother had died a few years ago and she and her partner had decided to emigrate. They just wanted to make a fresh start somewhere else. The problem was, the girl had suffered a breakdown as a teen and as a result was denied entry to her new 'home'.

That was the final straw and she had a complete and utter mental breakdown.

It was incredible to believe that a person could just give up on life but she had. She hadn't spoken in years, not a word. She wouldn't feed herself, she wouldn't get up and her joints were atrophying. She sat in her wheelchair all day, refusing to move, refusing to live. Her mind had literally switched off.

Every day her dad came in to see his daughter. He'd talk to her, stroke her and comb her hair. In nice weather he'd push her outside and let her look at the beautiful lawns of the golf course that surrounded the building. He couldn't have been more loving. I think he blamed himself.

The saddest thing of all is he had no idea how his beloved daughter was being treated by the staff he trusted to help her. Most days she was dragged out of her chair and left on the floor. Then just before he arrived after work they'd lump her back in, try to spruce her up a bit and stand around smiling.

I learnt the meaning of hate watching that. I wished I was brave enough to tell him. I despised myself for not stepping forward. But I had my reasons. They were cowardly but they made sense to me.

If I interfere they might do that to me. With drugs they can do anything.

And I couldn't afford that. I was going back to Cassel. I hadn't had my closure.

I was in bed one day when I was told I had visitors. I was led into the TV room and Barbara and Cathy were waiting for me. I couldn't believe it. They'd bothered to come all that way just to see me!

It was lovely catching up with them but after they'd left I felt lower than ever. It tells you everything you need to know about the Cassel versus Warlingham when patients from one have the freedom to go and visit the other. As much as I'd loved seeing my friends it was a real slap in the face.

At least they'd bothered. Mum didn't come to visit me at Warlingham. I didn't expect her to, not after last time. Lorraine showed her face a couple of times but it was obvious she was uncomfortable. Anyway, now she had a little mouth to feed it wasn't a good environment. I couldn't wait to meet my new little nephew Ben. I did think all the baby business was making Lorraine a bit weird, though. One of the first things she said to me was, 'The weight's falling off you, isn't it? I wish I was so lucky.'

What an odd thing to say.

She'd just had a baby. Of course she was a bit bigger than me.

Dad said a couple of things like that as well. I didn't pay any attention. I hadn't put on a pound or lost any since I'd come in. I didn't have to weigh myself to know that.

It was when the nurses and orderlies began to start going on about it that I got really annoyed. Everyone was always trying to get me to eat things. 'We need to get your weight up.' Things like that. I suppose I must have eaten whatever they gave me, I can't remember. Why wouldn't I? I love food. I remember they gave me eggs again. I assumed someone from the Cassel had told them about the trick they'd played on me there. It didn't seem right, to me, to laugh at a patient like that. I can take or leave eggs. I didn't see why I should have to eat them when everyone else was having a roast.

It's not fair.

But they wouldn't let up. I began to dread mealtimes. Thinking about them at the end of the day I could never remember the actual dinners, or breakfasts or lunches. Or in fact actually eating. But I did know I wasn't dieting. I didn't need to. I was lucky like that.

I was lucky as well because I knew I was going back to the Cassel. Every day I looked at the dribbling, screaming patients in the beds near mine, or skulking lifelessly around the TV room, and I thanked my stars I wasn't in their position.

Or so I kept thinking. Then every so often my hope was punctured and I remembered the section. I wasn't going anywhere until the doctors said so. It was quite out of my hands and it made me shake just contemplating it. What was the point of behaving well when no one had the power to release me anyway? Every day that passed I got angry. Things I'd accepted one minute now sent me into a rage.

That was the irony. Just being there was enough to drive you crazy. And if you act crazy you get the drugs, which in turn make you crazy. And I did not want the drugs.

I remember walking over to the garden door and trying the handle. I knew it would be locked. All the doors were locked. Our dormitory door was locked, the bathroom door was locked, the TV room was locked. There was even a secure door leading onto our floor.

I'd always known this. Yet knowing when you don't want to get out and knowing when you do provoke different reactions. As I stood looking out, watching the shadow of the building's giant clock tower flickering across the golf course, I just wanted to throw a chair through the glass and flee. Knowing that I couldn't just made me want to try harder.

But I didn't. Maybe they drugged me. The next thing I remember is being back in bed. I thought again of the section. I was still angry but scared as well. Just as my fury had heightened with the sense of being trapped, so had my fear. I'd been wandering around, I realised, in a psychological cocoon. The promise of imminent release had protected me. That's how it felt. Now I accepted I was trapped with the psychos and the deranged and I wanted to hide. Some of them looked like they wanted to hurt me. And they were always shuffling around at night, going through my things. I didn't belong here.

I have to get out. I have to do anything to get out.

A meeting room. Dad is here. A nurse also. Normal visiting time? We'll see . . .

'Are you happy now?' Dad was saying. 'Are you? The least you can do is answer me.'

Okay – not a normal visit, then.

'I don't know what to say to her,' he told the doctor. 'What can I say to her?'

'About what?' I asked, utterly perplexed.

'For God's sake, about why you did it, of course!'

'Did what?'

Maybe this is normal. We've had this argument a hundred times.

Dad reached over and flicked the collar of my gown. Instinctively I raised my hand to my neck.

'This!' he spat, and I winced as he spoke. Not from his word – it barely registered. But from the burning, lacerating pain in my neck.

I shot an accusing look at the doctor. 'What have they done to me?' Then back at Dad, back at the man who had signed the section. 'What have you let them do now?'

He looked genuinely shocked. Speechless.

'They saved your life,' he said finally. 'They cut you down. They stopped you hanging yourself.'

That wasn't the closure I was expecting ...

CHAPTER TWELVE

You've got ink all round your mouth

It all looked so delicious.

Sonia surveyed the mouth-watering feast before her. Cream of tomato soup to start. Succulent roast chicken with all the trimmings, coated in a rich gravy as the main. Then an array of lavish chocolate cakes. Some with icing, some with cream, some with extra chocolate. It was such an amazing spread. She wanted to savour the moment forever.

She was tempted to go straight to the dessert. She loved cakes. She missed them. It was so unfair. Other people ate them without putting on weight.

But even she was allowed a little treat. Just every now and again. She deserved it.

Where to start? Soup, roast or cake? It didn't matter: she wanted all of it.

Oh, but that chocolate looks so enticing.

It was decided. Cakes first. Cakes second. Cakes third. The rest would have to wait. Sonia was relieved to have made the decision. Now she could relax and enjoy her meal.

Then she tore the page out of the magazine, shredded it into tiny pieces and began to chew.

A child when I entered 'the system', I was seventeen now. I didn't know how I'd got that old. As they say, time flies – but I wasn't having fun. The latest ignominy heaped on me was that I'd tried to hang myself. Another lie. Obviously someone had attacked me in my sleep. If I was lucky it was another patient. Either way, it was a cover-up by Warlingham. They were lying to my dad like they were lying to the father of the wheelchair-bound woman.

Who knows what lengths they'll go to to keep me here?

The lies were coming thick and fast. Not only did I have dissociation, now they said I had anorexia. That was just ridiculous. Eating wasn't my problem. Getting enough food was the problem. I was always so hungry. *And whose fault is that? Why won't they feed me?*

As my month in Warlingham grew to a close I feared the worst. How would the 'hanging' count against me? This anorexia business had been blown out of all proportion as well. What would Dr Picton-Jones do next? *Lock me up for six months or let me go back to the Cassel?*

At the end of the section I had a review meeting with her. She went on about progress and effort and this and that. I couldn't concentrate. The pressure was killing me. In the end I had to blurt it out.

'Are you letting me go back to the Cassel?'

The doctor looked over her glasses. I scrutinised her for any signs or clues. Two years of therapy had taught me there's more to a conversation than words. Slowly she put her pen lid back on, adjusted her papers minutely and took a breath.

'No, Kim,' she said slowly. 'I'm not sending you back to the Cassel.'

'Don't keep me here! They'll kill me.'

'Kim,' she said calmly. 'Listen to me. I'm not sending you back to the Cassel – because I'm sending you home.'

It took a moment to sink in.

Home?

I barely dared say the words.

'*My* home?' I asked nervously.

She nodded. Some of her colleagues had argued for an extended section but they'd been overruled. My hanging – as unfortunate as it was – was a sign, she felt, of how much I loathed my body. In other words, a classic demonstration of the demons driving my anorexia and bulimia. Yes, she said, there *were* grounds to keep me locked up for the next six months or six years or sixty years. But what I really needed was treatment for my eating disorders.

I didn't know whether to laugh or cry. Laugh – because I was getting out of that hellish prison even though they claimed I'd tried to hang myself. And cry – because still the lies persisted. Anorexia and bulimia? I wished they'd play another record because this one was getting tiresome. How could a non-existent eating disorder drive me to a non-existent suicide attempt?

Apparently my diagnosis of dissociation was still relevant because it was often a factor in eating disorders – especially when I was claiming not to remember my behaviour at meal-times (amnesia being a symptom). But that, and the anorexia and bulimia, would be sorted out once I started outpatient visits at the Maudsley Hospital. That was the condition on which I was being released. Failure to attend would see me hoiked back into Warlingham Park the same day.

Eagerly I agreed. She could have set the bars at any height and I'd have jumped them. Or injured myself trying.

I only needed one clue to know where I was this time. My sister's smiling face. She was holding a small bundle. My nephew. Ben. Behind her was her new boyfriend, Lawrence – or Lol – the lad's father. It was like looking at a family photo.

Lorraine and her new family were in Nan's old room. My things were in the box room. I didn't mind. At least it was mine. There were no locks on my door, no one would follow me to the loo in the night and the only person I had to worry about going through my things was a curious little boy.

'Well, you'll be needing a job, then.'

Mum was as blunt as ever.

'You're an adult now. You need to be paying your way.'

It was fair enough. I was seventeen. Unfortunately I'd missed the last few years of education. What job was there out there for me?

'At least you can sign on until you find something.'

Before I knew it I had an Unemployment Benefit number and fortnightly payments coming in. I wasn't exactly earning but I was able to give Mum a few pounds for my bed and board, as she called it – especially as we no longer had Dad's wages to support us. After seven or eight unsuccessful years, it had finally happened. Dad had moved out. One day he'd just waited until everyone was out of the house, then packed his bags, left a note and walked out the front door for the last time.

With Dad gone money was tight. That wasn't the main

issue though. Mum was the hardest-working woman I ever knew. She believed that everyone should pull their weight in the world. And that included daughters fresh out of hospital.

Mum was right. It might only be dole money, but if I had my own income I'd be able to put some distance between me and my dark past. I could make a fresh start. Unfortunately that was the last thing the authorities wanted me to do.

Because of my hospital history I was registered on the 'Green Card' system – basically to show a disability. That was the last thing I wanted. It's one thing being locked up in a mental institution. It's another thing having to carry a card that tells the whole world.

'Put it this way,' the guy at the job centre said. 'If you're on the Green Card there's a lot less pressure on you to find work. And if you do find work it means they have to let you have any further treatment.'

Actually the card didn't specify why I had been in hospital. I suppose it could have been for an ingrown toenail. But I knew what it meant and every day I saw it in my purse was another reminder of the treatment I'd been subjected to.

Lots of people. Machines. Terrible, loud whirring noises.

I was in some sort of factory, sitting at a bench alongside dozens of other women. There were a few men milling around as well. They were wearing overalls, like foremen at a depot. Some had clipboards. Everyone was talking. I hadn't heard so much chatter since Warlingham. But here people were answering. Listening and answering. That was something you didn't get at the other place.

Suddenly it was my turn to listen.

'How are you getting on, dear?'

My godmother, Bette, was leaning over my shoulder.

Quickly. What do I know about Bette? She works in a factory. She works in a factory where they make something. Where they make optics for pubs!

That's where I was.

'Do you want me to show you again, dear? It's a bit tricky at first, I know.'

I smiled. 'Yes please.' A minute later I was picking up the small bits of plastic and inserting them into their moulds. It was simple, straightforward and incredibly dull – and I had no idea why I was doing it.

Still, I suppose I'm being paid. That will keep Mum happy.

Part of my deal with Dr Picton-Jones when I left Warlingham was I had to go back for regular outpatient sessions. They were easy enough. I trotted along and the therapists or doctors there told me about my depression, my anorexia, my bulimia or my dissociation. I just sat and nodded. Whatever they wanted to tell me, I wasn't going to disagree – even though it sounded like they were plucking random words out of a medical dictionary. I knew they were wrong. I knew it wasn't about me. And I knew the best way to play it.

Bite your tongue, nod your head – then get out of there as fast as you can.

I didn't need their advice. I didn't need help from anyone. I had discovered my own therapy: alcohol.

I can't remember when I first had a drink but know I liked it. White wine was my tipple. I began to have a little glass at home with Mum. Sometimes I went out with her and Lorraine on one of their regular sessions. In most of my memories from this period I was holding a glass.

I didn't always drink alone. One of my visitors at Warlingham had been a girl called Jennifer. We'd known each other at school and then lost touch. She bumped into Mum one day and discovered where I was. It was lovely to see her, although she looked too terrified by what she called 'the nutters' around her to speak much. Once I was out, though, we hooked up. She'd moved back into the area after a few years away. We got on so well that we decided to go on holiday together. After a few months of working I'd saved enough for a week away. It was so exciting poring over the holiday brochures. In the end we settled on Greece and had a great week. Well, I say week – it seemed to flash by in a blur. *But,* I thought, *that's the wine for you. It affects the memory.*

I used the same excuse when I started doing the weekly shop for Mum. 'It's the least you can do now you're earning.' She sent me to the supermarket with a list and off I trotted. When I got back, Mum opened one of the bags and just stared at me.

'What's all this?'

'It's what you asked for,' I replied.

'I don't think I ordered a carrier bag of sweets.'

Sweets?

I tore open the other bags. They were all full of cakes and goodies.

'I must have picked up the wrong basket,' I said. But I could tell Mum wasn't convinced.

In a fairly short time after leaving Warlingham I'd managed to put down some sort of roots: I'd got a job which gave

'Pratt' by Ria Pratt

To find out more about each artwork featured in *All of Me*,
please turn to the back of the book.

'Ken' by Ken

'The Art of Starvation' by Judy

'Lost in Play' by Ken

'Thinking Man' by Abi

'The Naming' by Dawn

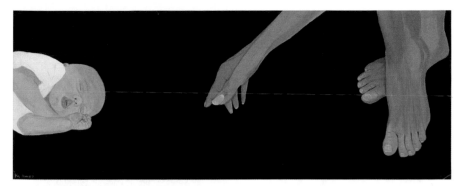

'Reaching Out' by Bonny

'Aims' by Suzy

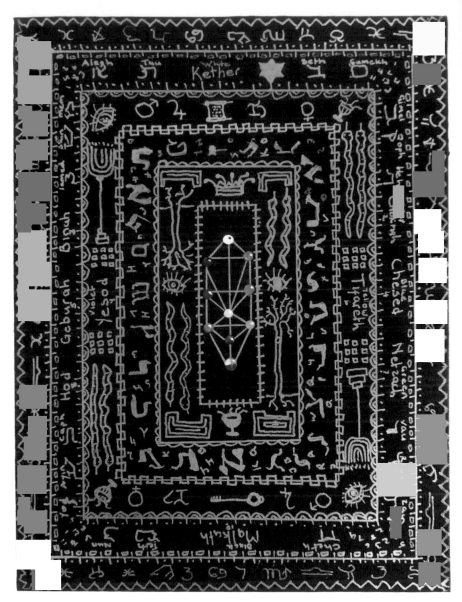

'Golden Kabbalah' by Key

'Longing Rose'
by Judy

'Mystery of the
Prayer' by Anon

'Hangman'
by MJ

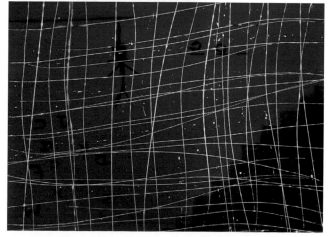

'Oh!' by Suzy

'Silent Blue' by Patricia

me a small income, I was socialising with friends and I even enjoyed being at home. Mum was still devastated that Dad had gone – despite everything she was that classic 'one-man woman' – but without him there I didn't have to put up with the constant bickering. If anything, she was back to the normal, kind, funny woman that I'd seen so little of for so many years. Yes, things seemed to be working in my favour for once.

I even started seeing boys.

It began when Lorraine bought me driving lessons for my eighteenth birthday. I don't know how it came about but I ended up dating the instructor. Every night Joe and I would end up in a pub somewhere and usually I'd drive us there, although I don't remember actually ever having a lesson. Luckily for me he didn't drink.

Everything seemed to be working for me, but it didn't take long to get back to situation normal: out of the blue I was told I'd lost my job – I knew people sometimes seemed fed up when I asked what I was meant to be doing, but firing me seemed a bit extreme. *No,* I decided. *There has to be another reason.*

It's because of my Green Card. Someone must have found out.

But that wasn't the reason at all. Apparently I just hadn't shown up a few times and they'd assumed I'd quit. This was news to me, although, on the plus side, it was a relief to learn I hadn't been fired at all.

Bette later told Mum that on the days I had appeared there'd been reports of my disappearing to the toilet to throw up. Mum denied it to Bette but as soon as she was gone turned on me.

'For God's sake, Kim, you know what will happen if you don't stop this stupid behaviour.'

I didn't – but I soon found out.

'My name is Dr Simons. I'm in charge of the eating disorder unit here.'

I looked around.

Who's he talking to?

There was no one else in the room.

Where am I? It's not Warlingham. Too smart, too clean, too friendly. So far, anyway.

His words sank in.

What does he mean, 'eating disorder'? There's nothing wrong with my eating.

True, I couldn't remember my last meal, but that was normal. *Blame the wine.*

'Now, here at the Maudsley we believe in therapeutic treatment.'

The Maudsley. I knew that place. A huge redbrick psychiatric hospital in Denmark Hill, near Camberwell. I didn't know why I was here but, I'd learnt, it paid to go along with their ideas. Or at least appear to.

'When do I have to come in?'

The doctor looked surprised.

He didn't expect me to say that.

He certainly didn't – any more than I predicted his response.

'Oh you don't have to come in,' he beamed. 'You'll be staying here for a while.'

Oh no you don't. I've got my life. I'm happy. You're not ruining it again.

'I'm eighteen. You can't keep me here if I don't want to be here.'

He shrugged. 'Technically, I'm recommending you stay with us for a while until we get your eating under control. However, if you choose to walk out that door I will apply for a section.'

'A section?' My mind was reeling.

What for?

He nodded. He was serious. I slumped in my seat.

'You win. Where do I go?'

The Maudsley, I'd heard, catered for all sorts of nutters and weirdos and psychos.

And me.

I was on Ward 3, the therapy ward, with a complete range of oddballs. The ones with eating disorders were the worst. Anorexia, bulimia, you name it. Half of them wouldn't eat anything; the others cleaned the plate, then threw it up within minutes.

What's wrong with people? Who would want to live like that?

The same accusations had been levelled at me, I remembered, so it was best to take them all with a pinch of salt. In my experience my fellow patients turned out to be some of the sanest people you could meet – with perhaps a few things to work on. Funnily enough, though, no one else denied their diagnoses. That was weird. Why was it just me who was locked in by mistake?

The ward was split in half for group therapy. Half a dozen of us went with Dr Young, the registrar, the rest with someone else. Overall control for the ward came from Professor Julian Leff.

I don't think a lot of the patients had much experience of

therapy prior to those sessions. They struggled with the rules and the incessant questioning and analysis, whereas I'd seen it all before. If anyone had asked, I could have predicted the therapist would sit there, nodding, umming and ahing, and peppering everything with 'I see, I see' and the classic 'And how did that make you feel?'

I was right. But I still had to get through it and try to convince these idiots that there was nothing wrong with me so I could go home.

Mum didn't come to visit, although Jennifer did and so did Dad. The Maudsley wasn't too far from his new house, so he was a regular sight. He was never as embarrassing to talk to as Mum – who sometimes struggled to hide how uncomfortable she found being among my fellow patients – but we'd been through the whole patient-and-visitor role for so long there wasn't much left for us to talk about. Still, at least he wasn't weird. One of the other girls in Ward 3 was regularly visited by her dad but, if you ask me, he was the one who should have been a patient. He'd barely say a word. He'd just stand in the lounge, near her chair, and pose like he was a ballet dancer caught mid-dance. It was fascinating to watch. He had such grace, such poise, like a bird, but what the hell was he doing? I wasn't surprised to see him on television years later but he was a painter, not a dancer.

The Maudsley has had its share of celebrity patients, actually, and while I was there I shared therapy groups with someone with royal connections. I wondered if she was being kept there by the same lies as me.

No one looked exactly pleased to be there but some coped better than others. We were all sitting around doing nothing as usual when there was a big fuss out in the corridor. That wasn't new. But the screaming was worse than anything I'd ever heard in Warlingham.

There was a crowd blocking the door by the time I got there. But I was just in time to see a man outside completely on fire. He'd obviously tried to kill himself but I don't think he'd been prepared for the slow pain. He was haring up and down, flames pouring off him like the Wicker Man.

Oh my God, he's going to die!

Then out of nowhere a nurse shoulder-charged him and they both went down. A second later he was wrapped in a blanket being rolled over and over. The fire was out. He was alive. It had taken about five seconds.

It's only in an emergency that you see what people are really capable of. Who'd have thought Ward 3 staff knew what to do when someone immolates himself? They also had a procedure to prevent escapes.

The Maudsley was a big hospital and you were allowed to wander, by and large. The entrance to Ward 3 was at the top of a flight of stairs, but if you got through the door there was room to roam. With permission you were even allowed to venture down to the shops. Dare to touch the stairs without clearance, however, and the flags went up. I saw a lad flash past once. He was young, athletic and really motoring. I thought, *There's no way these staff are going to catch him.*

A nurse came flying out of her office but she didn't even try to chase him. She just ran to a button on the wall and hammered it. A second later alarms pealed throughout the building. That was the lockdown signal, I realised. That was the cue for certain staff on every floor to drop what they were doing and head into the corridors – to stop whoever was making a break for freedom.

It was an incredible sight to behold. Staff in white coats appeared from every corner and literally jumped on the poor guy. We called them the 'A-Team'. Nobody ever got past them although plenty tried.

I was accused of it once. As if! But I suddenly found myself being manhandled back up the stairs by two giant orderlies. They were hurting my arm.

'Get off me!'

'And let you try to run away again?' one said.

'You may as well let her go. She won't get far at that speed.'

'Yeah, you'll have to be quicker next time, love.'

Nod and smile. Nod and smile.

Three weeks, four weeks – I don't know – but some time later I found myself back at home. I didn't feel healthier. I didn't look any different.

What was the point of that?

Still, I didn't have time to waste on worrying about my weight. I had things to do, starting with finding a new job.

Sometimes things just fall into place, don't they? No sooner had I thought about it than I discovered I had a new job – even if I didn't know how it had happened. Still, you can't look a gift horse ...

That smell! The bodies, the urine, the Dettol.

The familiar claustrophobia of panic was overwhelming.

No, not Warlingham!

Where else could I be? I took a second to study the room. The patients looked older. The layout was different. The TV was newer and bigger. It wasn't George Ward. I wasn't in the peep-hole cell. That made a change. So where was I? And why was one of the older ones asking me to help her up? And how did she know my name?

Weird.

I think I'd been there about ten minutes before I realised I wasn't a patient – I was a member of staff. It was an old people's home – which explained the smell – and I was a carer. For once I'd be following other people, making sure they were where they had to be. This time the boot was on the other foot.

I was excited, actually. Warlingham had shown me how these institutions shouldn't be run. I had the chance to make a difference. I really thought I'd found my vocation. That didn't last long.

One of my jobs was getting the old dears washed and bathed. I just had to run the bath, help them with their cloth-ing if necessary and then hang around in case they got into difficulties. The old ladies were really sweet – senile as you like, but lovely. Some of them reverted to kids in the bath water. It was really lovely to watch.

The men, on the other hand, just reverted to evil so-and-sos. The first old boy I took there, Eric, told me he was too decrepit to wash himself. His words, not mine. 'Beverley, your predecessor, always washed me,' he said pathetically. Like an idiot I believed him.

I got hold of a sponge and told him to stand up. While he held onto the safety rail I scrubbed his back, legs and stomach and arms as briskly as I could. When I finished I threw the sponge back into the bath and dried my hands. In the mirror I noticed Eric was still standing.

'You've missed a bit,' he said.

When I turned round I noticed something else was standing as well!

It was staggering how many randy old buggers there were in that place. They all tried it on at one time or another. The home leader just laughed in my face when I told her what I'd been doing. 'They're having you on,' she said. 'If they can't wash themselves then they don't get washed. That's the rule.'

There was one exception. One bloke had some sort of infection and his testicles had swollen up like tennis balls. I was told by a nurse that I would need to wash them for him. I agreed but when the old boy took down his pants I nearly gagged.

No way!

I hated working at that home. I think the patients were treated well enough but I'd spent enough time in institutions. It wasn't pleasant being there, especially with the familiar stench of wee and bleach. More than that, there are only so many times you can have your backside slapped by an eighty-year-old. So one day I just threw my blue tunic on the supervisor's desk and walked out.

It felt good leaving. I literally just walked out the door and never returned. How many times I'd wanted to do that at so many other places. The only problem was what to tell Mum.

The next morning I was in my car. I don't remember getting there. I don't remember driving to the top of our road. But I do remember waiting until nine o'clock and thinking, *Mum will have left by now.* Then I drove back home and went inside. When she returned nine hours later she assumed I'd been to work.

We carried that on for about three weeks. I'd leave for work, wait for Mum to go past, then shoot back home. My cover was only blown when Mum asked for my housekeeping money and I had to tell her why I didn't have any.

Not again.

I recognise some of the walls, the beds, the nurses – even some of the patients. I was on Ward 3 at the Maudsley. Dad was next to me, talking to a doctor. They were discussing my weight. I tried to tune out but it was impossible. I needed to eat more, they said.

Yeah, yeah.

I needed to stop being sick.

Heard it before.

I needed to focus on being healthy.

Same old story, same old lies.

If I didn't I could look forward to a lifetime of institutional care.

Now I'm listening!

I promised I'd behave. What other option did I have? The only problem was not knowing what I'd done wrong in the first place. If you don't know that, how can you avoid doing it again? I became a bag of nerves. Making my bed, brushing my teeth, contributing to the therapy sessions – were any of these acts on the 'mustn't do' list? Was I doing them right? It was like walking on eggshells and knowing one of them was really a mine primed to go up at the slightest touch.

Worst of all was the suspicion that when the mine went off I could be nowhere near and still get the blame – and that's exactly what happened.

'Well, that won't fill you up,' the nurse laughed wearily. 'You'd better spit it out.'

Where did she come from?

'Spit what out?' I replied. 'I haven't eaten anything.' That was the God's truth. I hadn't had a crumb all day, not even breakfast, I suddenly realised.

'Come on, you know what I mean. The paper. Don't tell me you've swallowed it.'

She held one hand out under my mouth and with the other picked up a magazine from the table in front of me. It was open at an article on food. There were scraps of pages screwed up all over it.

Someone's been having fun, I thought.

Then I looked back at the nurse, who now had both hands on her hips.

'Look, Kim, you've got to stop eating paper.'

So that's what this is about. She thinks I made this mess?

'I haven't eaten any paper. Don't be stupid!'

'Kim, love, you've got ink all round your mouth.'

The paper episode got me kept in another few weeks. They said it was part of my disorder. Not my depression or my dissociation or one of those other made-up diagnoses. My anorexia or bulimia – I can't remember which. It didn't matter to me. They were both as untrue as each other.

There was no point in fighting it. I knew how it worked. They accused me of something, I promised to behave, we had therapy for a while, then they let me out. Over the next few years this happened, on average, once or twice a year. When I wasn't inside the hospital I was visiting Dr Murray Jackson in out-patients, listening to one wild claim after another. Trumped-up charges every time, from having breakdowns at work to claiming the television was giving me signals. When Professor Leff had told me that one I just laughed in his face. He didn't flinch, just wrote something in his notebook.

Trying to juggle a normal life knowing that at any moment I could be scooped off into the Maudsley was almost impossible. Almost – but not quite. I still found time to have a drink. Of course, when Dr Jackson found that out, his notebook received a new load of scribble. The next thing I knew I had a new diagnosis to add to my collection: alcoholic.

For once I couldn't disagree. In the outside world I always seemed to have a glass of Pinot Grigio in my hand. It wasn't the best tag to have on my medical records but, I realised, it was better than being called bulimic.

Nobody has ever been sectioned for being drunk.

But they have been locked up for schizophrenia – and that was coming my way next.

CHAPTER THIRTEEN

My own place

The delivery van thundered down the congested south London street. Parked cars were lined bumper to bumper as far as the eye could see. Pedestrians flitted in and out of shops and houses. Julie had to be alert. Any one of them could suddenly dart out in front of the van. It happened all the time.

As she pulled up at traffic lights, Julie used the red light's pause to sift through the paperwork on the passenger seat and double-check the pick-up address. Just as she thought. She'd been there a hundred times. The van could probably find its way without her.

Amber. Green.

Van into first, then through the gears to fourth, Julie crawled away. She needed the third turning on the right. Ready to indicate any moment.

Then she noticed the car in front. It was trying to tell her something. She studied the number plate. It was as clear as day. It was saying 'turn left'.

Change of plan!

The squeal of tyres trying to cling to the road as the van skidded into a sudden turn brought shocked stares from passers-by. A cacophony of horns joined in a second later and there was angry swearing from a man who'd been halfway across the road.

Julie heard it all and didn't care.

She had to obey the messages.

She pulled up behind another car, a blue one, and waited for further instruction. It was there, in the registration plate as usual, the letter 'R'.

That means 'right'.

So that's where she turned, less suddenly this time but still without warning the car behind.

Julie had forgotten about the delivery. She was following a more important mission now. The messages were coming through loud and clear. The next one was the most unmistakeable of all.

'C.Y.E.'

It could only mean one thing: 'close your eyes'. Without a second thought Julie obeyed.

She was travelling at almost thirty miles an hour.

Cars have played a regular part in my life. The sound of Dad roaring up our road and those tense moments afterwards wondering if he'd make the bend at that speed is one of my clearest, earliest memories. Mum's accident changed the dynamic in the house for ages. She was the strong one, the one in charge. Having her out of action made everything wrong.

Then there was the fact I was given a driving licence without ever having taken a lesson – although I was going out with the instructor at the time.

Speaking of boyfriends, I was going out with another guy when my next four-wheeled memory occurred. My little car had a problem so I called a mechanic to come and have a look. He was a good-looking chap and so when he asked me out I said yes. Of course, he turned out to be married – although that wasn't the only reason we only saw each other once.

He picked me up in his car – even though he'd fixed mine now – and we drove out to Epsom. It's a bit more picturesque than certain parts of south London but I'd have been happier with somewhere closer. I thought maybe he was trying to impress me – although he probably wanted to get far away from being possibly spotted by his wife!

We had a nice night actually. My wine glass was always topped up, which was the main thing. As we drove back along these narrow lanes through Banstead, the road was so twisty, it was bend after bend. There were no streetlights and either side of the road there was a high grass verge that made it look narrower still. If anything came the other way both cars had to slow down to make sure we didn't touch.

Everything was fine, romantic even. Then we saw the headlights.

It happened so quickly I couldn't even scream. There was a car on the other side of the road – and another one overtaking it and heading straight for us.

Where could we go? There was nowhere. Everyone slammed on their brakes but it was too late.

The next thing I remember is scrabbling for the door handle. I had to get out. I was sure the car was going to explode. That's what happened in films. It was pitch black; all the headlights had been smashed. I didn't even know where I would run. I couldn't make out up from down.

Come on! Open!

The handle turned but the door wouldn't budge. It had been smacked too hard. Then I realised we were up against the grass verge. Panicking I shoved it with my shoulder, hard, and felt it give. I did it again, and again. Finally there was just enough of a gap for me to squeeze through. I just managed to get through, oblivious to the nettles and damp grass scratching my face, and pulled myself out. I didn't give two hoots about my date, that much was clear. I just wanted to get away.

Half running, half staggering into the darkness I heard screaming and crying. It was like being back in Warlingham. Like being in the dreaded lock-up area on George Ward.

Suddenly there were lights and the sound of an engine. A car pulled up. Instinctively I went over but when the doors opened I froze. Three terrifying-looking punks were clambering out. They were dressed in black from head to foot with studs and pins sticking out of everywhere. There'd been a lot of bad press at the time about people like this. I looked behind me. Was it too late to run back?

I learnt a lesson that night. Never judge a book by its cover. Those kids were so sweet. They took me to their car and made me sit in it while one of them ran to the nearest house to call an ambulance.

'Are you sure? I'm bleeding. It will get all over your car.'

'Don't worry about it. Get in.'

I think they thought a bit of blood might have improved their image!

I was taken eventually to a hospital and patched up. My face was lacerated, my arm was battered and I had a gammy leg. They wanted to keep me in overnight but I discharged myself. I just kept saying, 'I need to get back to Mum.'

I clearly wasn't ready. Two days later I was back in hospital. I don't know how I'd arrived – nothing new there. I'd been found, they said, wandering around and couldn't remember my name. Eventually someone recognised me – not surprising considering the amount of time I'd spent there. They produced my notes and deduced 'hysterical amnesia' – apparently a 'classic example of dissociation', they agreed. I wasn't convinced.

I've just been in a serious road accident, you idiots. Don't you think that might have had something to do with it?

I mentioned Mum was on her own. That was true. Lorraine was pregnant with her second son, Alex, and had decided it would be best if she, Lol and Ben moved out to stay with Lol's mum round the corner. After Dad had gone Mum clung to Lorraine. She was her rock, she'd given her a grandson – and she took Mum out drinking every week.

Indirectly, a car was about to make her life worse – not that the doctors ever admitted it.

It started when she went to the opticians for her annual check-up. There was nothing wrong with her eyes but it's best to be on the safe side, she always said. The optician told her she had a leaking blood vessel in both eyes – which we think was caused originally during the accident. He booked her into hospital and said they'd seal it.

The operation went perfectly. Lasers were fired into Mum's eyes, then they put patches on her and said, 'By tomorrow you'll be back to normal.'

She wasn't.

'I can't see anything!'

Mum was truly scared. 'It will be all right,' I said. What else was there to say? But Monday turned into Tuesday, which quickly became Friday. A week after the operation we returned to the hospital to be told Mum was permanently blind.

I can't imagine being told that. She'd gone into the operating theatre with 20/20 vision and come out unable to see. Nothing prepares you for that.

Weeks later we got to the bottom of it. The doctor with the laser had said, 'When it gets too uncomfortable let me know and we'll switch it off.'

Mum took it as a point of pride to endure it way past the discomfort stage. In the end they turned it off without her asking.

Stupid, stubborn old woman. Her and her warped ego. It was the same as that business with the dentist removing my teeth. She cared more about what people thought than what was good for her.

The result was two burnt eyes and 98 per cent blindness. She could make out light and shade but that was it. It must have been horrible for her.

Even with her near-to-total blindness, Mum actually found it easier to find work than I did. Because she worked for the Department of the Environment they found a job she could still do. Apparently, my Green Card wasn't exactly what employers were looking for. Rejection letters arrived at the house thick and fast – many of them from jobs I had no recollection of applying for. Fortunately, family and friends rallied round.

Aunty Ivy found me a job with her at a bookbinders in Norwood. It was pretty menial stuff – putting this here, taking this there – but it paid, although not for long. When demand died down I was let go.

Then my friend Jennifer's sister stepped up. Jill worked at Croydon Council and managed to persuade them to take me on at Taberner House as part of the Housing Benefit team.

'It's only a temporary post for six months,' Jill explained, 'but if you're any good I'm sure you'll get the job. They're looking for someone to fill it permanently.'

Six months? If I lasted that long it would be a record.

But I did. In fact the reason for my leaving half a year later had nothing to do with me. Jill couldn't have been more apologetic but they were hiring another temp on the same contract. They were doing it to save money. Temps are cheaper, apparently. So the job was never on offer, really.

Once more the dole stepped in to plug the void between posts. Finding something when you've as good as got 'disability' stamped on your forehead wasn't easy. Ironically, the next job I found myself doing came as a result of the company actively searching for Green Card holders. I think there must have been tax breaks or some other incentive. I don't suppose they were doing it for the good of their souls. Either way, they seemed to be keen because I appeared to be taken on without even applying. One minute I was at home; the next I was there. I didn't question how – as I hadn't with the washing-up job and the shop position or any of the others – I was just interested in discovering what, where and with whom.

First impressions: two people. In navy blue uniforms, white shirt and tie. Talking to each other – and me. They know me so I must know them. They're laughing. We must be friends.

That was what I took in during my first couple of seconds with them. A moment later I noticed the vans. Five or six white courier Transits parked alongside one another in a pen. Instinctively I looked down. I was wearing the same outfit as the other pair – and the logo on the breast pocket matched the sign on the side of the vans. I worked here.

But doing what?

There was a pause and then the other two headed across the road to a cafeteria. Inside there were half a dozen other people wearing the same thing. The woman who'd led the way introduced me to a few of them. I realised she must be my supervisor.

'This is Kim. She's driving for us now.'

Oh, am I? There's that driving thread in my life again.

But at least I knew. I looked out the window at the vans across the street. I'd never driven anything that big before.

I had a fun lunch, just watching everyone, listening, trying to pick up clues about what I was delivering where. When we'd all finished I had it explained to me. I was a courier for a large company. It was my job to take internal mail around town from one division to another. Weirdly, the supervisor claimed I'd been doing it all morning. I wasn't going to argue, not on my first day, not even if she was the maddest woman on Earth. And besides, there was a perfectly logical reason:

Maybe I'm not the only one in on the Green Card ticket.

I did that courier job for five years. Five years! It couldn't have been easier. In fact every lunchtime we'd all meet up at another café to compare work loads. The goal was to always have had everything done by midday. Then you could tell your boss you were still going and pretty much doss for the remainder of the day. It felt naughty but everyone else was doing it. *Why shouldn't I?*

Socialising was just as good after work as well. At the end of each day I'd park up, hop out, then go for a drink with my colleagues. More accurately speaking, I'd just go for the drink. I rarely remembered actually driving the van at all. Obviously I did because that was my job. It was like the eating thing. I got into so much trouble for eating too much or too little or too infrequently and I really argued about it. Honestly, though, I could rarely recall a single meal. And if I couldn't remember them, how did these other people think they could? But I knew I did it. Just as I knew I was having baths although I could never remember actually getting in one. I was clean every day. Mum complained about my taking time in the bathroom for my entire life. There was the proof right there.

Maybe if I didn't drink so much I'd remember more.

Life had never been busier or more fun. I dated a couple of guys from work; nothing serious, just an excuse to get out and have a glass or two of wine. Then, after a short while of working I managed to save enough money to finally leave home. I was so excited. It felt like I was taking charge of my life for the first time. My own place! In my wildest dreams at Warlingham I could never have imagined that.

It was more of a bedsit really. I don't remember viewing it. I picked up the keys from the guy who ran the launderette below, handed over an envelope of money I was carrying and he let me in. It was a bit of a tip to be honest, furnished with a load of flea-ridden tat. But it was somewhere for me to go. Somewhere for me to call my own.

The problem was, I didn't dare tell Mum. Her health had been deteriorating since she'd lost her eyesight. In the first year or two of my driving job she developed quite severe arthritis which caused problems at her own work until eventually she was grateful to retire. Mum was the hardest-working person I've ever known and she hated twiddling her thumbs at home. She received decent support from social services – meals on wheels and a cleaner and eventually a daily carer – but nothing seemed to cheer her up like visits from Lorraine or evenings in front of the telly with me. Mum liked a vodka and a natter so I'd happily have a drink with her and then help her to bed. Then I'd slip out, back to my own place. I had to leave for work before Mum got up anyway so she never noticed. Other nights I'd go out straight from work so she wouldn't expect to see me then either. I should have been a spy. It's amazing how easily I led a double life without even really trying.

If I'm honest, it would have been better for Mum if I didn't have my own place, especially when a few years later she was ravaged by both rheumatoid arthritis and osteoarthritis and getting about was getting harder and harder. But I needed space to myself, to grow. In any case, I think I did all right by her. In fact, Mum often thanked me for helping her out when I hadn't even been round there. I put it down to our friends in the bottles. Either she was drinking too much or I was.

Things could have been a bit more straightforward, I suppose, but by the time I reached my mid-twenties I'd been spinning plates for as long as I could remember, trying to keep so many things going at once, that it was almost second nature. I was busy, I was trying to cram as much in as possible – that's how it felt, anyway – but I can honestly say I was happy. I was independent, I had boyfriends, I had a job and I hadn't been inside a funny farm for ages.

And then my delivery van was completely written off in a collision with two parked cars on an otherwise deserted street. *Cars again – the bane of my life.* Witnesses said I hadn't even attempted to make the bend, just ploughed straight ahead, without braking. My body was found slumped over the steering wheel and then taken by ambulance to A&E. I didn't remember that. I didn't remember any of the accident. The first thing I knew about the whole affair was a concerned new doctor, Dr Peters, leaning across his desk at the Maudsley and his chilling words.

'You could be here for a while.'

CHAPTER FOURTEEN

The psychotic shuffle

It made perfect sense at the time. If you feel unclean, you have a bath.

Julie excused herself from the session and skipped along the corridor to the bathroom. It was locked, as expected. Standard practice during daytime, but worth checking anyway.

Doesn't matter, she thought, pushing open the door to the ladies' lavatories. Selecting the end cubicle, she went in and stood on the toilet lid. This was the stall that backed onto the bathroom. If she was lucky, when she looked over the low wooden partition, she should see the row of baths and sinks.

Bingo!

One foot balanced on the cistern, Julie hauled herself up – and over. It wasn't a dismount to win gymnastic medals but she didn't twist anything. Anyway, she didn't have time to worry about it now. In a few minutes she'd be missed. The dogs would be set on her trail.

They'll never find me here, she thought as the water slowly filled the bath.

It was a shame to rush. She was looking forward to this. Then, having tested the temperature, she stepped in, absolutely fully clothed.

They call it 'the psychotic shuffle'. You can spot sufferers a mile off. They drag themselves along, barely lifting their feet, like ice skaters in slippers. The men normally have hair sticking out all over the shop and bad dress sense. With women the tell-tale sign is the makeup. It reminds me of a kid's colouring-in, where he can't stay within the lines. There's usually lipstick all over the lower face; anywhere but on the lips. As for eyeshadow, it's always bright blue, always all over their eyes, like a colourful panda.

One glimpse of this bunch and you know the backstory: 'mental health problem'. They may as well stamp it on their foreheads – although they'd probably miss.

You don't need to have been in and out of mental institutions all your life to recognise the signs. But you do need that experience to realise that it's not their illness that causes patients to act like this.

It's the medication.

And that's exactly what they wanted to give me.

Mum and Lorraine. They're here. I'm at the Maudsley. What have I done now?

Professor Leff was very apologetic. He said, 'I refuse to diagnose this lightly. Some of the episodes were years ago but I prefer to wait. Now though, what's this? Six psychotic episodes? I think we've held back long enough. We'll keep her here for the twenty-eight-day observation but I'm afraid there can only be one diagnosis.'

Schizophrenia.

Mum and Dad were in shock. Lorraine was petrified it might be hereditary. She was a mum now. Anything like that could affect her family. And me? I just wanted to scream.

But that's playing into his hands, I thought. So I bit my tongue. As usual.

There would be no option, the professor explained, given my most recent episode, which could so easily have injured or killed innocent people, but to take me on a six-year section as a ward of court after that. If my parents wouldn't sign then he could find the necessary social workers who could.

'I'm afraid your daughter needs long-term, monitored help. And,' he said, producing a little pot from his drawer, 'she will have to take these every day for the rest of her life.' That was the final straw. I couldn't take any more.

'I'm not being drugged up. I'm not schizophrenic!'

The professor gave a look to my family that seemed to say, 'See what I mean?' and I backed down. It was the wrong tactic. As I let myself be led to a ward I was annoyed with myself for my outburst. I'd been sectioned before and got out. I just had to keep my nose clean. That shouldn't be hard. Then they'd see I was fine and, hey presto, I'd be out before I knew it. I just needed to bite my tongue, whatever the provocation. That was the plan.

I can do this.

But then they gave me my medicine and all plans flew out the window. In fact, everything flew out. After a couple of days on the schizo pills I could barely remember my own name. I thought, *Is this your way of curing people? Making them unable to walk ten yards?*

Even as I swallowed the pill as a nurse looked on, I could see what they were doing.

You don't want to make me better. You want to make me behave.

That was it, I was a fully paid-up member of the psychotic shuffle community. I didn't think I would ever be getting out.

The medication prescribed to me was an anti-psychotic. It was designed to cancel out the lure of hallucinations. Side effects, as I already knew, included listlessness, dribbling, incoherence and general inability to live life. To combat these I was also given tablets used to treat Parkinson's disease. As I didn't suffer from anything I knew neither pills were going to help. They could only make me worse.

I think my parents were quietly happy with Professor Leff's diagnosis. No one wants a schizo in the family – certainly not Lorraine – but there was a general relief that the root of my behaviour had been identified. The first step to curing a problem, after all, is admitting the problem. That was the logic. That is how it works in the therapeutic community, anyway. The only problem was, I wouldn't admit the problem.

As far as I was concerned I wasn't depressed, I'd never suffered from amnesia, anorexia, bulimia, dissociation or, the latest accusation, schizophrenia. The only diagnosis that I had any time for was alcoholism. I didn't think I had a problem but I could see my drinking was causing the occasional memory lapse and, to be fair, I did like a tipple now and then – more usually 'now'.

Intransigence in the face of the medical community never goes down well. Therapy or not, the hospital's ethos was simple: either my way or the highway. I chose the highway. Day after day they shoved these pills into my mouth. Then the nurse, or sometimes lovely Kingy, the orderly, would wait until I'd swallowed and even check my mouth afterwards. It was horrible. I could feel the results but I was helpless to prevent them. It was like someone else had taken control of my body.

As my body shuffled and dribbled its way through the day, my mind at least tried to remain active. *You have to focus, keep focused.* The last thing I wanted was to succumb to the effects of the pills. Once you start on that slippery slope there's no way back. I'd seen it with my own eyes. In fact I could see it all around me. People who'd been like me once and now, weeks, months or years later, looked like gibbering vegetables, all nervous energy and restless legs making them jump up then sit down every five minutes. A lay person would understandably recognise them as ill, without knowing it was the medicine making them appear that way. Most psychiatric patients give no outward clues either side of an episode. Everywhere I looked there were lives ruined on the off-chance that someone might make a mistake in the future. It was terrifying.

I don't want to be like them.

But I was locked in tight. What choice did I have?

Actually, I realised, I did have a choice – but only if I acted quickly. One morning I watched as the medicine trolley made its way down the ward, dispensing pills and potions to my fellow inpatients. Only when the nurse was confident the tablets had been swallowed would she move on to the next bed. By the time she reached me, I knew what I had to do.

I'd been taking my medication for quite a few days by now so I knew the drill. Pill in one hand and little drink in the other. Pop pill in the mouth and take a quick gulp of water to wash it down. Then, finally, present my open, empty mouth to the nurse for inspection. The whole procedure took less than a minute and it was already second nature – which is what made me so sure I could fake it.

The nurse handed over the pill and drink. I tossed the pill into my mouth and a second later took a gulp of water. As soon as I'd swallowed, I opened my mouth like I was at the dentist and waited for the nurse to peer in. She nodded approval and pushed the trolley around to the next bed. Then, as soon as her back was turned, I spat the tablet out from underneath my tongue. I'd done it. I'd beaten the system. I would never have to take another pill again.

Day after day I carried on the same act of pretending to take my medicine. At first it gave me a kick, knowing that I had some of the finest medical minds convinced they were controlling me. Then I realised I was still, to all intents and purposes, a prisoner. There had to be a way out, I thought. And then I discovered it. I wish I could have seen the staff's faces when they discovered I was appealing the ward-of-court order.

Yes, crazy, old, schizo me was taking them to court.

'No one's ever won a tribunal.'

'Have you got a solicitor?'

'The last person to fight it was never seen again.'

News of my legal intentions was spreading all over the building. The patients on Ward 3 who could still think for themselves were especially excited.

When you're sectioned, you're given a bunch of papers explaining your legal status. Everyone is allowed the right of a tribunal. In the Maudsley there was a box where you could post your completed dispute form. I don't think many people did it with much conviction. Once on the medication, they were lucky if they could concentrate long enough to tick the right box.

It can't have been that hard, though, because I seemed to appeal without even realising it.

The first thing I knew was when doctors and patients started talking about it. Then Mum said my appeal date had been set.

Odd, I thought, *that they're talking as though I applied for this.*

Even more so that they implied I'd already informed them I would be defending myself and not using a solicitor.

It was confusing but I decided to go along with it even though I didn't have a clue what to say.

Tribunals were held at the hospital. A three-person judging panel, comprising one layperson and two doctors who are not your own doctors, hear the evidence and vote. The hospital then sends its representative and you send yours or, in my case, represent yourself.

Where on Earth had they got the idea that I could do that? I wondered. *Is it some kind trick to make sure they win?*

Realistically, though, I would never have been able to afford a professional so it was a relief when I found myself sitting outside the tribunal room with my father a few weeks later. It only took a second to work out where I was and what was going on – and just a second more to become absolutely petrified about going in to make my case.

What am I going to say? I haven't prepared anything!

I'm glad Dad was there because he knew his way around the social services world, thanks to his job, although this was new territory for him. Luckily he wasn't the only one experiencing a tribunal for the first time. Professor Leff couldn't make the appointment so he sent a young registrar to represent the Maudsley. This doctor had never attended a tribunal before and he was desperate to look the part in his dickie bow but I could tell he was a bundle of nervous energy.

He looks how I feel.

We all sat outside the tribunal room silently. No one dared to make eye contact. Then we were called in. The doctor went through the justifications for my long-term status as a ward of court: I was a danger to myself and to the public at large and my continual refusal to accept the assessment of schizophrenia meant I was likely to not take the medication, which in turn would lead to further psychotic episodes.

It was a persuasive argument, even when put by a perspiring, stuttering bag of nerves. The enormity of the situation suddenly hit me.

What am I doing here? I'm out of my depth. Why did I agree to come to this in the first place?

The funny thing is, I came out later not remembering another word. And yet there was Dad saying, with genuine pride beaming from his face, 'You really put it up them.'

Did I? I don't remember.

The letter saying I would no longer be detained under

the Mental Health Act confirmed it. Apparently I'd sat round the table with all those professionals and addressed them as if I'd been at the bar all my life. I had – although it was a different type of bar.

My tactics of rebuttal apparently had been pretty straightforward: there's no point arguing with the doctors because they have evidence on their side. The best you can do is just go in and agree as much as you can and say the action you are going to take. So that's what I'd done. I'd confessed that while I had originally challenged the diagnosis of schizophrenia, I had now come to accept it as being accurate. I'd also accepted, therefore, that without medication I would become ill and pledged to continue taking the medicine. While that was the case, I'd concluded, there was no purpose to be served in becoming a ward of court or by being sectioned indefinitely.

I had to agree, it did sound persuasive. I just wished I could have remembered it to have basked in the moment with him.

A decision had been made that afternoon and I left the tribunal as the first alumnus of Ward 3 to ever win.

I wasn't fighting the hospital's diagnosis, just its right to strip me of my freedom. The verdict didn't mean I was cured and there was still the little matter of taking the tablets every day once I got home. I had, after all, admitted to suffering from schizophrenia. Miss even one tablet, a nurse warned me, and the punishment would be severe.

'If we discover you're not taking your medication then we'll call you back in and administer the drug via injection every month. Mess around after that and you will be hospitalised until the end of your section.' She shrugged. 'It's up to you.'

I was so delighted to be released I'd have agreed to anything at that moment. But the second I left that austere old building I was searching feverishly for a plan. There was no way I wanted an injection and I certainly didn't want to be locked up again. But there was also no chance of my taking one more tablet now I wasn't being watched over by some scrutinising nurse. That would be like asking to be turned into a zombie. It would be the end of my life as I knew it.

It might be chaotic; it might not be everyone's cup of tea. But it's the only life I've got.

To make it harder to cheat, the hospital handed over a certain amount of tablets and told me to return when I ran out. That was a pretty devious trick. Keeping track of which pill I was meant to be on was harder than it sounds. I spent a good portion of every day worrying, 'Have I taken today's one out of the packet or not?' To really keep the façade of co-operation going, whenever I returned to Denmark Hill I did my best to appear as I remembered the drugs making me – although I did draw the line at dribbling.

Months went by and I didn't take a single, solitary pill. Eventually the hospital discovered what was going on. I didn't know how. Kingy claimed I'd admitted it to her but that was a lie. Why would I?

I really thought my days of freedom were up. It turned out I might have accidentally done myself a favour. Professor Leff passed a note to my nurse to the effect that if I had genuinely not taken my medicine and still hadn't had an episode then there was an argument to be had for desisting with the treatment. I couldn't have agreed more and later that afternoon I skipped out of the Maudsley a free woman once again.

Now to rebuild my life. Now to get back to work.

Unfortunately, as I was soon to discover, my troubles were only just beginning.

CHAPTER FIFTEEN

It's a crime scene now

Hayley smiled as the man poured the coffee.

She could hear men's voices. It sounded close and yet muffled. Hayley shook her head. Was it suddenly foggy in there?

I must be more tired than I thought.

She didn't fight it when the man with the coffee helped her up. She didn't resist when he led her down the stairs. In fact, without his help she wouldn't have made it.

What's wrong with my legs?

She didn't even try to prevent it when two other men appeared and all three of them lifted her into a box raised on a long table.

She giggled. Am I in a dream?

Could there be another explanation? She felt so listless, like a toy almost out of battery life, barely going through the motions. Nothing seemed to be working. She just wanted to close her eyes.

But then she recognised the pink, quilted fabric.

My God – it's a coffin! I'm in a coffin.

Suddenly alert, Hayley's heartbeat must have been off the scale by now. Still, though, she couldn't move.

What the hell was going on?

Adrenaline surge fading, she fought hard to concentrate. She needed to be awake. She needed to see everything. She needed to be able to tell the police every last detail.

But I'm so tired.

The fog in her head was settling lower and thicker. It wasn't a dream, she knew that. It was a nightmare. But this was worse.

Worse than anything she had ever seen.

Because of the children.

She heard them first. The sound was unclear, like a badly tuned radio, but slowly she recognised it as singing. When her eyes focused she could make out five little ones. They were dressed in long shirts, holding hands, chanting 'Ring-O-Roses'. The children weren't smiling. They were young but Hayley could read in their faces they knew it wasn't a game. None of them dared look at the men in the grotesque animal masks standing at the back. None of them smiled. They just gripped each other's hands as tightly as possible, sang as well as they could and tried not to look at the man filming it all.

'**M**y name is Patricia – and I am an alcoholic.'
I never uttered those words at an AA meeting but maybe I should have. I needed to do something. I'd entered my thirties full of optimism for the future. Life was going my way, for once. I had a flat, a few potential boyfriends sniffing around, nice lads actually, a job I enjoyed and somehow I'd even taken on the medical establishment – and won. For the first time in my memory I felt truly independent. But there was a problem and I could only think that the drinking was to blame. If I wasn't at work or hospital I always seemed to have a glass in my hand.

I never felt drunk or out of control but things were happening to me that I couldn't explain any other way. I was losing huge chunks of time. Afternoons, evenings, sometimes entire days. How was that possible? I'd close the door of my flat, turn round and find myself somewhere completely different. Ping – ping – ping. Now I'm here, now I'm not. It was like flicking through a film on fast forward. You whizz on a bit, pause to view a few seconds, then press 'FF' again to skip to the next scene.

I could only put these events down to alcohol-related blackouts. I hated thinking I'd drunk so much I couldn't remember so many things or passed out for such long periods of time – even though there hardly seemed to be any empty bottles at home – but it was easier than coming up with any other explanation. Somehow I was losing days on end and, shameful as it was, no other reason made sense.

As I sat down to analyse it one day, after another episode where I seemed to have 'lost' half a week, I realised everything had got worse since I'd started a new job. The gaps in time seemed to have begun then, and my memory problems had worsened. All the things in my life that had always been confusing but manageable had begun to escalate around the time I'd switched from the courier job to an admin position. Of course, when I say I switched jobs, I had no recollection of doing it and – like with so many other new jobs I'd found myself in – it had actually taken me a while to realise what was going on. That, at least, was normal for me . . .

I'm in an office. I've been here before. I've delivered and dropped things off here. But I'm not wearing my uniform. And I'm sitting behind a desk. There's a pad, a computer and a small calendar that says it's five years since I started my driving job. Where does the time go?

'How are you settling in, then?'

Good, a familiar face. The penny started to drop. *This guy's been on at me to apply for a transfer to a desk job for ages.* Had I actually done it? Had they actually given me the post without any interview or forms to be filled in? Surely I would have remembered.

I smiled. That always seemed to help when I was buying time, trying to figure out what was going on.

'Glad to be out of that stupid truck, I bet,' he continued. As he spoke he came over and perched on the corner of my desk. 'Remember, anything you want, anything at all, you come to me. Okay?'

'Thanks.'

I wonder if he winks at everyone.

A girl on the desk across the room came over. I'd met her before. She was the one I usually picked up from. What was her name?

Carol!

'He thinks he's God's gift,' Carol said. 'Lord knows why to look at him.' I smiled again as I searched her face for more clues. Carol gestured again at the man. He wasn't what anyone would call a looker. 'He's married, not that you'd know it.'

We chatted for a while. Then I just had to ask: 'Carol, remind me again what I should be doing.'

Was it my imagination or did she look at me a second longer than was comfortable? Had she already told me this? By the look of it, she certainly thought she had, and recently too. Then she relaxed and went through a few things. It wasn't hard, mostly paperwork and filing. But I could tell what she was thinking.

Bloody Green Card employees. More trouble than they're worth.

*

There's more to sussing out a job than just getting on top of your office duties. Somehow you have to learn your hours and, more importantly, learn how the hell to find your way back there the next day without annoying too many people. Not for the first time I felt like I was trying to board a spinning carousel.

It didn't help that work wasn't the only thing that kept me on my toes. Trips to the Maudsley remained a regular occurrence in my life – although I never seemed to remember travelling there. Luckily I only seemed to go for outpatients appointments but even so it was still such a pointless exercise. There are only so many times you can hear a doctor talk about your so-called weight problem before you start to drift off. Listening to them go on and on about this or that eating disorder – when they only had to look at me to see I was perfectly fine – made me actually wish I could have a blackout for once. Unfortunately it doesn't work like that. I didn't know how it worked but it never seemed to do me any favours.

And was it my imagination or had I started going to the Maudsley more often since I changed jobs?

Appearing at the Maudsley when I least expected it was disconcerting but at least familiar. I opened my eyes and there I was. I recognised the chairs, the waiting room, some of the faces. It was still absolutely confusing to be going to get a coffee or think about nipping out to the shops and then the next second suddenly appearing there, but at least I was used to it. Even if I couldn't explain it – how I'd got there, when I'd had time to change, all those regular questions – at least it only took me a moment or two to adjust, to get my bearings. It was only when I found myself one day mysteriously in another hospital that I really began to panic.

This isn't the Maudsley!

A sickening fear swept through me. Anxiously I looked around for clues.

Check the walls. Check the doors. Check the staff.

Check my clothes!

I was in my own things.

Thank God – I'm not in Warlingham.

It was my worst fear to realise I'd appeared there again. There'd never been any warnings in the past. Why would there again? Even after the tribunal, I never doubted that I could be spirited back there at a moment's notice. I hadn't realised it before, but I suppose it was my biggest fear.

If I wasn't in Warlingham then where was I? And what did they want with me?

I'm in a chair, next to a bed. But wait – the bed's not empty. I don't believe it, I'm a visitor!

I got another shock when I saw who was asleep in the bed: it was Mum. The arthritis had been getting worse and worse and finally she'd had knee replacement surgery. She would be in there for a few more days.

'Then,' a doctor appearing next to me said, 'she would need round-the-clock help for a couple of weeks. I understand you live together?'

'No, I don't live there.'

'Really? I thought you told me … Never mind. Perhaps if you could pop round. Your sister says she will help as well. Otherwise we can call on social services.'

Mum wasn't very good at being helped by strangers. She

hated anyone else knowing her business. That part of her personality hadn't changed. She was always cancelling the meals-on-wheels people or telling the cleaners not to bother returning. I decided that perhaps it would be better for her if I moved back home.

And maybe it would help me settle down as well ...

Even though I'd never told Mum I'd gone, I think she was grateful to have me around more. She'd always given me a lot of credit for helping her out when, I had to admit, a lot of those times she'd said I'd helped her to bed I really hadn't. Still, I could do it more now.

I enjoyed being back home but it was horrible seeing Mum suffer. Even with new joints she was so immobile and in such a lot of pain even if she tried to do simple things like pick up a bag or turn herself over in bed. At least once a week – although of course Mum insisted it was more like every night – I'd hear the thud of her walking stick on the bedroom wall and I'd stagger in to help her roll over and get comfy again.

Apart from weekends now, Mum was still on her own during the day because of my work, so a home help used to come in every morning and wash and feed her and look after the house a bit as well. What I didn't know at the time was that the woman used to bring her kids sometimes, and even her boyfriend. They'd all hang around the entire day, watching telly, using Mum's things, generally carrying on like they owned the place. Loads of stuff went missing during that time and naturally I blamed Mum. I thought, *She's blind, who knows where she's put it?* It was years later when I learnt how she'd been terrorised by the people employed to help her out.

Mum's health really deteriorated. She'd suffered a serious

stroke. After she was released from hospital she needed twenty-four-hour assistance. Social services supplied some care. Other than that it was down to the family. My boss said I could change my hours to get off earlier so I was home when the help left.

I'd worked as a courier for five years and it seemed like a couple of months. I realised now, with Mum's operation, that I'd been in my new job for three years already. I honestly couldn't put my finger on where the time was going. Days, weeks, months and maybe even a year or two seemed to be slipping through my fingers like dust. No sooner had I got up some mornings than it felt like I was already climbing back into bed. Sometimes I recalled having a glass of wine, sometimes I didn't. The weird thing was I never really had a craving for a drink. If booze was the problem, shouldn't I have at least wanted it more?

Between looking after Mum and trying to track down my missing minutes there hardly seemed to be much time left for work. If it weren't for the money in my bank account at the end of the week I would probably have questioned whether I was even going in some days.

But if they are paying me, everything must be okay.

Except everything wasn't okay. Far from it. I couldn't put my finger on why but the mood in the office had changed. In fact, the atmosphere around the whole building was completely different – and not in a good way. First of all there were the whispers. People were talking about some really unpleasant things. Not openly, but I'd hear snatches of conversations in car parks or toilets or occasionally in the pub after work. There were rumours that a certain member of staff had complained of being sexually assaulted by others. No one told me directly, and they certainly didn't mention who the victim was. I felt sorry for whoever it was. They were just whispers, not much better than gossip really. But people seemed to be taking it seriously and, day after day, that was the secret topic of conversation behind the work façade.

The worst thing about the rumours was not having a name. I realised, *Anyone could be involved*. Everyone who came into my room was suddenly a suspect. Relationships generally appeared strained.

How is anyone meant to get any work done like this?

Even though I seemed to be going into work less and less frequently – or so I remembered – the atmosphere was getting worse. Paranoia was in the air, you could feel it. Was I imagining it or were people staring at me? Did it go quiet when I entered the room?

Pull yourself together, I told myself. *You've got nothing to do with it.*

People were also talking about a paedophile ring which had been discovered. I'm not even sure I knew what that was. When I found out, my stomach turned. I couldn't imagine a worse crime. I still can't.

The biggest blow for me was realising Carol, who always helped me, had disappeared – literally just walked out one day. I'd gone to her house but she'd moved. It was really odd. Was it something I said? Carol and I loved a night out. Had I let the vino get the better of my tongue?

Or was she something to do with what everyone was talking about?

I really hope not. I wouldn't wish that on anyone.

Even though I didn't have a clue what was going on, I had a sense of things building to a head. The final straw came when I found myself turning up to work and the lass on reception saying, 'I thought you were on sick leave.'

I just stared at her. Sick leave? What for? I wasn't ill. I'd just come to work, hadn't I? But she insisted I'd been signed off indefinitely by a doctor. Usually I just play along with whatever people tell me and try to join the dots as I go but this time I was stumped.

'What's meant to be wrong with me?' I heard myself ask.

The receptionist started to reply then changed her mind.

'It's probably best if you just go home, isn't it?'

Just at the point I really needed time to get my head clear and start collating all the various strands of information I'd learnt over the last few weeks – or was it months? – I found myself getting shorter and shorter on time. As usual I put it down to the wine. Stress from work, I reasoned, was obviously making me drink even more than usual and as a consequence I was blocking out a lot of memories. But I never seemed to have a hangover. And I never seemed to be drunk, either. But something was happening to me, even I could see that. For the first time in my life I even began to wonder whether the doctors had been missing something every time they locked me up.

I'm not an alcoholic, I know I'm not, I told myself. *So what is the matter with me?*

I was none the wiser, when, what felt like the next morning, I casually rested my chin on my hand while I was watching television.

Ouch! That hurts.

It felt like my face was on fire. What on Earth had I done? Gingerly I ran my fingers along my cheek. The slightest touch was like a dozen pinpricks and yet the skin didn't feel cut. In fact it felt like I was one massive scab.

My mind went into overdrive. What was the last thing I remembered? Nothing rang any bells. Reluctantly I considered the only possible cause.

Had I fallen? Too drunk to walk? How embarrassing.

I just hope it was a good night . . .

I was annoyed with myself for joking about it but what else was I going to do? My life was a mess. What the hell had I done to my face? I couldn't even bear to think about it. Just too much to take in. It had been too much for a long time. I needed to get out, find somewhere to sort out my life. I needed some fresh air.

I grabbed my coat and marched to the door. 'Just going out!' I called up to Mum. I snatched the handle, flung it back and nearly jumped out of my skin. Two men, dressed head to foot in black, spun round, almost as surprised as me.

'All right, Kim,' one of them said. 'Going out?'

'Er, yes.'

'Do we need the car?'

Who the hell are you?

'I was going for a walk actually.'

They looked at each other and shrugged.

'Shouldn't be a problem,' one of them said.

Ten minutes later I was marching angrily through Croydon's shopping area with Tweedledum and Tweedledee about ten feet behind. It didn't matter which shop I went into, they followed. If it was a small place then one came in and the other hogged the doorway. They were big buggers, too. You wouldn't want to mess with them.

On the way back I couldn't bear it any longer. I'd worked nothing out for myself. I needed to know who the hell they were.

'How long will you be here?'

I thought that was pretty clever.

'Until we're called off,' the talkative one replied, 'or they find the maniac who threw acid in your face.'

Usually after a hospital visit I knew it had all been a waste of time. I shouldn't have been there in the first place and, far from curing me, normally it was the doctors and their team who were subjecting me to painful tests and so-called cures. This time was different. I could feel my face had changed. It was rough, like crêpe paper. And even a week afterwards it still hurt like an open wound. Just smiling felt like I was ripping my own face. Laughter was completely out of the question, although, for obvious reasons, there wasn't much chance of that.

Learning that I'd been attacked was a lot to take in. Initially I'd denied it. But having a couple of security guys on twenty-four-hour duty outside my front door pretty much won the argument. These men cost money. From what I knew about the world, you had to be in pretty deep trouble for anyone to put their hands that far into their pockets. I wanted to argue, to say it was all a mistake, a bad dream, a misunderstanding. But then I would touch my face and have to admit there was no other explanation.

I just wished somebody could tell me why.

*

Answers had been in short supply for most my life. In the months after the mysterious acid incident they were virtually non-existent. In fact, although I would eventually discover why it happened, by then I had greater problems to deal with. At the time, however, I had no information about the cause or the culprit. I wasn't even told that the security team would be taken away. One day they were there, the next they weren't. I could cope with that. Compared to somebody else who suddenly went missing, they were nothing.

I remember sitting at home, staring at the TV one day. The house was so quiet and I realised the television wasn't even turned on. How long I'd been there I didn't know, although there wasn't a glass near me. I hadn't been drinking.

I looked at the time and decided to check on Mum. Then I remembered.

She's gone.

The pain never got any easier to bear. Mum had died. I was alone – and distraught that I couldn't even remember the funeral. I must have attended. It was inconceivable that I would miss it. But I couldn't recall her dying or saying goodbye. It was as if I hadn't even been there.

I had to blame the wine. There was no other explanation. I'd obviously drowned my sorrows at the wake as though there were no tomorrow. But even so, you'd think I would remember some of it.

Mum's death wasn't the only thing I missed. A few days – or maybe weeks, months, I don't honestly know – later I remember coming home, being on my road and stopping outside the house.

This isn't right, I thought, and stared at the blackened windows. Policemen were coming and going through the front door like it was the local station. A dozen or so neighbours were milling around. The smell of burning, even drenched by firehoses, was unmistakeable.

I felt sick.

Mum!

It was instinctive. I had to get to her, rescue her, make sure she was all right.

Then it came flooding back. She wasn't in there. She'd gone.

I forced myself to look back at the charred walls. What had happened? Did I leave a cigarette burning overnight? Was I drunk again? Who else could have started a fire in my house if it wasn't me? Apart from Mum's Airedale, Alfie, no one else lived there. I don't think he smoked forty a day.

I sniffed my clothes. I didn't recognise what I was wearing but at least it didn't smell of smoke. Obviously I hadn't been involved in the fire. Thank God.

I moved along the path. A uniformed arm stretched across the door.

'Sorry, Miss, it's a crime scene now. We can't let you in.'

'But I need to collect some things.'

'I'm sorry, Miss, but I don't think there's much left. So, if you wouldn't mind stepping back out onto the pavement.'

Without thinking I did as I was told. Every step that I took, though, resonated with the same thought.

He said 'crime scene'. Did I not cause this fire?

The alternative was almost too much to process.

First the problems at work, then the acid and now this. What the hell is going on with my life?

I didn't have the answer. I didn't know anything. The only conclusion I truly drew for sure was that my problems had nothing to do with alcohol.

But if it's not the wine, then what is it?

CHAPTER SIXTEEN

Please help me

The woman collected her papers from the lectern, gave a brief, self-conscious nod of recognition and headed towards the anonymous safety of the stage's wings. It wasn't like being at a concert or the theatre but the speaker's audience applauded heartily all the same. And no one clapped with more gusto than Hayley.

What a day, she thought. *Applauding alongside her, Hayley's friend Ann looked just as rapt. No one, they agreed, could possibly leave that hall without feeling empowered after hearing these incredible women speak.*

The event was a conference about women and violence and the speakers on the bill included some very famous names. Susie Orbach was the headliner, familiar to many the world over for her book, Fat Is A Feminist Issue. As one of Britain's most distinguished lawyers, Helena Kennedy was someone who'd built a reputation for championing victims' rights. But it was another speaker, one Hayley hadn't heard of before Ann had mentioned her, that had truly struck a chord. Valerie Sinason, a therapist from London, was a wonder to listen to, from start to finish. By the end of her speech Hayley couldn't imagine ever being a victim of men again.

As the hall emptied, Ann led Hayley towards the event's social area. Unlike at theatrical performances, conference stars were happy to

mingle afterwards. As they reached the area where fans waited for Susie
Orbach's signature on well-thumbed copies of her book, Hayley began to
drag back.

Noticing, Ann laughed.

'Don't go getting cold feet now,' she mocked gently, and gave her
friend a comforting arm to hold through the throng. Even then Hayley
was reluctant to go further.

'Tell you what,' Ann said. 'You wait here and I'll give it to her.'

Relieved, Hayley found a chair and sat down. Ann had been a good
friend, especially with all the troubles at work and then the acid and the
fire. It had been her idea to come here today. Just the recollection of the
acid saw Hayley's hand absent-mindedly stroke her cheek. The physical
wound had long stopped hurting but Hayley could still feel the burn with
every touch. That would stay with her forever.

Moments later, Ann returned.

'I've done it,' she said. 'I gave her the letter.'

'What do we do now?' Hayley asked.

'We wait.'

Standing outside the darkened shell of my house I thought
of all the times I'd blacked out, all those unaccounted-for
hours and days of my life that just seemed to be lost however
much I tried to call them back.

And how I wished I could have blacked out there and
then.

Everything I owned was in that building. Now a policeman was calling it a crime scene. There was a chance they were
still looking for clues and in my heart I knew I couldn't guarantee I hadn't caused the fire. But there was a chance, albeit a
small one, that it had been started by someone else. The more

I dwelled on it the more scared I became. If there was even a 1 per cent risk that the fire had been started deliberately by someone else then I was in more trouble than I could cope with.

What on Earth am I supposed to do now?

I never thought that the answer would lie at Kingston train station.

I don't remember how long after discovering the house it was. I just recall staring at the sign and looking for a station clock.

According to the timetable, the next train is in twenty minutes.

I checked the platform numbers. I was on the side heading away from London. *Where the hell am I going?* Then I noticed the herd of people funnelling towards the exit. Maybe I wasn't going anywhere. *Has a train just left? Did I just get off here?*

I scratched my head, desperate to remember. Why was I in Kingston? Who did I know there? What was I doing? In the absence of any better plan I decided to follow the masses to the exit. Hopefully something outside would jog my memory.

'Kim?'

It was a woman's voice.

'Hello?' I said warily but if she picked up on my nerves it didn't show.

'My car's over there,' she gestured. 'Shall we go?'

I didn't have a clue who this woman was but she obviously knew me. That gave her the advantage but at that moment it was just a relief not to be on my own.

During the course of the journey I discovered I was on my way to a women's refuge. The address was top secret. That's why she'd met me at the station rather than sending a cab. For the sake of conversation I asked if security was an issue. 'It's our number one priority,' she replied. Even if someone found the refuge's telephone number, the woman assured me, they would always be answered with 'never heard of anyone of that name'.

They seemed to have thought of everything – but it still didn't explain why I was there.

'Just until you get yourself back on your feet,' the woman explained. 'We can't have you going back home until the bastards who set fire to you and your house are brought to justice.'

She looked embarrassed at her choice of words but I didn't mind. I could only fix on one thing.

You mean it wasn't me?

You can play that moment over and over in your head all day and night and it will never sound any better. Every which way I considered it made me feel more and more afraid.

Someone had tried to burn down my house. With me inside. Why? What had I ever done to hurt anyone?

For the hundredth time in what felt like as many minutes I couldn't help thinking, *What the hell is happening to me?*

My own problems paled into insignificance when I met some of the other women at the refuge. There were people there afraid of their own shadows. Others were so close to tipping point I was impressed how they got through each day. And then there were the ones who just looked relieved to be somewhere safe. I suppose I fell into that category.

I had the usual problems of playing catch-up during conversations but generally it was refreshing to find women who had been through similar ordeals to me and had come out the other side. We weren't encouraged to share our problems unless we were comfortable doing so, but I heard story after story that gave me faith in womankind's ability to overcome adversity. When it came to my turn I felt a bit of a fraud. I knew so little of what had happened to me that I'm sure it didn't quite ring true. Still, it wasn't an audience who would judge.

Generally I think I would have taken my own problems over most of the other women's. There was just one area where I considered myself disadvantaged. Everyone else at the refuge knew full well who had caused them pain. Each woman had a name or a face etched indelibly on her memory.

I had nothing.

I could pass my attackers in the street and not recognise them. The man who threw acid into my face could be my taxi driver, my postman or anyone else in the world and I'd never know. The person who set light to my house could buy me a drink and I'd be none the wiser. That not knowing was almost unbearable. I'd had a lifetime of confusion but this was threatening to eat away at me unless I came to terms with it. But how could I square these acts if I couldn't remember them?

And why couldn't I remember them? Was my memory trying to protect me somehow? *You read about the brain doing things like that.* Something I did remember, actually, was that old diagnosis of dissociation. The doctor at the time had said it carried the possibility of amnesic moments where you suppressed experiences you didn't like. Was that what I was going through?

I honestly didn't know – but very soon I would meet someone who did.

*

I'm not at the refuge. There are chairs, people, posters on the walls. It's
a waiting room and a door is opening.

I didn't know where I was but I could tell that I was about
to have a meeting with the woman extending her hand towards
me. She was leaning against a door to what looked like a con-
sultancy room. If I had a pound for every bad experience I'd
had inside one of those ...

'Hello, my name is Valerie Sinason.' Her voice was calm
and soothing. 'You can call me Valerie or Ms Sinason.'

Just her manner put me at ease. Then she smiled – a genuine, welcoming smile – and said, 'What would you like me to
call you?'

No one ever asked that.

It still didn't explain why we were meeting. Then Valerie
explained that it was because I'd been brave enough to get my
friend Ann to pass on a letter at a conference on women and
violence.

It was all news to me, although I did recall a female coun-
sellor called Ann who had popped up at the various homes
I'd stayed in since the fire and I liked her. She was on my side,
I knew that. Against whom God only knew, but it had felt
good to have an ally.

I learnt later that Ann had written to Valerie asking her
to give me an appointment. Together with Dr Rob Hale, a
consultant psychiatrist and psychoanalyst, she was researching
severe abuse and ritual abuse with funding from the
Department of Health. I wasn't entirely sure how I could help
her work or what she could do for me – yes I'd been attacked
by strangers but the only abuse I'd known was people in authority messing with my mind and locking me up against my will.

Yet there was something about Valerie and, when he joined us later, Dr Hale that gave me confidence. As I listened to them speak so passionately about their work I cast a critical eye over my own past. Too much of it was a mystery to me and what I did recall, judging from the reactions of the women at the refuge, was out of the ordinary. Acid and arson attacks weren't normal, were they? Other people didn't get locked up in asylums when there was nothing wrong with them. People like Lorraine, my sister, weren't always forgetting where they worked and what they were meant to be doing there. As each realisation hit me I felt my shoulders slump. I was tired. Life had worn me down. I'd always told myself I was a fighter, that I was coping, that no one would ever get the better of me. But who was I kidding? After years of fighting against meddling doctors and medics and psychiatrists it was time to put my hand up and say the very words I thought I'd never hear myself say.

'Yes, please help me.'

I didn't know what they could do for me but anything was better than the way I was living.

The deal was simple: I would attend the Portman Clinic in Swiss Cottage every week for separate sessions with Valerie and Dr Hale and talk about my problems, and they would ask me the questions they needed to. It was a win–win situation: they got their research and I got to share my confusion with someone. The arrangement had the added bonus of their not wanting to force-feed me medication, or lock me up or, in particular, spy on me when I sat on the loo.

Those sessions would have to wait, however, because until

my house was repaired I was still homeless. I needed to explore other options. Having made the psychological leap that – yes – I was ready to talk to Valerie and Dr Hale, I decided to pursue further help. Someone at Kingston told me about the Arbours crisis centres in Crouch End, north London, and so I got in touch. Arbours owned a number of houses in the area called 'therapeutic communities', like the Cassel, where patients could live and enjoy in-house therapies of various kinds. For the first time in my life I found myself asking for treatment. I was so keen that even when my local health authority refused to fund it because it was outside their borough, I decided to find the money myself. Fortunately I had received a cheque along with a letter saying it was compensation for the attacks on me. Not only did I not recall those, I had no memory of asking for compensation. But it was welcome.

Like the Cassel, it was round-the-clock therapy sessions of one kind or another run by either our residential therapist, Lizzie, or various visiting ones. It felt weird knowing I'd actually chosen to be there but I still found it hard to get into the spirit of the thing. One of the visitors in particular seemed to be barking up completely the wrong tree with me. Whenever I arrived at sessions he'd say, 'So, who have we got today? Baby Kim, Angry Kim, Teen Kim, Giggly Kim or Adult Kim?' He seemed pleased with himself with that.

I thought, *I don't know what you're expecting. It's me. Who else did you think was going to turn up?*

A lot of people get a kick out of talking about their feelings in front of other people but I hated that. Like the Cassel, Arbours came up with all sorts of ways to tease confidences out of you. Art therapy was on the agenda, which bored me. There had been an art class at San Martino's, which the therapist, Jeff, and a few of his friends took part in, but it had never been for me. Here, Lizzie would produce a painting and we'd all have to give our opinions on what it was saying to us.

How am I meant to know what it means? It's a painting, not a letter.

I never knew what to say but it didn't matter. If you admitted you liked a picture they'd say, 'You like the dark colours? Interesting,' and that obviously meant something. Or if you didn't they'd find a way of remarking about that that made me think I'd got it wrong.

Even though I was actively seeking help, I wasn't ready to give up my own form of alternative medicine. Again like the Cassel, Arbours didn't believe in administering any form of drugs. It encouraged patients to be as healthy and unfettered by chemical influences as possible. I couldn't have agreed with them more. The only problem was, their definition of drugs included alcohol.

And mine certainly did not.

Every day I'd slip out to the local and have a glass or two, then sneak back into the house ready for my next session. The very first week I did it, I was rumbled. They weren't particularly large rooms so I guess it wasn't that hard to smell the wine in the air. But that didn't mean I had to admit it.

'I see Drunk Kim's turned up today,' one of the lovely visiting therapists said suspiciously. 'You know alcohol is strictly forbidden at Arbours.'

'I haven't been drinking,' I replied and gave him what I considered my butter-wouldn't-melt face.

'Well, I think you have,' he said, moving his face so close

to mine he reminded me of the Childcatcher in *Chitty Chitty Bang Bang* trying to sniff out Dick Van Dyke's kids. 'Lizzie, come and check her breath.'

I shut my mouth firmly.

'Really,' the other therapist admonished him. 'I can't smell anything – and if Kim says she hasn't been drinking then she hasn't been drinking.'

Thank you, Lizzie!

After four months in Arbours, which felt to me like a fortnight at most, my money ran out. I'd hoped that by the time we reached that point my health authority would have stepped in but they had been utterly intransigent, which is a polite way of saying they were complete bastards about it. There was no way they would pay. After all the places they'd locked me up in against my will during my life, now here I was showing some interest, yet they wouldn't lift a finger.

At least my house was finally fit to move back into, after the insurance company had paid for some redecoration and repairs and the fire brigade had given the all-clear. And finally I could get going with my weekly meetings with Valerie Sinason and monthly appointments with Dr Hale at the Portman Clinic.

The meetings came and went very quickly, like so much of my life. I was sure Valerie said she worked in fifty-minute blocks but I barely seemed to arrive before I was home again. The conversations while I was there seemed the weird end of bizarre, as well. I didn't really know what the therapists' agenda was but I quickly got the feeling they were trying to nudge me down a particular path. I couldn't put my finger on it so one day Valerie came out and said it.

According to her I shared my body with dozens of other people.

I waited for the punchline but it never came.

Even so, I think I still must have laughed in her face. Anyone would, if a so-called professional came out with nonsense like telling me there are other people who take control of my body sometimes.

If this is what your research is for, I'd pick another career!

Obviously I accused Valerie of being mad but I didn't exactly storm out of the room. People had always spun me the most fantastical lies. Every so often, like with the acid and the fire, the stories seemed to be based in truth. But this one was too ridiculous for words. Valerie was testing me somehow – I just needed to work out how.

The next time I saw her she was pushing the same line about strangers sharing my body. I was disappointed when Dr Hale started going down the crackpot road as well. According to him I had something called Dissociative Identity Disorder.

'I've been diagnosed with dissociation before,' I said. 'And that was wrong as well.'

Dissociation is different from DID, he explained. Lots of people – people you'd consider 'normal' – suffer from dissociation to varying degrees. People who block out pain or bad memories by forgetting or compartmentalising their problems are dissociative.

'What you have is far more extreme,' he said. 'Your dissociation is so great you actually have different personalities living inside one body. Your body.'

It was too ridiculous for words. Yet, I couldn't just walk away. I owed it to Dr Hale to listen – even if I couldn't see the point.

'You're telling me there's someone watching me when I go to the loo?'

My old experiences of Warlingham left deep scars.

'It doesn't work like that.'

A worse thought then struck me.

'Or when I have sex?'

'No, it's not like that,' Dr Hale said. 'You are not here all the time. Other people take control of your body. They have their own separate lives, just as you do.'

Ridiculous as it all sounded, I couldn't help asking questions.

'So where do I go then?'

He shrugged. 'It's as if you go to sleep.'

'So why don't I fall over then?'

'Because someone else is awake and keeping the body going.'

We went round in circles like that for ages every time I saw him. Sometimes I played the game. On other occasions I wished he'd call it a day.

Seriously, man, change the record!

I don't know what he expected me to say. 'Oh yes, I get it, I'm just a figment of my body's imagination. I don't really exist!' But I didn't mind. I'd been accused of anorexia, bulimia, depression, attempted suicide, schizophrenia and so many other things I couldn't remember, and I'd managed to prove all those wrong. So what difference did it make if he accused me of having multiple personalities as well? It was just another name. But what a waste of time it was hearing it, month after month.

If they keep this up, I'm going to pull out of the sessions. Deal or no deal.

But I didn't. I don't know if I was intrigued or amused or too offended to quit, but something made me keep returning to the Portman.

Despite his wild claims, I got the impression that Dr Hale was worried about me somehow. Perhaps that's why I kept going back time after time.

It was no different with Valerie. It didn't matter how long passed between sessions – and sometimes it did seem like ages between our meetings – we would always come back to the same sorts of circular conversations:

'How did you get here?'

'Through the door. How did you get here?'

Whatever the provocation, Valerie never rose to the bait.

'Do you remember coming through the door?'

That's a good one.

'No I don't. But who remembers boring details like that?'

'Okay, can you tell me what you did last night?'

'It's a bit fuzzy.'

Valerie gave that smile that told me absolutely nothing.

'It's because you weren't around last night, were you?' she suggested.

Not this again.

'No, I was probably too drunk. Do *you* remember everything when you've been drinking?'

'You blame drinking for everything.'

'I drink a lot.'

'Do you? Because I don't think you do.'

That was interesting. I'd been thinking for ages that I

didn't really drink as much as I thought. But how else, then, could I explain the gaps in my memory?

And as for her other theory . . .

According to Valerie's diary I attended her weekly clinic for just shy of two years. According to my memory, though, it was more like twenty or so sessions, no more than that. Predictably, Dr Hale tried to blame the discrepancy on my not being around all the time.

'Obviously I wasn't around or I'd have made the meeting,' I said. He'd have to be quicker than that to catch me out.

Annoying as the pair of them were sometimes, the day came after two years when Valerie announced their research project was drawing to an end. In other words, funding for my sessions was about to be withdrawn. Both she and Dr Hale agreed it was not right for me to have no ongoing treatment, so Dr Hale and the Contracts Manager wrote to my local Primary Care Trust.

Would the authorities listen?

Absolutely not.

I couldn't escape the irony that after years of trying to escape from the system, here I was now desperate to get a finger-hold back into it. The difference was, I was driving this treatment. This time I had asked for help.

So why wouldn't they give it to me?

Arbours put me in touch with a solicitor who said he would take my case to the health authority and paint a picture of me as someone totally unfit to live unshackled, someone who would benefit from the help of a trauma therapist recommended by the Tavistock and Portman – at the council's cost. This wasn't the worst lie that had ever been told about me and, I figured, as long as it got what I wanted, it was okay.

I thought we were making headway, I really did. Big organisations like councils are always thrown when you play them at their own game. By bringing in a solicitor I was forcing them to show their hand. They didn't like it.

After several months of negotiations we had almost cracked it. Then my solicitor rang me one day to say he was resigning from the case.

I was distraught. 'What on Earth for? We're so close! Is it the money? I can pay you more, I'll find it somehow.'

There was a pause.

'It's nothing to do with money.'

'Then what is it?'

What would make him abandon me so cruelly after such a long fight together?

'Kim, it's my professional opinion that if we continue to portray you as unstable then it will harm any hope you have of winning your other case.'

'What other case?'

Another pause.

'Winning your daughter back.'

CHAPTER SEVENTEEN

This is Aimee

There must have been a dozen people in the room, all wearing gowns and masks. Two of them pulled a little screen along Dawn's body and fixed it just below her chest. It wasn't very high, but lying down there was no way she could see her feet, let alone her tummy. Dawn smiled when she thought how suddenly her bump had quadrupled in size. For seven or eight months she'd been so small that most people hadn't believed she was even pregnant. Then – whoosh – it was like she'd ballooned overnight. And she couldn't have been happier.

And now, in ten minutes, all the morning sickness, the exhaustion and the nervous anticipation was about to pay off. Her baby was coming out.

Dawn closed her eyes as the surgeon and his assistant began their incision. Even though she couldn't see beyond the screen, knowing that a man is cutting into your skin is the most unnatural feeling in the world – not that Dawn could actually feel anything physically, thanks to the epidural in her spine.

It was true what they'd said. It didn't hurt, it was just like being tickled from the inside, like a sock drawer might feel with someone rummaging through it.

The surgeon was as good as his word. He'd promised it would all be over in ten minutes and it was. Soon he was lifting the baby. Any second now Dawn would see . . .

Her!

It's a baby girl!

'Congratulations,' the surgeon said, handing the tiny creature to a nurse. Dawn watched like a cat following a ball on a string.

Come on, *she thought*, it's my turn. Let me have her!

A second later she got her wish. Dawn could barely contain herself as the nurse unfastened Dawn's gown then placed the little bundle onto her chest. So many sensations coursed through her body at once. Her daughter was wriggly, hot, sticky and so beautiful. Her tiny little gasps for breath were the loveliest sounds Dawn had ever heard.

The nurse hadn't left their side. She was smiling. There was no more perfect vision in the world than a mother and her newborn child. They'd been together for less than a minute but the new mum was already showing the instincts of a mother of five.

'Do you have a name for her?' the nurse asked.

'Oh yes,' Dawn said, pulling her robe gently over her daughter's back. 'This is Skye.'

'That's lovely.'

'She is, isn't she?'

It was a wrench to hand Skye back to the nurse but the baby had to be weighed, measured and subjected to all sorts of other tests. Dawn followed it all while the assistant surgeon completed her sewing.

I can wait a few minutes. Soon I'll be able to hold her forever.

Just thinking that made Dawn want to burst with joy.

It seemed to take an eternity but eventually the nurse started walking back over. Skye was dressed this time, in a little white outfit. It was all Dawn could do not to cry as her baby was handed back. As far as she was concerned, at that moment she had the whole world in her hands.

With so many emotions surging through her, Dawn only vaguely acknowledged the comings and goings of all the gowned doctors and anaesthetists who'd populated the operating theatre just half an hour earlier. It even took a few seconds for one of the nurses' next words to sink in.

'We're just going to take Skye for a few more tests.'

Dawn was in a hospital. She knew her baby was in safe hands. Even so, it seemed like hours until Skye was returned with a clear bill of health. As Dawn hugged her child to her chest, she could not have been happier. Then she noticed the suited strangers standing next to her. One of them was starting to speak.

'Miss Noble, we're from social services. We have a court order, to remove your daughter from your care, effective immediately.'

They went on but Dawn's head was spinning too fast to take it in.

'Take my daughter? Why?'

Was this a dream? Was someone playing a trick on her? Was Lorraine going to step out in a minute with Jeremy Beadle?

The nurse had come back. She looked devastated. That's when Dawn knew the strangers were deadly serious. Without a second thought she clutched Skye tighter and turned her body as far as her epidural would allow. They weren't taking her daughter anywhere!

'Come on, Kim,' the nurse said, 'you have to hand her over.'

'No! No, no, no! She's mine. She's my baby!'

Two other nurses arrived, each looking as glum as the first. What they were being asked to do was completely unnatural, an abhorrence of the natural order of things. But the law was the law.

There was nothing Dawn could do. She had just had an operation. She could barely move, let alone fight. But she could scream.

'They're taking my baby! Give me back my baby! Skye! Skye!'

Skye was born at ten o'clock on 18 August 1997. Twenty-four hours *later she had left the hospital, en route to unknown foster parents. As for Dawn – she would never see her daughter again.*

How could I have a baby? It was the most ludicrous, implausible idea I'd ever heard – and I'd had a lot of wild accusations hurled at me over the years.

I may have done a lot of stupid things when I've been drunk but I think I would have noticed if I'd given birth.

It was so ridiculous. I hadn't even been pregnant. Did I look like the Virgin Mary? A woman would notice these things.

Absolutely ridiculous.

I'd never felt more frustrated or more alone. Normally I would have jumped straight on the phone to the Portman. But what was the point of that? Valerie had probably put him up to it anyway – after all, she'd been spouting the same old guff for ages. I remembered our last conversation:

Valerie: 'Do you accept you have a daughter?'

'No.'

'Why not?'

'Because I haven't got a daughter. I would know if I'd had a baby.'

'What do you think the scars are on your tummy?'

'I had an accident.'

The words tripped naturally off my tongue.

'It must feel much easier to think that,' Valerie said carefully. 'It's so much harder to have a look and see they are actually scars from a caesarean section.'

These pie-in-the-sky theories were a joke. It's true I couldn't remember the accident but there had to be another explanation.

I did not have a child.

'You know that until you accept what I've been telling you, until you accept that you have a child, the social services will never let you have her back?'

I shrugged.

I don't have a child. I don't need anyone back.

One of the things Valerie and Dr Hale used to try to convince me of their multiple-personality theory was my time management. It was their claim that I was only ever 'out' for a certain portion of any given day. Sometimes, they reckoned, I didn't come out at all. That was why, they concluded, I often couldn't remember doing things, travelling to places, being with people or so much else.

My answer was always the same: 'if you drank as much as me, you'd struggle to remember everything as well!'

Even so, away from their offices even I was beginning to question some of the places I found myself. Despite the therapy, nothing had changed. I still found myself literally appearing in various locations, with no idea of how it had occurred or why. Usually I could put two and two together. Usually, but not always …

I remember being in a strange room – nothing new there, so I ran through the usual checklist.

What can I see? People standing around. Not dressed as nurses but they definitely work here. Quite a big room, nicely lit and with comfortable furniture.

And a little baby on the rug!

I was so used to deducing where I was that I didn't always

take in the important details first. You'd think the baby would be the first thing I spotted. I guessed it was a girl as she was dressed in pink. She was sitting in a little inflatable tyre to keep her upright. She looked really cute – but where were the parents?

One of the people in the room came over.

'Do you want to hold her?'

Won't her parents mind?

'Yes, please.'

The woman scooped the little pink bundle up and handed her over. I was completely nervous but somehow I seemed to know exactly how to tuck her into the hook of my arm. An unusual, content warmth washed over me. It was like I'd known this little creature forever.

'She's lovely,' I said. 'What's her name?'

'This is Aimee.'

Aimee? That's what Valerie and Dr Hale said my so-called daughter was called. Was this something to do with her? Bliss turned to rage. I'd been conned.

What are they playing at?

Whatever I thought of some of Valerie and Dr Hale's methods, I couldn't deny they were looking out for me. I didn't know how it had happened – or, more importantly, who was paying for it – but their campaign to find me a permanent therapist eventually paid off. Dr Evelyn Laine, another trauma therapist, was also undertaking research into the severity of the after-effects of trauma. Whether I accepted I needed her or not at the time, to this day I still see her every week.

As part of my treatment, Dr Laine also introduced me to

a psychology researcher called Professor John Morton. I shook his hand and waited to be patronised.

He didn't do that.

Instead he asked if I'd be interested in taking part in a project he was researching. All I would have to do was have my regular sessions with Dr Laine, then afterwards pop over to his office for a debrief. He also wanted to run a few tests on me, if I didn't mind.

It was so refreshing to find someone who actually asked permission rather than just subjecting me to the sorts of procedures I'd endured at Warlingham and Mayday that I couldn't say no. Basically after every session with Dr Laine, Professor Morton would have some task or other. Sometimes I would have to learn a list of words, or sentences. Other times I did intelligence tests, solved puzzles, looked at pictures, tried to remember things from the past. Week after week, month after month, even year after year this went on and, I have to admit, it made such a change from hearing all that nonsense about multiple personalities.

In between, there's not really much I can say. I didn't work – although I wouldn't have been surprised to find myself in a new job one day, as usually happened – so money was tight, but I did recall spending a fair amount of time socialising, shopping and drinking – your average pastimes, I suppose. And I also seemed to devote an inordinate amount of time babysitting that little Aimee girl. Don't ask me why, but her mother was always dumping her at my house. It was nice watching her grow up from a toddler to a little girl, especially when she learnt to say my name, but having her around was really restrictive.

Dr Hale and Valerie might have disappeared from the scene but Dr Laine and Professor Morton were obviously working from the same script. It wasn't the only thing we spoke about – having the same conversation for three or four years would be too much – but rarely did sessions pass without their insinuating to some extent that I'd been away and another personality had done this or that. Every single time I laughed them off, or agreed sarcastically or had an argument for the sake of it, just to see how far I could push it.

Nothing ever fazed them. No matter how angry or sceptical or rude or patronising I sounded, they still pressed ahead, gently pointing out their latest piece of evidence proving I was living a shared existence.

It didn't matter that so much of what they said made logical sense – or that I couldn't find any more plausible alternatives. I didn't have multiple personalities, I just didn't – and that was that.

And then one day, several years after our first meeting, I walked out of Professor Morton's room and thought, *What if he's right? What if there are multiple personalities living in this same body?*

Suddenly, for the first time in my life, the whole world began to make perfect sense to me.

PART TWO

CHAPTER EIGHTEEN

Pandora's box

Bonny studied the picture on her screen.

This has to be some kind of joke.

The cursor hovered over the image as Bonny's hand rested gently on the mouse, index finger poised. A mixture of trepidation and intrigue.

One click.

That's all it would take.

One click, then she'd know the answers: why she was staring at a photograph of herself. Why it was on an online dating site.

And why her name was 'Abi'.

One click.

Bonny fought the urge to run. Turn off the computer, walk away, and never be troubled again.

That ship had sailed. It was too late. She had already seen too much.

Bonny felt ill. Her stomach was churning, crippled with nerves. Trepidation had turned to dread. Intrigue to panic.

In her heart, Bonny already knew the answer.

Oh God, *she thought.* It's happening again!

And then, sick with nerves, she clicked on the image.

I magine the moment when you realise that the six-year-old
girl you have known all her life is actually your own daughter. What do you say? There's nothing to prepare you for that.
I'd known Aimee since she was four months old. She was always
in my house. In fact, usually I was the only person with her. The
clues were all there.

But I never joined up the dots. I always came up with a jus-
tification for it. There was always some logical reason why I was
in charge of a friend's little girl – even though I'd never actually
met that friend.

Looking back, it was obvious. Something, in my own mind
was preventing me from making the link. The brain's a funny
thing. It's also very clever and mine was protecting me. Because
if I ever accepted that Aimee was my baby, then I had to accept
other things – things you wouldn't wish on your worst enemy.

And obviously it didn't think I was ready. Yet.

My initial response on being told I suffered Dissociative Identity
Disorder all those years earlier had been denial. I'd denied it to
Rob Hale, I'd denied it to Valerie Sinason, to Evelyn Laine and
John Morton. You could have lined up everyone from Lady Gaga
to the Queen of Sheba and I'd have denied it to them as well.
There was absolutely no way I shared my body with other
personalities.

It was nothing personal. As far as I'd been concerned this
new diagnosis was no different from doctors telling me I'd
taken overdoses, or I had bulimia or I was schizophrenic – I'd
denied all of those too, and I'd been proved right. To me, DID
was just the latest in a long, long line of lies that the medical
profession wanted to make me believe.

So what changed? It was a gradual process. It couldn't have been the volume of people talking to me or the length of time they spent doing so, because I'd had a lifetime of ignoring doctors' opinions. Instead, every so often, I looked at the things troubling me on a daily basis – my blackouts, being mistaken for someone else by strangers, losing things around the house – and just wondered if there was another explanation. Rob Hale had diagnosed me with Dissociative Identity Disorder soon after meeting me. Valerie had agreed and jointly they'd pursued a campaign to help me understand. Two years later they might just as well have been talking another language because I certainly wasn't listening. Even if I wanted to believe them, it was too much to process. It sounded like the plot from a science fiction film, not something that happened to real people. I was as likely to accept I had alien DNA or super powers as I would that I had multiple personalities.

Then slowly, very slowly, in fact over a period of another two or three years of sessions with Dr Laine, I entertained the idea. Tentatively at first, by researching the subject at home – although I never admitted this to them! Then I started asking the question 'What if . . .?', but every time I'd quickly dismiss it as a childish fantasy. A few months later I would wonder again, then again, and slowly I realised that my denial had turned to something else.

Fear.

Fear that they might be right.

It's a short trip from being scared to being disgusted at the idea of sharing your most personal moments with unknown personalities. I'd been confused on and off for most of my life.

Now I was running the gamut from fear to loathing and back to disbelief every time I had a spare moment.

The funny thing is, the more I dwelled on the possibilities of having DID, the more time I seemed to have to do it. For what seemed like forever, and certainly for the last few years since the acid and fire incidents, days had rushed by in a blur. It was strange to admit but I suddenly seemed to have more time to myself.

It's incredible to me now, looking back, that Dr Laine and Professor Morton showed such patience with me. By the time I finally admitted to them that, yes, I accept your diagnosis of DID, I was expecting anger and shouts of 'About bloody time!' That couldn't have been further from the truth. They were both genuinely delighted. I could see that professionally they were happy but they also seemed relieved for my sake.

'Your life is going to be so much easier from now on,' Dr Laine promised.

I don't see how. I've just admitted I've got God knows how many people living inside my head!

It had been such a long journey, from originally meeting Dr Hale to finally admitting his diagnosis, and Dr Laine didn't feel any need to rush this stage. But now I was desperate for information. I was like the kid who can't wait for Christmas.

In hindsight, Dr Laine was right to take things slowly. Eager as I was emotionally to learn everything, mentally there is only so much that your brain can take in. It didn't take me long to find my head spinning – again.

'I'm sorry it's taken so long,' I admitted one day to Dr Laine. 'You've been trying to tell me this for years.'

She laughed. 'Don't worry, you're not the last one to come to terms with it.'

That sounds weird.

'The last what?' I asked.

'The last of your other personalities, or alter egos, "alters" or self-states – whatever you want to call them. There are only a couple who understand the DID.'

I'd heard all the jargon dozens of times – the 'alters', the 'personalities' – and dismissed them. Now they all took on new significance. They were no longer just words or ideas or theories.

They were people.

Dr Laine told me about a woman called Hayley and another called Bonny.

I recognised both names instantly. I'd seen letters addressed to both at the house. I'd always just assumed poor postal service as usual, or that Mum or Nan had kept them for some reason. Then the shutters had come down and they were filtered from my thoughts.

Self-defence again.

'And they both live inside this body?' I asked, already knowing the answer.

'They do – they all do.'

'All? You mean there are more?'

'With all the names Kim, Hayley and the others have given me it adds up to over a hundred. Maybe even double that.'

You can be as open-minded as possible and still be nonplussed. I didn't know a hundred different people. Even though some of them were only 'fragments' of a personality, how could that many exist in my tiny body? My faith in this business was beginning to slip.

'That's impossible. It must be a trick.'

'They're as real as you are.'

There were so many questions I didn't know which to ask first. Fortunately Dr Laine took her time, explaining everything in as much detail as I could bear. In the back of my mind, of course, was this new realisation that I might 'disappear' before she'd finished speaking.

'Will I know when I'm going to switch?' I asked Dr Laine.

'You don't appear to.'

'So I could go any moment?'

'That's right.'

'And will you be able to tell who's replaced me?'

'If I've seen them before then yes. But every so often I meet new personalities and I have to introduce myself and start again from the beginning.'

Incredible.

'So you really have the same conversations with two or three people who look exactly like me?'

She nodded.

'Don't you feel embarrassed repeating yourself like that?'

'Not at all,' Dr Laine said. 'Remember, I'm not saying the same thing three times to you. I'm saying it once to three different people.'

That would take a while to sink in. At least it explained my history of people looking exasperated at work or school or even in shops when I sometimes asked questions. They'd obviously just gone through it with someone else who looked exactly like me!

On those occasions, Dr Laine explained, I was most likely being confused with either Hayley or Bonny.

'How can you be so sure?' I wondered.

'Because Hayley and Bonny are the ones who are most like you. If they left a room and you walked in, most people might not spot the change.'

'Whereas the others?'

'Oh I don't think anyone would ever confuse some of the others with you!'

My similarities to Bonny and Hayley, she explained, had just got greater. Those were the only other personalities who were aware of the DID diagnosis. At least, those were the only two who accepted it. I was glad to learn that I wasn't the only one who'd rejected the idea – but shocked to imagine all those similar conversations going on between the therapists and the various personalities. When the Prof revealed he'd also been giving them the same memory tests as I'd been doing for the last couple of years – to see how much information leaked through from one to another, in spite of the fact that none of us was conscious of anything that happened to the others – I was blown away.

'When did you test them?' I asked, still in shock. 'I only come here once a month.'

'Remember that sometimes you didn't always come to my sessions?' he replied.

I nodded. There had been weeks when I hadn't remembered attending.

'But your body always made it. Bonny or you managed to find your way here and I tested whoever was out.'

The reliance on Bonny and Hayley was no coincidence, I

learned. The body may play host to multiple personalities but, Dr Laine explained, if that body was to function normally in the wider world then there had to be one personality in control, what she called the 'dominant personality'.

'So I'm the dominant personality?' I assumed, completely unprepared for the answer.

'I'm afraid not,' she said, adding it was her role to encourage me to reach my potential.

As if discovering you share your body with 100+ other personalities isn't embarrassing enough for your ego, it's nothing compared to the blow when you realise you're not even the main one!

It took a while but eventually Dr Laine explained it in a way I could accept. When Kim Noble had faded into the background, as Dr Laine put it, Hayley had taken over. She was the one who took charge of getting us from A to B, of generally keeping our life on track. As an adult, she was the one who found us jobs, paid bills and handled the day-to-day bureaucracy. None of the rest of the personalities – myself included – had any input in this. I didn't even realise it went on. At some point, which she said she would explain later, Hayley had grown tired and faded. At the same time, the personality most like her, a woman called Bonny, stepped forward. From just coming out for portions of the day, like I was told I had been doing, Bonny now appeared for the lion's share of the time. And because she was similar in behaviour to Hayley it had been a fairly seamless transition as far as the outside world was concerned.

'And now,' Dr Laine said, 'you might be needed more and more as there is so much pressure on Bonny.'

Bonny, she feared, was beginning to fade away as Kim and Hayley had, and the body was already looking for her replacement. It wasn't just bills and admin that were in jeopardy once she went. Without a dominant personality at the helm, the body's daughter was at serious risk of being removed. For this reason, Dr Laine had identified me as a potential dominant personality years ago. Now, it seemed, the body was agreeing. The final piece of the jigsaw was getting me to realise it for myself.

'How do you know I'm going to be the dominant personality?' I asked Dr Laine.

'Well, have you noticed yourself being more present recently?'

I considered it. Yes, it was true. I had seemed to spend longer and longer periods with Aimee and I'd even noticed that the time I dedicated to thinking about the DID hadn't flown by like when I did so many other things.

'I think you're coming out more because you're being selected,' the doctor said. 'The body thinks you're its best bet for coping with the future.'

I don't think I'll ever understand the full workings of the human brain, body and consciousness. I was heartened, however, to realise that even old hands like Professor Morton were still capable of being surprised as well. The tests I'd been undergoing for the last few years had been designed to check how extreme a case I was. The results intrigued even a man who'd been interested in the disorder for decades.

'This is really significant, Patricia,' the professor said. 'You might say you are the gold standard for DID!' he smiled. 'You are one hundred per cent not co-conscious.'

'What does that mean?'

'It means there is absolutely no seepage between person-alities. The majority of dominant personalities in people with DID have some level of awareness of the other alters. Some hear voices, some can see what's going on when they're not in con-trol. Some can even talk to all the different personalities in their head.'

'I can't do that.'

'No,' he agreed. 'It's remarkable, isn't it? I've never met anyone like you.'

On one level, accepting that I was one of several – possibly hun-dreds of – personalities turned my head inside out. It was like trying to catch your breath standing under a waterfall. There was too much information to take it all in at once. I needed time to process – but time was the thing I was always missing. On the other hand, it explained so much I felt a weight rise from my shoulders. It wasn't like the diagnosis for schizo-phrenia, which I'd always instinctively known was wrong.

This feels right.

As hard to conceive as DID was, it was such a relief to learn that my blackouts weren't caused by alcohol. I wasn't some drunk struggling to get by in life. My apparent memory lapses were actually gaps in my knowledge and they had a med-ical reason: I genuinely wasn't there at the time.

Even though I knew it made sense, coming to terms with being a bit-part player in my own body's life took a while. No one likes to think they're not important. Yet, when I looked back at some of the most dramatic moments of my life, I realised I hadn't really been the one pulling the strings.

Hayley, for example, was the one who had fought the

tribunal at the Maudsley. She was the one who had got us off the schizophrenia charge. She was the one who'd filed the application, done the research, then got up there and made such a powerful presentation that she became the first patient on Ward 3 to have ever beaten the system. She had done all that – and I'd taken the credit. Dad had told me how impressive I'd been and I didn't even question it. At the time it seemed normal for me. All the while it was Hayley doing these things.

But at least I wasn't drunk. I didn't black out. The simple reason why I had no memory of the tribunal is because I didn't attend.

Hayley sounded a very dynamic person. Not like me at all, really. I think I would have been intimidated to meet her. Unfortunately, as far as Dr Laine could establish, the pressure of the acid and fire had taken its toll. Hayley stopped 'coming out' as often.

At that point Bonny stepped up. She'd always been around, apparently, just like me. The only difference between us, Dr Laine said, was Bonny's temper. She would only put up with things for so long and then she'd explode.

'Have you ever blacked out when you were getting cross or agitated about something?' Dr Laine asked.

It did sound familiar. I remembered times just being penned in in Warlingham, feeling so claustrophobic about the locked doors, and wishing I could force them open. I never would, I was too timid. The next thing I remember, though, is being told off by the staff for trying to break out when I knew I hadn't left my bed. I'd thought, *What tablets have they put me on? Can they actually read my thoughts?*

Now I knew: Bonny had taken it further. She had shaken

those doors. She'd kicked them until the hinges rattled. And
then she'd been manhandled back to bed.

Which is where I took over again!

It's a slow process opening your perception to something so massive. First I needed to appreciate that I wasn't
always in 100 per cent control of my body or its actions. As
much as I wanted to accept that blindly, it takes a while to
come to terms with. Then I needed to be aware that other
people inhabited the same physical space as me. This was the
tricky one. I just felt dirty. I couldn't shake the suspicion that
other people had been spying on me. Understanding that this
isn't how it works wasn't easy. Dr Laine kept saying, 'But you
can't see what the others are doing when they come out, can
you?' and the answer was no, I just seemed to vanish. Even
so . . .

On paper I'd accepted what the therapists were saying: I suffered from Dissociative Identity Disorder. That was a big leap to
take. The epiphany really came, however, when I started to look
back and apply my new knowledge to my life.

That was my eureka moment.

Forget the blackouts. I'd learnt to live with those years
earlier. To a certain extent it didn't make much difference
whether I'd passed out from overindulging on wine, or been
parked because a different personality had taken over.

The bombshell realisation for me was all those other
things during my life that I had been accused of doing. What
was it I used to say as a child?

'It wasn't me.'

And now I knew I was right. Such a huge weight lifted

off me. I always knew I hadn't done those things. How many innocent men are imprisoned on the strength of overwhelming evidence? How long had I lasted before I stopped denying everything? Looking back, that annoyed me. Why didn't anyone work it out? Why did they all just assume I was a liar and move on?

As I said, coming to terms with an epiphany of this magnitude is not something you do overnight. It took months of sifting over my past to get a little perspective on everything. Even then I'd barely scratched the surface. Every day new memories flooded in and I tried to work out what had really happened. Sometimes I was left wondering. Sometimes Dr Laine had the answers.

The black paint episode at school – my earliest memory. That *had* happened. That was Bonny. She'd spilt it.

It wasn't me.

Trying to climb out of the Orange Room and being caught? Bonny again.

It wasn't me.

God, it felt good to know I hadn't been mad, to actually feel vindicated after all these years.

Playing detective, having to work out where I was and what I was up to, had always been part of my daily routine. Now, though, I felt like an investigator working on a cold case. I was surrounded by unsolved mysteries from ten, twenty, thirty-odd years ago – and I was determined to solve every single one of them.

Every spare minute available, I raked over my past, trying to piece together exactly what had happened. The only problem was: spare minutes were thin on the ground. I'm still learning now. Watching *Oprah* taught me things I didn't know about my body. Writing this book has been a revelation as well.

Knowing about DID, even accepting I had it, didn't change anything. It wasn't as though I'd been handed a 'cure'. The blackouts remained as frequent as ever. I was still disappearing for hours or days at a time. I still found myself wondering, *Where the hell am I now?* And I was doing the usual process of trying to slot the evidence together. The only difference now was it didn't scare me any more. In fact, I even fantasised about the next 'switch'. That took time but, yes, I really found myself thinking, *I wonder what I'll get up to today without knowing it. I wonder who's coming to take my place.*

Among all the crimes I was wrongly accused of were a few where I had to plead guilty. All those occasions at school where I'd been accused of talking had happened. Sometimes it was Kim or Bonny or someone else doing the yapping. But if I suddenly found myself in a room with one of my friends I'd naturally start talking to her – before I realised I was in assembly or class.

The more I delved, the more trouble these 'alters' seemed to have caused me. It never occurred to me to wonder what predicaments I ever put them in. I wasn't ready for that yet.

There were funny things, too. I discovered that at the time I had my own flat – so did Hayley. Bonny, meanwhile, lived with Mum. That explains why she never noticed when I left home and why she was always so grateful for the help I was giving her when I hadn't even been there – it was Bonny putting her to bed, looking after her.

Can you believe that our body was living at three separate addresses at the same time? Imagine how much more money we would have had if we'd all shared!

While we had different addresses for that period we also signed on with different local GPs. It probably couldn't happen now, but my body was registered on the NHS at three different surgeries. Bearing in mind the amount of times I'd spent in the profession's care, you'd think someone would have noticed.

Learning about DID was life changing, of course, but the full reach of its effects didn't hit home overnight. No fairy godmother waved a magic wand and sorted everything out. Coming to terms with the disorder was such a gradual transformation that for a while I wondered if much had changed at all. In fact, I soon realised that nothing would ever be the same again.

It wasn't as simple as saying that DID suddenly answered all my questions. If I'm honest, I wasn't aware I had any questions. All those odd incidents and inexplicable events had all been explained away at the time. I never felt I was seeking answers.

That was just as well. Knowing about DID actually created more questions than it answered. It wasn't an instant thing: I didn't wake up with a head chock full of problems. But like an avalanche, it built, slowly, from the occasional thought until before I knew it every preconception I held had been destroyed – starting with some very fundamental things, like my age.

For as long as I'd been seeing her, Dr Laine had always tried to get me to look in the mirror. I always refused.

'I don't need to. I know what I look like.'

'What do you think you look like?'

Stupid question. I pointed to my face.

'Like this.'

'How old do you think you are, Patricia?'

'I'm twenty-one.'

'And when were you born?'

'Twenty-one years ago.'

'What if I told you that you were born in 1960?'

'Then I would say that must be twenty-one years ago.'

Honestly, Dr Laine must have had the patience of a saint to deal with me!

It's not Dr Laine's nature to keep pushing the same buttons so it was a while before the subject came up again. By then I had been aware of the DID for a couple of months.

'Would you like to look in the mirror, Patricia, and tell me what you see?'

For the first time I didn't say no. It was only a mirror, for God's sake.

So why was I so nervous?

I went over to the mirror, took a glance, then spun round. There was no one behind me. I looked again and couldn't help checking over my shoulder for the second time. There was still no one there. Was it a funfair mirror – is that why Dr Laine had been so desperate for me to look in?

I couldn't understand it.

If there is no one else behind me, then who is that old woman staring back?

As far as I was concerned, my name was Patricia and I was twenty-one. Now, though, I realised I'd been stuck at that age for more than twenty years. It was like looking with fresh eyes. When I stared in that mirror I wasn't seeing the reflection of a young adult – I'd literally doubled in age. And why did my skin look so thin?

This was going to take some time to work through.

The avalanche continued its slow descent. My age and appearance were just two of its early victims. More discomfort was to come when I began to think about those times at the Cassel when Dad would turn up to collect me and insist I'd called when I hadn't. How many times did that happen? I've lost track. Or sometimes I'd ask to go home and then he'd be angry because he said I'd asked to be taken back. I can see what happened now. A different alter ego asked to be picked up. I don't know who. And then of course I'd know nothing about it and be unprepared.

On the other occasions I was the one who wanted to go home – and then one of the others demanded to go back. Dad used to say I'd get hysterical about it, screaming and shouting the house down. I hadn't believed him – until now. Looking at it from the other personality's point of view, they – whoever it was – would have been as stunned as me to find themselves somewhere else. They'd be doing the 'where am I now?' jigsaw puzzle. It was numbing to think I wasn't alone playing that particular game.

The real victim in all this was my father. Poor Dad – no wonder he always seemed so angry. *And why he called me a liar.*

It was a happy day when I solved that particular mystery. However, as one door marked 'Question' was closed, others just kept opening. It was a few weeks later and I suddenly woke up with a single question on my mind:

Why were the other personalities so determined not to stay at home? Was there something there or nearby that they didn't like? *Very strange.*

Thinking of the Cassel reminded me of why I was there and all the other places that had held me captive for so much of my life. Analysing these was a lot harder than mulling over a bit of spilt black paint or the odd 'I didn't do that' argument. Did I really want to know?

Dr Laine was a great help. She'd spoken to another personality. Like me for so long, this personality, Judy, refused to believe she suffered from DID. To this day she still denies it. Hearing about her, it's like listening to the old me: she's got an excuse for everything. If not an excuse, a reason. Judy, I was told, was fifteen.

That sounds familiar, I thought. *I was twenty-one for long enough.*

Unlike me, though, Judy was quite overweight.

That drove me back to the mirror. If I could convince myself I was half my age, could I lie to myself that I was thinner than I was?

I studied the reflection of the woman before me. No, I was confident the image was as slim as I remembered. It was me. Older than I liked, but me. The size tags in my clothes confirmed it.

Judy, though, was convinced she was overweight. As she told Dr Laine, 'I deserve to be. I'm always eating.' She always had a bun or a chip or a knife and fork in her hands. It stood to reason that she was massively overweight if all she ever did was eat.

Except – she may always have been eating, but the body wasn't. I don't know why, but Judy only ever 'came out' when there was food around. This made sense to me. I was in my forties and I couldn't remember more than a handful of meals in my entire life. Why hadn't I ever realised that before? I could see it all suddenly: food arrived and I disappeared. Judy was the one who did all the eating! Of course she thought she must have an eating problem.

That realisation brought me to focus on my own situation. What was it that therapist at Arbours used to say? 'Is Drunk Kim here today?' I went along with it, didn't I, because I always seemed to have a glass of wine in my hand. Every single weird thing that happened to me I merrily chalked down to drunken passing out or similar stupidity. But the truth was, yes, I did often seem to have a glass in my hand. But that was because I always appeared when there was some partying to be done. Some personalities get the bed-making and cooking and I got the drinking – it wasn't a bad deal, I realised. But it did confuse me.

It also made me appreciate that perhaps I really wasn't out as often as I would have liked. My biggest memories of my driving job were the lunchtimes and drinks after work. If I was honest, actual recollections of doing the job itself were few and far between. I'd seem to go from tea to the pub, nothing in between. How the hell did I convince myself that this was normal?

So I wasn't an alcoholic – that was another diagnosis that had been wrong – and neither was Judy overweight (although pictures from when we were fifteen do show us plumper than I remember – so that's obviously where her paranoia is rooted).

But she did have a problem: she was the one who was eating and then running off to the toilet to throw it up again. She was the one with bulimia.

She was the reason we were under lock and key in the Maudsley.

Judy was also the one who'd tried to break out of the Maudsley. No wonder we were caught – she probably thought she was too overweight to run!

When I learnt about Judy I assumed she must be the reason I was accused of anorexia as well. Not so, it turned out. Anorexia was suffered by a girl called Sonia. Whenever I felt hungry it was because Sonia had turned down another meal. She was the one who the Cassel had been trying to feed eggs.

The bigger picture is so much clearer. It's just such a shame the others couldn't see it. What often used to happen was that Sonia would appear and reject her food – then she'd disappear. So, as far as she was concerned, she was not eating. She might make a big fuss of this and leave the room, anything.

But Judy would appear and she would devour everything in sight, feel guilty and go and get rid of it.

If it weren't so tragic, if it hadn't ruined large chunks of my life, I could laugh.

Another way of understanding DID, I learnt, was to picture peeling an onion – and not just because it leaves you in tears. I'm told I could excavate layer upon layer for the rest of my life and still never reach the bottom. Living with multiple person- alities is not something you just wake up fully understanding. For months, maybe years after I first accepted the diagnosis, I was still discovering new nuances, fresh areas I hadn't considered. Infinite questions, infinite problems – some more palatable than others.

Like: sex. Men. Strangers.

The moment this aspect of a shared body occurred to me I felt such nausea I thought I would faint. It was one thing imagining poor Judy stuffing her face on the body's behalf but this was serious. Had other people touched me without my consent?

I felt the bile rising in my throat just thinking about it. According to Dr Laine – yes – some of the older ones had been interested in having a partner and might have had physical moments.

I don't know why it hadn't occurred to me sooner. Men, strangers, touching my body, being intimate with me, doing things to me that only my lover should do – the very idea made me retch. I can understand it better now and empathise and knowing it would have been consensual is the most important thing. But my initial reaction that my body had been touched without my knowledge was instinctive.

It's disgusting.

I still don't know how many personalities were – or are – sexually active, although since things have calmed down a lot since I became the dominant one, I think the chances for others these days are few and far between. About five or six years ago, however, a new personality with hopes of finding a partner was discovered – quite by accident. One of Bonny's friends had asked her why she was advertising on an internet dating site. Bonny had denied it of course, then at the first chance she'd gone to the site and clicked through the various members.

To her horror there was a photograph – and the profile – of someone who could only be her. But since Bonny knew it wasn't her,
it had to be one of the personalities. At that point, I think, she
went through the horrible thought that I was experiencing
now – that moment when you realise someone else is using
your body for sex.

Bonny had gone straight to Dr Laine, who in turn had
visited the site and sent a message to the personality, called
Abi, via her profile. The next day she received a wonderful
reply:

'Hello, Evelyn, thanks for getting in touch but I should
make it clear – I'm looking for a man. I'm not a lesbian!'

Poor Dr Laine. She eventually managed to persuade Abi
that she wasn't a stalker and to come into one of her therapy
groups, but it wasn't easy. Abi seems headstrong, to say the
least, although I know she has been given all the information
she needs about DID for when she is ready to 'hear' it. For
now, though, she doesn't accept the diagnosis and, to be
frank, that's why I have a mistrustful feeling about her. If
I'd met Abi before I learned about DID then we'd probably
have got on like a house on fire. But I'm a mother now – and,
of course, so is she. I've put a large part of my life on hold to
concentrate on bringing up Aimee. There's so much more to
take into account with every decision than 'do I fancy doing
that?'

It took a while to come to terms with this other, physical
side of my body's life. Of all the things I'd had to contend with
so far, the moment this dawned on me rocked me hardest of
all. It was one thing envisioning another personality eating –
as long as I was the one doing the drinking, who cares? – but

another entirely to have let my body be subjected to God knows what.

I had a sudden flashback to being in a man's flat one morning. He'd spoken as though we'd known each other and we'd arranged to meet that night. At the time I'd made my excuses and left. But now ...

My God, had we just had sex?

Was it possible that another personality could have a partner I did not know about?

There are only so many times your head can spin. I sat on the floor, beaten and hurt, and picked through the mess. How I wanted to scrub every inch of my body. To sand my tongue, Dettol my skin and spit out every last drop of moisture from my mouth.

What good would it do?

I realised it wasn't just my problem. It was the body's problem. *Our* problem.

After months of resistance I obviously began to embrace the truth. I didn't notice it happen, but suddenly I was talking about my body as 'our body', and myself as 'us'. It wasn't planned, it just happened. Gradually, I was joining my other selves. I was accepting them.

By accepting them, however, I had to accept certain other things. And how I wish I never had.

It was Hayley who had won us the driving job. For all I know it was her who had passed the driving test – I'd never taken a proper lesson. She was the one who applied, using the Green Card, took the interview and was handed the company uniform.

She was the personality who dragged us out every morning and, I assume, did most of the work. I say 'assume' because at this point I didn't know better. I knew from Dr Laine that it wasn't Bonny and it certainly wasn't me. I popped up for the fun times – I wasn't daft.

There could have been other personalities, Dr Laine told me. At this stage she hadn't met many. Of the ones who had made themselves known, several were children and incapable of driving.

Of course, even those who could drive had their moments. Our car crash – the episode where I'd been told I'd crashed into five parked cars – that was Julie. As far as we know, Julie had never tried to drive before. (Nor has she since – the body won't let a non-driver have control of a vehicle.) But for that moment Julie had believed car number plates were communicating with her. She believed TV aerials were beaming her instructions.

And she truly believed she could steer with her eyes closed.

Julie was the reason we were diagnosed with schizophrenia. I don't know if she suffered from this or not. Most likely she was just scared and confused – her mind didn't protect her from the blackouts as well as mine had. Whereas I had come up with the catch-all defence of alcoholism hers had gone for a more extreme – and dangerous – option.

Learning about Julie I discovered things I'd never known. Crashing the van hadn't been the end of her adventures. Travelling on a bus one day she'd pulled out a canister of fly spray and started showering the other passengers in insect-killer. She honestly thought they were in danger of being stung. From what, who knows?

It's funny to recall that now. It has nothing to do with my life – I may as well be reading about a boy in Berlin doing it, that's how much of an impact it has on me. And yet, it was our body that did it. There were people terrified out of their minds because of things we did. That doesn't feel nice. What if I ever run into one of those travellers? You wouldn't blame them if they got their own back, would you?

You might think that what happened to Julie, and the things that she made happen to us, should have had greater impact on me. That would make sense. It's the same body, after all.

The truth is, my alter egos and I may as well be on opposite sides of the Earth for all the influence we have on each other. I know that my car crash would have befuddled the others. I was the one who suffered the collision, who injured my arm and face. My alters would have had to explain those pains away to others and themselves just as I'd done so many times.

The greatest impact my alters' behaviour had on me was not in the acts themselves but in the telling. And some of those tales I just was not prepared for. Opening my mind to DID was like opening Pandora's box. The demons that emerge could not be put back again. They were out forever.

Success at the driving job that Hayley had fought so hard to win had seen us promoted to an office position. I remembered working that out when I found myself at a desk.

What I never worked out was what had happened to make work so difficult.

Hayley had informed police of being a witness to a recording of a film involving child pornography. I read all of this years later in police papers. I could barely comprehend the words.

For the first time I cursed my DID. How dare it let me witness something so hideous and let me do nothing about it.

Perhaps if I had stepped forward then I wouldn't be here now to tell the tale. By blowing the whistle on this depraved paedophile ring, Hayley had angered some very dangerous people, people in authority who had too much to lose to go quietly. As the court case drew closer, the suspects' acquaintances were getting more and more desperate that we shouldn't testify. I couldn't believe how far they were prepared to go: one day we'd been attacked on our way home from work, resulting in a black eye and twisted arm.

That was nothing. Our local newspaper received threats for giving the case coverage. Other witnesses were cowed into walking away. Hayley had refused – and we had all paid the price.

One day she had answered the front door at home to be met by a man holding something. As soon as the man was confident it was us, he'd thrown something into our face. It was acid. I can't imagine anything worse. Obviously we ran inside and threw water over our face but the damage was done. To this day I still have papery-thin skin as a consequence. I'm lucky to have any face left at all.

On hearing this, part of me wanted to just scream, 'Stop making this up!' It was too horrific to be true.

It sounds like something from a Martina Cole novel.

But I remembered the long blackouts round about that time. I remembered discovering my face was a giant scab and not daring to look in the mirror, not daring to enquire why lest I discovered something I didn't want to. I remembered all that and knew it was true.

That, however, had only been an attempt at intimidation. Our assailants' next move was designed to shut us up once and for all.

It was a Saturday night, early 1995. Hayley was at home alone. It must have been late because she was in bed, sound asleep. It was the dampness that woke her, from deep sleep to deep discomfort in seconds. Then as she roused, the unmistakeable stench of petrol assaulted her senses. That was what was soaking through her duvet.

Then she saw the man standing at the foot of her bed. It was so unreal, she couldn't move. Not when he struck a match, not when he flung the flickering flame towards her bed, not even as he thundered back out of the room. Only as the match hit the duvet and burst into a terrifying ball of fire did Hayley leap out of bed.

What to do now? Hayley was frozen with fear. The man might be out there on the landing. Could she risk it? Then the heat from the fire told her she had no choice. A crack of wood splitting in the darkness sent her diving out of the room. By the time her television exploded against the wall, she was tugging at the front door, which slammed shut immediately afterwards – trapping our dog, poor Alfie, inside.

Firemen later revealed the man had broken in via the back door. More importantly, they rescued Alfie. In the end no one had been injured although the house would take months to put right.

It was a horrific tale, made worse by the later discovery that the police had eventually dropped the case – due to evidence going missing and witnesses changing their stories. All that suffering for nothing. Whatever the outcome, though, hearing it was like being told it had happened to a friend of a friend. The thing that connected most with me was the memory of the charred house. All our clothes had been destroyed and we'd been forced to flee to, first, the women's refuge and then Arbours. At least now I knew why.

Thanks to my mind's unique defence mechanism, I'd missed the abuse of our body and at least two murder attempts. Believe it or not, however, that wasn't the worst of it.

Although I'd got to the bottom of the anorexia accusations, I realised there were several other loose ends as far as my hospital history was concerned. I didn't know why it took me so long to query it – although obviously it was that self-defence mechanism again – but one day it suddenly came to me:

Why was I always having my stomach pumped?

Dr Laine held the answers here. She'd met a personality called Rebecca. Rebecca had taken the overdose of pills that saw us rushed to Mayday that first time. And the next time, and the time after that. Each time, though, Rebecca followed the same pattern. She would gulp down Dad's pills, then stagger downstairs and inform Mum or Nan or Lorraine or Dad what she had done. They had called an ambulance and the medical process had taken its course. What was obvious was: she didn't want to die.

It's a classic cry for help.

The overdoses had continued. She'd considered crashing the car and also throwing herself from the top of a local multi-storey car park. Then, at Warlingham, she'd managed to hang herself. Hearing that made me reach instinctively for my neck. In my mind the burn felt as fresh as it had all those years before. Again, there was enough chance of being discovered that assured me it was not a serious attempt.

But there was another episode. This one was in Lewes during the time we'd been assigned round-the-clock protection from those two guards. Somehow Hayley had given them the slip and gone to visit a friend in Lewes. Once there Rebecca had taken over and popped a canister of pills in the sanctity of our hotel room. Before they could kick in, the police – alerted by the security guards – had discovered her. They arrived just in time to call an ambulance.

Hearing these stories was just that: they were stories. I'd already dealt with the fallout from Rebecca's actions – did I want to dwell on the suicide attempts again now?

But then I realised I still wasn't taking in the full picture. There was one very important question I hadn't asked. Even when I realised, I hesitated. Did I honestly want to know the answer?

Yes, I decided. *Yes, I do.*

Okay: exactly why did Rebecca try to kill us?

Now I was at the crux of the matter. This was why I had been in denial for so long, in the face of irrefutable evidence, that I suffered from DID.

This is what my mind had really been protecting me from.

Because, as Dr Laine was sad to explain, to accept that I had Dissociative Identity Disorder was to accept that our body had been abused.

As a child.

Again and again and again.

It's enough to drive anyone to suicide.

CHAPTER NINETEEN

That's not Skye

Was she there?

Dawn pressed her palms against the shop window. Even with the glare of the sun behind her she could make out the customers, all those mothers with their little tots, pushing them around without a care in the world. Some of the prams were open, their little occupants wide-eyed and smiling. One by one Dawn ticked them off her mental list. The closed pushchairs, where the little passengers were sound asleep, were another matter. Dawn peered harder.

Was she in one of those?

She ran round and stood in the doorway.

Is she one of them?

Is one of those babies my Skye?

Discovering the truth about DID and what my mind had been protecting me from all these years was hard to process. I'm sure it was the hardest part of Dr Laine's job, informing me how my body – our body – had been subjected to the worst kind of abuse at such a tender age. From therapy sessions with Hayley and Bonny, Dr Laine had assembled the bones of our background. Then she had encouraged the dominant personality at the time to step aside and let other alters emerge during those sessions. Dr Laine and Aimee both seem to have the power to summon other personalities – although only if those personalities are willing to appear, and if the dominant alter doesn't 'block' or fight it. One by one she met the poor victims and learnt their stories.

Not all of the victims were coherent – some were too young, frozen in time as toddlers, small children or even babies, doomed to remain at an age where the pain was still as raw as the day it had happened. We all seem to have stopped ageing at a certain point. For me it was twenty-one, I don't know why. For two-, three- and four-year-olds I think it's obvious. That's when their childhoods were taken away. Some of them are still too paralysed to speak. Most of them haven't even revealed their names. They're all scared, all scarred, all ashamed – and I just want to hug them and say, 'It's not your fault!'

The luckier ones had had the chance to age and try to put some distance between them and events. Other older personalities denied the abuse although their own lifestyles indicated their suffering. Eating disorders, along with other symptoms, is a tell-tale sign. Self-loathing, especially the wish to die, was another. Judy, Sonia, Julie and Rebecca are all likely victims.

Part of me didn't want to know the details for fear I would never recover. But another part was desperate for any information. It may not have happened to me, but this was my body. If I couldn't share their pain, I felt an obligation to my fellow alters to know as much about it as possible.

Dr Laine never discovered all the details but she learnt enough. As my parents both worked, they had entrusted Baby

Kim to various local babysitters on those occasions when Nan couldn't look after her. Sometimes the childminders took Kim into their own house. On other occasions they would look after her at ours. This wasn't as cavalier as it might sound today. You have to remember this was the early 1960s. Communities were tighter. Children would regularly be passed around a network of babysitters who, today, probably wouldn't even be asked. As far as Dr Laine was concerned, my parents had acted as anyone else in their position would have.

What they didn't – what they couldn't – know was that one or more of these sitters took advantage of his or her position. I don't know who the guilty party was and I don't want to because it would disturb me more if I remembered being alone with them – especially if they were abusing Kim when they were at our house. But it's enough to know that it happened, again and again and again.

Unable to cope with the physical and mental pain, Kim Noble's mind had fractured. In her place had appeared hundreds of others, all as innocent as Kim. Some suffered as she had suffered and some, like me, Hayley and Bonny, had been lucky.

Learning the truth made me somehow feel I was dishonouring Kim. After all, she would have done anything to forget what had happened to her and here I was wilfully drawing those memories out from the others who suffered like her.

Without the help of Dr Laine I probably couldn't have coped. With every new revelation I questioned whether I had to go on, whether I needed to know everything. But for me to fully accept DID, to fully take on the responsibilities of becoming the dominant personality, it was essential. Yes, it was the worst feeling of my life – but knowing everything about our body's past was a very small price to pay to keep our daughter.

Other personalities weren't as lucky. One in particular was stuck in time for another reason altogether.

Through Dr Laine I learnt that a personality called Dawn had given birth to Aimee six years ago. She was the one who'd endured the caesarean section, although I share the scar. She was the one who had just cuddled her little baby Skye when the officials from social services had come in to remove her. I can't imagine what that must have felt like. If I had to make a choice between suffering what my body suffered as a child and losing my daughter, I would take physical suffering every time. There can be no greater loss for a woman.

The more of the story I learnt, the worse the ordeal sounded – not just for Dawn but Hayley and Bonny too. And of course for Aimee.

It had begun during a routine visit to Dr McGilchrist at Mayday, when he told Hayley he had to inform social services of any women with mental health problem who were pregnant. *Fine*, Hayley thought, and understood why. A social worker, called Christine Impy, came to the house to do an assessment which, again, Hayley completely endorsed. Hayley couldn't have been more co-operative. As she told Christine, 'If there is any danger to this baby from the inside or outside, then she has to be taken away and protected.' Further assessment appointments were booked to take place at the social services offices and Hayley didn't miss one. Christine couldn't have been more impressed; not only was Hayley attending all her antenatal appointments but everything at home looked exemplary: there was a pram (bought by our dad) and a cot, clothes, a high chair, car seat, Moses basket, bottles, bath, nappies and toys – you name it, Hayley's baby, as far as Christine was concerned, was going to have it. Even the nursery was all beautifully decorated well in advance in Le Pig trimmings. Nothing was being left to chance.

Christine was equally as thorough. A pre-birth appointment was arranged which Hayley, a solicitor, a policeman and thirteen other interested parties attended. It was agreed by all that Hayley and her baby should be transferred to a mother-and-baby unit after the birth for monitoring. There Hayley would have support and Christine and co. would have final confirmation that she was more than capable of being a 'normal' mother.

If only they'd stopped there, a lot of heartache could have been avoided. Two personalities' lives might not have been scarred forever.

Social services decided, as a final safeguard, to get an independent DID specialist to assess Hayley. Two weeks before Aimee was born Hayley attended a meeting with Dr Elizabeth Hall at 9 a.m. on a hot August day. By the time it finished at five, Hayley was exhausted. But, she reasoned, the more time she spent with Dr Hall, the easier it would be for her to see that Hayley was going to be a fine mother. Certainly it should be clear that her baby would be in no danger.

After the meeting was when things began to go wrong. After months of attention, suddenly it was hard to get information out of social services. Pre-arranged appointments with Hayley were cancelled and when she phoned to find out which mother-and-baby unit she would be going to they said it had yet to be decided.

But my baby's due any moment ...

Days went by. Finally, three days before the scheduled caesarean operation, Hayley was informed a social worker would meet her at the hospital. Little did she know that the social worker had instructions to remove Aimee the moment she was born.

Nobody told Dawn anything. Even when Aimee was taken away minutes after birth, Dawn was still kept in the dark.

'Where's my baby?'

'She's been taken to intensive care for tests.'

'Can I see her?'

'I'm sorry, no.'

Dawn wasn't the only one denied access. The visiting room was packed with friends and family bearing balloons and flowers. My Dad had been there for ages and now Lorraine and her sons, Ivy, and our neighbours had all arrived as well. They were all told the same thing: you can't see the baby and you can't see Kim. As one, they all had the same fear: is there something wrong with the baby?

For Dawn, separated not only from her child but also her well-wishers, the not-knowing must have felt even worse. If her baby was having tests, it stood to reason doctors thought she must be ill. What was wrong with her? What wasn't she being told?

The answer, it turned out, was *the truth*.

Dawn's baby was not having tests at all. Social services were trying to get an order allowing them to remove the baby. They assumed it would be a matter of minutes before it came through. In the end, the order wasn't granted until five o'clock – a full day during which child and family were separated.

When a doctor suddenly appeared with her daughter, Dawn could have been forgiven for thinking everything was going to be okay. Feverishly she grabbed her little girl and hugged her for dear life. She barely looked up when her visitors were allowed in for the first time. She certainly didn't notice the social worker appearing at her side – but she would never forget the next few moments for as long as she lived. As Dawn screamed, the baby was removed once again from her mother. Her life with foster parents would begin the following day.

I can't imagine how traumatic that must have been for Dawn. Like me, she hadn't been party to the prenatal assessments. She didn't have a clue why social workers were involved or why any of this was happening. She just knew it was wrong and it was unnatural. Even her body was telling her that. As she lay there sobbing through the night, Dawn felt the milk forming in her breasts – milk meant for Skye, milk that she would never be able to have.

Dawn has had to live with the memories of the actual removal but it was Hayley, appearing soon afterwards, who had to face the trauma when she discovered what had gone on.

'Ask Dr Hall,' she begged a social worker. 'She'll tell you I'm fit enough to look after my baby. Check her report!'

'That's *why* your baby was taken,' the social worker replied. 'Dr Hall made it clear you would not be able to cope.'

Hayley was shocked. She thought the pre-birth meeting had gone well. She didn't know what Dr Hall had said but hadn't thought there was any problem. Although Christine had always been efficient and kind, Hayley felt betrayed by the system that had allowed this to happen. She accepted that having commissioned a report from an expert, social services were duty-bound to follow the recommendations.

I've since seen the report. It makes me sick reading it years later. How must Hayley have felt when she saw Dr Hall's instructions to social services which effectively said: 'Remove baby at birth – arrange adoption, mother will never cope, so do not let any bonding take place.' It sounds like some evil punishment but there was more, the worst bit of all: Dr Hall had thought that if I had any contact with the baby, I might hurt her.

Hurt the baby? Hurt our baby?

How could they believe that? After everything Hayley had been through, her track record of risking her own life to protect anonymous children, she honestly felt she'd been stabbed in the back.

No wonder she faded away soon after.

It wasn't just Hayley who had cause to feel upset by the report. Dr Laine had conducted her own risk assessment of each of the alters and their separate attitudes to the forthcoming baby. She had been very moved by Hayley's transparency, especially when admitting she would be the first to ask for the baby to be taken away in the event of any risk. Professionally Dr Laine felt accused of being so biased towards her patient she would not see the danger to the unborn baby. She thought her own ethics regarding child abuse were being called into question. Dr Laine was quite certain that the alters she had met would all love and care for Aimee although extra help would be needed over some trigger areas.

Hayley, unlike Dawn, knew that Skye was healthy and alive. Tragically for her, it wasn't enough to keep her from taking a step back. Gradually as the legal fight to win our daughter back commenced, Hayley gave way more and more to the personality called Bonny.

Suddenly she was the dominant alter. She was the one in charge of finding our daughter.

Bonny's first step was to demand to see our file at the social services' offices. What better way to bring her up to speed? To say they were less than helpful is an understatement. However, by trying to hinder Bonny's progress they actually played straight into her hands. The standard procedure in this instance would have been for a social worker or other employee to have accompanied Bonny into the office while she perused the files. There was bound to be some harrowing reading matter in there. Policy was to protect the readers. But someone had left Bonny alone. That was a mistake. Not only did she not get upset – she stuffed page after page of notes into her bag and read everything marked 'private'. Everything about baby Skye was in there – foster parents, their address, how much they were being paid, plus social workers' diary sheets and reports. There would be no shortage of information when we reached court.

It's such a harrowing story, yet to a large extent I may as well have been reading it in a newspaper. I didn't feel that loss felt by Dawn and Hayley at all. I didn't meet our baby until she was four months old. By then she was called Aimee. That had been

Lorraine's choice after a solicitor had advised Bonny that if she was serious about pursuing legal action to have her daughter returned then 'Skye' might seem a little too hippyish. Bonny's attitude was 'I'll change whatever you like to get my daughter back', so she agreed. I don't know how it came about, but Bonny had actually chosen the name 'Ben' for Lorraine's son and so she thought it would be a nice gesture to return the honour to our sister. So that's where Aimee came from. Bonny chose the middle name, Melissa.

I don't know if Lorraine was aware of the irony or if Bonny had worked it out. Thirty-seven years earlier we had been named 'Kim' by a nurse. I had always sworn I would never let that choice be taken away from me. And here we were, decades later, and our daughter had gone through exactly the same thing. Was it fate? Damn bad luck? Had we wished it on her somehow? I still have no idea.

Actually, it gets even more complicated than that. Before we got her back, Aimee's foster parents went against all procedure and renamed her Daisy – and even gave her their own surname! That's the name that appears on the front of her red medical book.

So before the age of one Aimee had already been given three different names. And I thought I was the only one with identity problems!

The foster parents should have done lots of things differently. Dawn, Hayley and later Bonny were told that we could expect regular updates and photos of our daughter. That never happened.

Luckily, we had our own source.

Lorraine was allowed to have contact with Aimee in a

social services office and brought home photographs for Bonny. At least someone was on her side.

The first time any of us set eyes on her again was nearly four months later after Bonny had started legal proceedings to get Aimee back. Aimee was brought into an NSPCC contact centre where they were set up to observe children with adults. There was a TV camera in every corner, two-way mirrors and hidden microphones, everything the scrutinising psychiatrists needed to make a judgement. I don't know how anyone was meant to act naturally in that environment but Bonny was allowed to go in. We have an amazing photograph of Aimee looking up at Bonny and you could see that she knew who it was. Aimee was laughing and the pride in Bonny's face is unreal. (I wish it had been me!) This meeting became a weekly ritual until finally the court inspector was content that there was a bond and that we were not a threat. Only then were we allowed to go into a mother-and-baby unit where we could be monitored with our baby over a six-month period. If we looked like we could cope, then the courts would consider letting us be reunited.

It was such a lot of pressure. In a way I'm glad it fell on Bonny's shoulders and not mine. She'd campaigned in court long and hard with support from Lorraine, our councillor friend Anna, and Dad. Some of our neighbours were amazing as well, Jean and her now late husband Stan welcomed us round there to talk or just sit, and Dad's sister Ivy was always there for us as well. I never appreciated why, of course, so from my point of view it was just nice to see them all. But they were a great help to Bonny.

The case went from magistrate's court to county court and

all the way up to the high court where the judge was appalled that it had reached that far without being sorted out sooner. It had been a gruelling four months but finally Bonny was getting to live with Aimee – even if it was under twenty-four-hour supervision.

All the while the court case was going on, we were having no treatment from Dr Laine. Not officially, anyway. Our solicitor had pulled out for a good reason – a conflict of interests. On the one hand we had been asking him to highlight our disability to qualify for free therapy from Dr Laine. Then Aimee had come along and we had to focus on the positive to convince a court that we were of sound enough mind to look after her like any normal person.

Obviously there was a conflict and only ever going to be one winner. But even after we had to drop our therapy, Dr Laine still kept in contact by phone, encouraging and doing as much as she could.

By the time I learnt the facts of this horrendous story, some months after finally accepting the DID, Hayley had already been superseded by Bonny as the main player in our day-to-day lives. Bonny, in turn, had become the true mother to our daughter, Aimee. Looking back, it feels criminal that I didn't accept our diagnosis earlier. If I had, I wouldn't have missed out on so many important years with Aimee. At that age every day is special and unique. You never, ever get them back.

It was at the mother-and-baby unit – basically a large house like an Arbours centre – that I first met Aimee. I realise now I'd been virtually mothballed for months. The last time I'd looked

it had been August – and now we were in December. In hindsight, the other personalities had had more important claims
on the body's time – and obviously it had shielded me from a
lot of the harrowing details. But here I was, at the end of 1997,
in a room with a little girl. There was no preparation, no run-
throughs with Dr Laine. One minute I was enjoying a glass of
wine in the summer, then it was winter and I was with a little
girl people claimed was my daughter.

Even with my ignorance, the monitors at the mother-and-
baby unit were impressed by how we got on. As I understand it,
three or four personalities had the honour of holding Aimee
that day. I think the body went into self-preservation overdrive,
naturally showing Aimee off to all its potential dominant
personalities, everyone likely to have a mothering role in the
future. Luckily, we all bonded instantly, even those of us with
no real idea why we were there. In fact, we obviously gave off
such instinctively positive maternal vibes that the mother-
and-baby unit officials didn't even realise we'd been separated
for four months. They'd assumed we'd been together all this
time. In the end, instead of being made to stay the full half a
year, we were released after just two months.

And so, in January 1998, completely without my knowledge, Bonny had carried our six-month-old baby daughter
through the door of our house.

Thanks to Bonny and friends we had custody of our daughter
but, Bonny was made aware, it was only a temporary measure.
We had Aimee under a care order – essentially the same as the
ward of court that the Maudsley tried to impose on us –
whereby if we transgressed one rule, broke one promise or

invalidated one condition then Aimee would be whipped away again. At that stage, as I didn't accept she was my daughter, I was blissfully unaware of the ruling hanging over the house.

But then the social services did something life changing: they did nothing at all.

One of the tenets of the care order was that Bonny had to agree to weekly or monthly house checks from psychiatrists and social workers. Obviously she would have said yes to anything. By the time Aimee had celebrated her first birthday and Bonny still hadn't seen anyone, she began to get twitchy.

As she told Dr Laine, 'They either check up on us or leave us alone – they can't have their cake and eat it.'

And so she went back on the attack. This time she put in a complaint and sent a copy to our MP, Malcolm Wicks. He was wonderful. He helped and supported her all the way and really put social services in their place.

Basically Bonny wanted to shame the authorities into admitting that she was taking better care of Aimee than they were.

'If my daughter is so at risk, how come you haven't bothered to visit her once?'

I wish I could have seen it!

Within a few weeks Bonny had the director of the social services fawning around our house because of the MP. 'Going to the press' and 'compensation' were mentioned and eventually she settled on a compromise. The local health authority would now take over funding of her – our – therapy with Dr Laine, even though she was outside our borough. In the circumstances it was the least they could do.

But still they refused to lift the care order. In fact,

bringing it to their attention actually made matters worse. From being ignored, Bonny was informed that she would now have six-monthly assessments to check progress. She'd agreed – after a fight, of course – but hated every minute of them. On paper the assessments might have had Aimee's best interests at heart. In practice they just felt like a bi-annual exercise in humiliation.

The problem was that most care orders are for children in foster homes. So, every six months there is a 'placement meeting' to decide whether a child should stay with his or her temporary carers. This is where child services can be so cruel. Even though Bonny was Aimee's actual mother, they refused to amend their terminology. Twice a year she would turn up for the meeting, tense and nervous, and listen to herself being described as a foster parent. At the end they always concluded in the same brutal terms: 'We agree the child can stay in its current placement.'

Bonny would sit there, fuming, *It's not a placement – it's her home!*

I think the pressure of those meetings contributed to her cracking up. So when I became the dominant personality a couple of years later, I swore I would get it fixed. I didn't care how long it took, I would do it.

I will get our daughter back.

During the court case, many experts had stood up to argue on both sides. A psychiatrist on Bonny's behalf told the judge, 'I work with mothers in the community who have killed their first child – and even they are given a chance with their second.'

Bonny was furious. She wasn't looking for a second chance – she wanted her first chance.

'How do you justify removing this woman's child at birth,' the psychiatrist continued, 'just because she has DID?'

They couldn't. So many people told Dr Laine and me they couldn't see how the decision had ever been approved in the first place. Still, it didn't matter now – in the end we got the result we wanted.

Unfortunately it came too late for one person.

Dawn.

Dawn had not come out since her baby had been snatched. She had gone through the operation, held our baby for the first time, experienced the maternal rush of first contact, seen baby Skye be weighed and measured and dressed, then held her again for what she imagined would be the rest of her life.

Dawn was there when social services snatched our baby away.

Dawn was the one who screamed and screamed and cried as she realised no one was going to help.

Dawn was the one whose world fell utterly and totally apart.

At some point our defence mechanism kicked in and Dawn switched. I don't know who replaced her but I do know that a year later she still hadn't been back. And then suddenly she appeared during a session with Dr Laine.

To Dawn, it was still August 1997. And her baby, lovely, beautiful little Skye, had just been taken from her.

To this day Dawn does not know that Skye was ever returned. Every time she appears, she's as distraught as ever, constantly searching for her missing daughter. Worst of all, she refuses to recognise Aimee.

I had never seen this with my own eyes for obvious reasons until we were filmed for the *Oprah* show in September 2010. Watching it back with Aimee I couldn't believe how brave she had been. There was Dawn, sitting next to thirteen-year-old Aimee on the sofa at Dr Laine's house. They were chatting away – they've known each other all Aimee's life, after all. But when the interviewer asked who the girl next to her was, Dawn replied, 'That's not Skye.'

'Then who is it?'

'She's the daughter of a friend.'

It was too much for Aimee. She has known the truth about Dawn, she knows the pain that Dawn is going through on her fruitless quest for justice, but to be rejected so visibly was more than she could bear.

To be honest, it was more than we could bear as well. I don't think our body thought I was up to seeing it and so for the first few times we sat down to watch a recording of the interview I disappeared and Dawn took my place. As you can see on the film, she's utterly bemused why Aimee is upset. After all, Dawn's the one missing a daughter. She's the one who should be crying. Then, however, you see Dawn's maternal instinct kick in. She leans in, hugs Aimee and sobs, 'You'd have loved Skye.'

And that just makes it worse . . .

The way our brain protects each personality is very impressive. With some of the suicide attempts, I think there was occasionally a switch at crucial times. Over the years Dr Laine has received calls from various personalities saying, 'I've just found a huge pot of pills in the car. What should I do?' One of the alters, Ken, discovered himself sitting on a multi-storey car park seconds from jumping. We assume it was Rebecca who climbed up there. The body must have realised there's no stomach pump that can reverse the effects of a high jump and intervened.

Some of its interventions aren't such matters of life or death but they can save embarrassment. Ken, obviously, is a man. (He is a gay man, as well, which means he only sleeps with men – something at least our body has physical memory of.) When Ken needs a lavatory, obviously he uses a gents' – but equally obviously we look like a woman.

Again, that's when the body steps in. I've lost count of the number of times I've discovered myself standing directly outside a door marked 'Men'. Occasionally I've actually seen a urinal before I've arrived. I'm sure it happens the other way round so Ken has near misses as well.

Watching Ken on the *Oprah* show was fascinating as well. Like Dawn, like Judy, like most of the others – like me for most of my life – he refuses to accept he is one of multiple personalities in Kim Noble's body and mind. When the interviewer challenged him he said, 'I'm a man. I haven't got breasts.'

When she pointed to his clothes – my clothes – he looked down and said simply, 'I'm gay. I'm not a transvestite.' Then he turned to Aimee and they shared the most wonderful look.

It gives me genuine pleasure to see the connection she has with him because I can see she's in such safe hands when I'm not there.

Some people are surprised that Aimee knows about the DID. (Bearing in mind its connotations – she's too young to be introduced to the idea of child abuse – we've only told her about personalities. The details she'll learn when she's ready.) In fact, Aimee knew about DID before I did.

Aimee was six years old when I began to accept I had what Dr Hale and Dr Laine had been trying to help me understand for so long, and closer to seven years old before I emerged fully as the dominant personality. Up until then she'd always called me 'Patricia', as I'd asked her, just as she called the fifteen-year-old girl who used to look after her, Judy. Then there was her little friend Katie, a three-year-old, Ken, Dawn, and of course Hayley. Only Bonny was called 'Mama'.

If you ask Aimee when she found out about our condition she'll say, 'I've always known.' And she has. Until Aimee reached school age Bonny would naturally take her to Dr Laine's. There she saw from a very early age all the different personalities coming out of Mama and talking. Just being in the room and seeing Dr Laine engage with them taught her not to be afraid when the different alters popped out at home. She learnt, almost subliminally, to accept each and every one of them as a person in their own right.

Even the child personalities.

DID poses a lot of questions for everyone who hears about it. Even after finishing this book I'm sure a lot of readers will still have some burning query they wish was answered. How do you do this? What happens when ...? One of the areas that seems to be a major sticking point for many, however, involves the existence of child personalities.

Okay, logically I can just about get my head around different
adults talking through one mouth, but you're a woman of fifty – how
could you possibly sometimes be a child?

Even people who've managed to get their heads around
DID can be floored by this. They suddenly think I 'regress' or
start crawling around on all fours when of course I don't – but
that's not to say the children don't. The switch from adult to
child is as total as from me to Bonny or anyone else. They are as
real as us too, and just as rounded. They just happen to be a lot
younger.

I know the most about a little girl called Katie because she
used to come out a lot when Aimee was young. Katie is stuck at
three years old, for reasons I don't like to think about, so I suppose it was a lovely change for her to have someone near her
own age to play with for a few years. I know Aimee loved playing with Katie, and Dr Laine, who saw a lot of them together
during sessions and on home visits, said it was absolutely no
different from watching any other pair of pre-schoolers.

So does that mean Katie talks with the vocabulary of a
three-year-old? Absolutely. She's yet to learn the language of an
adult or even an older child. And does she toddle around the
room, stumbling and leaping and climbing and falling and
starting all over again? All the time.

I used to be embarrassed thinking about what it must
look like, this adult body crashing about, playing with kids'
toys, but Dr Laine stopped me. In the time she had known
us, Katie tended to mainly come out when Aimee was around.
Anyone watching Katie and Aimee together probably wouldn't
notice anything more than a mother happily messing around
with her little girl, Dr Laine insisted. 'There isn't a parent out

there who hasn't got down on hands and knees and regressed temporarily when playing with their own children,' she said. 'With Katie it's just a little more authentic performance.'

Unfortunately Katie doesn't come out as much any more, which Aimee is sad about, especially as it's sort of her fault – because of course Aimee is much older than her now. Katie doesn't question why Aimee has aged and she hasn't. All she knows is that it's no longer fun playing with a thirteen-year-old.

If I'm honest, it's a relief, as the dominant personality, to know that a three-year-old isn't as likely to take over the body these days. Looking back, though, there are the odd clues that she did used to come out even before Aimee was around. During my stay at Arbours, one of the visiting therapists had various nicknames for me but I ignored them at the time – mainly because I was offended by the 'Drunk Kim' tag (even though it might have been true). I think actually this therapist had identified the DID without even knowing it, because he also referred to 'Giggly Kim', 'Angry Kim' and 'Baby Kim'. It's pretty obvious to me now that he had previously met some of the other personalities, just as it's clear Baby Kim was very likely Katie. In fact, Dr Laine has revealed that during our time at Arbours as well as the Cassel, Katie would hide in the wardrobe during some sessions. The clues were there!

Of course, it was the knowledge that there were child personalities likely to come out that fuelled social services' argument to have Aimee removed from us. *How can a child of three possibly look after a baby?* I can appreciate how that looks on paper. All I can say in defence, however, is that the body makes it work. In the same way it won't let depressed personalities go through with their suicidal plans – or it stops me walking into the men's toilets – I don't believe it would ever allow Aimee to be at risk. Katie would never come out when baby Aimee was being bathed, for example, or when they were out of the house. Whether the personalities appreciate she is their daughter or not, the bond between the child and the body is too strong to put her in danger. I really believe that.

While she had always been aware of the different personalities in our body, Aimee really came to formally understand the disorder when Hayley made her an amazing little book called 'Amy's Mama Had DID' (Aimee's name was intentionally spelt differently to protect her). It was a kiddy's story version of our condition, in language that Aimee could understand. From what I gather, Hayley wasn't around much at the time – Bonny was the dominant one – so it's lovely to think her connection with Aimee was still so strong that she would spend so much of her precious fleeting time on it. It was worth it. Aimee says she was so chuffed with it she took it in to show off at school and read it out in assembly.

    If you ask her what it's like to live with a mum with DID, Aimee will shrug and say what she always says, 'For me it's normal.' As bizarre as it might look on the outside, this is how she has been raised. It doesn't faze her a bit. In fact, she sometimes plays us off against each other. When she was thirteen, Aimee asked me for permission to get her ear pierced. I said I'd think about it. The following weekend, I switched with Judy and they'd gone out and got it done. I was so angry with Aimee. You can't blame Judy – she's only fifteen – but Aimee knew full well what I would say.

I suppose I'm just lucky Judy didn't get it done as well – or worse!

It's for reasons like that that Dr Laine had been keen to encourage me to develop to my fullest potential. Perhaps I would one day assume the mantle of dominant personality. Judy was too young – you wouldn't ideally have a fifteen-year-old raising a family, especially one as potentially erratic as ours. Many of the others had their own problems – for example weight, self-esteem or issues with their sexuality. By comparison, I'd like to think I had fewer hurdles to overcome. When eventually I was ready to reach my potential, however, it was nearly too late.

Bonny's descent from dominant personality to occasional visitor was gradual and sad. Like Hayley, who had withered under the pressure of fighting the court case, it was the long and arduous campaign to keep Aimee that got the better of Bonny. Even though she'd won, the effort meant she was soon showing signs of cracking up. Dr Laine spotted the tell-tale signals in her conversation. At home, however, it was when she began hoarding old newspaper that Aimee noticed. If Aimee had a new toy, Bonny would throw away the toy and keep the packaging. She became obsessed. Then one day Aimee went up to her room and on her pillow were several little wrapped presents. It wasn't her birthday, so what were they?

She pulled the ribbon, tore the wrapping and ripped open the boxes.

They were full of shredded newspaper.

I didn't know this but maybe the body was aware. Perhaps that was the moment it decided I was ready to accept the truth. Anyway, that's the time I admitted to Dr Laine that she was right.

Accepting the diagnosis of DID had its baggage, of course, and I had to deal with that. In due course I would have to take on the running of the house, and all the practical responsibilities that went with it. More importantly, though, it also meant I was a mother. I had a beautiful six-year-old girl whom I loved and who loved me.

My initial feeling, though, was one of abject panic. I hadn't been there to teach Aimee anything, I hadn't weaned her, potty-trained her or any of the other parental landmarks. Whenever I'd been out with Aimee I only remember playing. That was about all I could manage.

I remember saying to Dr Laine, 'I can't do it. I don't have a clue what to do!'

'You'll be fine,' she assured me. 'You've already done such a wonderful job without even knowing it.'

Had I? How had I? It's one thing looking after a child you think is a friend's daughter – it's another taking full-time responsibility for another human being. Especially when I was just coming to terms with the fact that I hadn't even been looking after myself for the majority of my forty-odd years on the planet.

'Trust me,' Dr Laine said. 'I would have no compunction in saying so if I thought Aimee was suffering in any way. You already have an amazing relationship with her. You're going to be an inspirational mother, I promise.'

It was a rousing speech, enough to fire anyone up. I left Dr Laine determined to make it work.

I'm going to be the best mother that little girl could wish for, I promised.

Unfortunately, that little girl already had a mother. Bonny

was the one she called 'Mum'. I knew it would take time for her to accept me – it had taken me years to accept her – but I hated seeing her upset. Every day she'd look at me and ask the same question:

'Is Bonny there? I'd like to see Bonny.'

She wasn't trying to hurt me – although obviously it was like a knife in the heart each time. She was just being a little girl who missed her mum.

CHAPTER TWENTY

Where did they all come from?

Patricia knelt down on the rug next to Aimee. Light was fading from the window. It would soon be time to turn on the lights and stop for dinner.

'How's the essay going, Aimes?'

The young girl glared up at her mum. 'It's impossible,' she replied angrily. 'Please will you do it for me?'

'I've told you, I'll help you, I'll look things up, I'll sit with you while you do it – but I'm not writing your assignment for you.'

That wasn't the answer Aimee was looking for.

'But my hand hurts.'

Patricia was tempted. She hated seeing her daughter so upset but, as usual, Aimee had left it to the last minute. Like any mum, Patricia would do anything to help – but she drew the line at actually writing the thing for her.

Unfortunately, Aimee didn't see it that way.

'It's not fair,' she cried. 'Bonny would help me.' Yes, Aimee thought, that's who I need!

'Mum, I want to see Bonny!'

After a lifetime of being tossed around like a cork on the ocean, it was unfamiliar to find myself in charge. I had a house to look after, a daughter to care for and a disorder to manage. And, for the first time in my life, I was coping.

Those early days with Aimee were perturbing to say the least. We were both finding our way from a relationship built on friendship to one that needed to go further. I was happy to – desperate to, really – but it was harder for Aimee. Bonny was the one she called 'Mum'. Even though Aimee knew about the DID, relationship-wise I was just a mate who looked after her occasionally. Just because I'd changed, why should she be expected to?

The assumption I'd made for all those years that I was around all the time was quickly exploded when we realised I knew so little about her life. I remember Dr Laine telling me, 'You need to take control. Aimee needs to go to school,' and I thought, *How am I going to do that? I don't even know where her school is!*

Luckily, Aimee knew, so on our first morning together we walked there. I recognised one or two of the other parents, not many more. They all seemed to know me. I got loads of comments like, 'Oh, you have got legs then?'

I looked at Aimee.

'Mum always drives.'

Oh, I thought. 'But it's only round the corner.'

'That's why they're laughing at you!'

There was so much I had to learn and to be honest I found it more than a little daunting. I guess a comparison would be a young single man being told by his girlfriend that she's accidentally pregnant. The guy's going to have mixed emotions, isn't he? Happy – hopefully – but also wistful at all the opportunities now closed to him. I admit an early concern was 'How am I going to go out for a drink if I've got a child?'

Then I remembered I'd had a child for years and somehow the body had made it work. Most likely I was only brought out when Bonny or one of the others found themselves in a social situation anyway. The only difference now was that I was the one with the responsibility.

Getting into the swing of things was a bit bumpy. If someone had handed me a baby at the time, I would have just about been able to hold it until it started crying and then, like most people I imagine, I'd be desperate to hand it back. It's not so dissimilar discovering yourself with an older child. She's great to hang out with, but what do six-year-olds play with? What do they talk about? What does she do at school? Which stores does she go to? The list was endless: mealtimes, bedtimes, homework, shopping, school holidays, friends, discipline, television, pocket money, even how to brush Aimee's hair – you name it, and I didn't know anything about it.

Things inside the house I just about got a grip on. When we stepped outside I felt really exposed, as if the whole world was watching, pointing its fingers and saying, 'You're not her mother.'

Just the thought of talking to one of Aimee's teachers sent me into a cold sweat. When I first had to go up for an open evening I felt like I was the one back at school. I'd never felt so intimidated. A lot of parents might think that, but I felt fraud-ulent, like they saw me as some Johnny-come-lately.

But I'd been in worse positions. I needed to remember that. Most of my life I'd found myself washed up in scenarios that seemed alien, and bit by bit I'd worked out what went where – and usually I'd had only a couple of seconds to do it. By comparison, I thought, getting to grips with a few logistics should be a doddle. *Should.*

Between sheer panic, overwhelming fear and simple frustration, I also experienced moments of happiness being with Aimee, the scale of which I'd never known. Everything was going to be all right, I knew it.

'I can't promise it's going to be a smooth ride, Aimes,' I told her, 'but I promise you we're going to make this work.'

If Bonny can do it, so can I . . .

I didn't know Bonny, obviously, but we had communicated. At Dr Laine's instigation, Bonny had opened a new Word document on our home computer and written a little welcome message and introduction about herself. When she'd finished she'd left the page open on the screen. The next time she'd returned to the machine there was a message from Judy. Then one from Ken. There was even one from me! That was before I acknowledged the DID. It's daft now but I convinced myself we were meeting on an internet chatroom – that's probably the logic the others still use. Obviously if I'd probed deeper I'd have discovered it was just a Word file – which could only have been added to by someone in my house! That realisation would have opened up a whole new can of worms which, I suppose, is why my mind never allowed me to make the leap.

Over the course of a few months we had regular chats. It's really helpful for me now, as the dominant personality, to be able to keep tabs on what the others might be doing with our body. These days I can leave notes around the house which sometimes get answered or sometimes get completely ignored – or sometimes even come back with rude messages (usually from Judy).

Many of them are also on email so we can communicate via that. This really foxed Oprah. Still not appreciating how unconnected we all are, she asked if I just left the messages addressed to someone else. When I told her we all have separate email accounts, separate passwords, I thought she was going to fall off her chair.

Even though I was told how Bonny and I were so similar, Aimee could tell the difference without a moment's hesitation. She can't say how she knows, she just does. Even when she was young, she could always tell the personalities apart, even if she didn't always know their names. *That's the one who shouts about God, that's the little boy who speaks Latin, that's the girl who can't speak at all . . .*

The logistics of my new grown-up life were complicated but doable with a bit of application. It's amazing how much you can pack in when you're around for the majority of the day. You don't always have to be in such a rush all the time. The most arduous change, in fact, was coming to terms with Aimee's love for Bonny. It felt stupid being jealous of someone who looked and sounded so much like me but I suppose it's the human response. I was in charge now. I was the one looking after Aimee, not Bonny.

I just want her to love me like she loves Bonny.

In time Aimee and I worked through our awkwardness. She went from calling me 'Patricia' and Bonny 'Mama' to calling her 'Mama Bon' and eventually me 'Mama'. I think school helped. It was easier for her to call me that when she was there and it just sounded right. You can't imagine a happier day for me than when that happened the first time.

Gradually we eased into our routine and I noticed the fears and the panic had gone. Now I was just left with true regret that I hadn't been around for the first six years of her life. I was like a man whose partner had kept news of their baby a secret. On the bright side, at least I had the future to look forward to. Bonny may have had the early years but she was missing out now. And poor Dawn had been missing out ever since Aimee was born.

Speaking of missing out, I remember watching Aimee playing in the garden – back when I didn't accept the DID – and she was singing at the top of her voice, 'I love my daddy so much'. Even as a family friend witnessing it, it was terribly upsetting. She was using a little doll as a microphone and really putting her heart into it. I thought, *It's awful that girl doesn't have a father.*

I remembered that years later. As soon as I appreciated that Aimee was my daughter, I knew instantly who the father was. It was my on-off boyfriend whom I'd met during my driving job. Baby Aimee was the spitting image of him – I don't know why I didn't make the link at the time.

Dawn, Hayley or Bonny or one of the others might have different views but I feel in my heart that I'm right. I may not have been there to give birth to Aimee but I did conceive her. That means the world. No one can take that away from me.

When I discovered the truth, I contacted the father. We had long ago drifted apart and the last thing I wanted was him in my life again. However, for Aimee's sake – and for his rights – it was the correct thing to do. He was shocked, obviously, that I'd shown up out of the blue, and nearly fainted at the news.

But he said he would marry me and we could make a fresh start. I said I didn't see a future for us and he said he would back off, just as I'd hoped.

But saying goodbye to me was one thing; he never even said, 'Can I see her?' If there was even a slight chance of our rekindling our relationship, his indifference to his child had killed it stone dead.

I've offered Aimee the opportunity to see him over the years and she's always said no. Lorraine is willing to take her over whenever she wants. If she changes her mind I'll be sad but I'll understand.

But I've never heard her sing about her daddy since.

Getting to know my daughter was a lovely, sometimes stressful but always rewarding process. Mainly, though, it was slow. I had been so used to dashing from one mystery location to another that I really struggled to adjust. Once I appreciated that I was around a lot longer these days, I could begin to calm and, gradually, everything slotted into place.

With my relationship with Aimee as secure as I could wish for, I finally turned my attention to getting to know other people in my life: the alter egos who share Kim Noble's body.

One of the personalities, of course, I knew very well.

It was me.

Coming to terms with the fact that I myself was an alter of Kim Noble was hard. What could be more unnatural? We all want to believe we come from the same place, we live the same lives, we are normal – otherwise we are just characters in *The Matrix*.

What was I meant to think? Were they saying I'm a figment of someone's imagination?

That I didn't exist?

No wonder my mind had protected me from the truth for
so long. It's almost too much for anyone to cope with. For me,
in a way it's been harder than discovering about the body's
abuse. Selfish as it sounds, that happened to someone else. This
was about me.

But I didn't have a choice. If I were to become the dominant
personality I needed to fully embrace the facts of my origins –
mainly that Kim's history and my history are not exactly the same.

According to the research I most likely wasn't 'born' until
Kim was one or two. Of all the things I've had to get my head
around, that has been one of the most taxing.

On the plus side, it does make me a few years younger!

Thinking about the process of facilitating my development – until I actually became the dominant personality – I
thought of Dr Laine's role. If I was worried about being a character in a sci-fi film, for her it must seem like *Groundhog Day*. All
the confusion, all the denial and all the resistance I was showing wasn't new to her. Dr Laine had seen exactly the same
responses from Bonny years earlier, and from Hayley before
that. I was just the next in line for the same treatment.

Even realising that hurt. *It's a bloody conveyor belt! I'm on a
production line!*

Therapy is meant to make you feel good about yourself but
realising your individuality is at stake is a bit of a body blow. Dr
Laine though, just like our friends, had one priority in mind.

The protection of Aimee.

What more incentive do you need?

Thinking about it from Dr Laine's point of view, I had appeared the most like Bonny and Hayley so I seemed the most capable of taking on the responsibility. Could Dawn do it? Could a woman so traumatised by the loss of her baby that she doesn't even recognise her today as the young teen she is? Could Judy do it? She's a teenager herself with low self-esteem and a craving for practical jokes. Could it be Sonia? Another youngster – she's fourteen – and a sufferer of body dysmorphia? Or could it be Ken, a gay man still struggling to come to terms with society's treatment of his kind? Julie, so convinced she receives signals from televisions and registration plates and sprays bus users with fly spray? Rebecca? Three-year-old Katie?

As I gradually learnt, however, there were many, many more candidates. All of them are instinctively kind and protective towards Aimee – Dr Laine never had any concerns there – but could they do the school run? Pay a gas bill? I suppose it was an honour to have been selected by the body but when I began to hear more about the others my pride was tempered. Yes – some of the other personalities seemed naturally fun, maternal and rounded. Others, I have to say, from what I know about them are like creations from a novel or a film. I just think, *Where on Earth did they come from? Someone must have invented them.*

When we go to see Dr Laine, it's for normal therapy. We don't go to discuss DID. So, before I was a believer, if you like, I went to discuss the issues affecting me: blackouts, people accusing me of things, why I had been locked up in institutions for half my life. These were the issues that needed resolving in my brain. Dr Laine took us on as separate patients, as individuals. There was a certain amount of trying to nudge us towards acceptance of DID. But that wasn't her primary goal in every session. We were sufferers, we were all victims of something, and she was there to help.

Having said that, part of her wider remit was to the body of Kim Noble – and to that body's daughter. She knew that the priority had to be to maintain as close to a 'normal' life as possible in order to avoid the attention – and intervention – of the authorities.

That meant taking on the more extreme personalities and finding ways to help them as well as serving the greater good – protecting Aimee.

I don't know Susan's history. I don't know how old she is, what she's been through or what she hopes to achieve from life. But I do know she has a problem. Whenever she came out, she would hit herself. She was like a member of Opus Dei from *The Da Vinci Code* – punishing herself for some unknown indiscretion. She can't sit for a minute without slapping herself on the head.

As far as the body was concerned, there was a risk of bruising or other injuries. I probably wouldn't notice unless my head hurt – mirrors and DID aren't natural bedfellows – although I would probably have blamed it on a drunken stumble. Worse than anything that could happen to us, however, was the effect on Aimee. There was never a concern that Susan might hit our daughter. Dr Laine would have acted had that been the case. The threats were more psychological: imagine if you saw your mother smacking herself. What would you do?

So, with Aimee present, Dr Laine spoke to Susan and as soon as she appeared smashing at her head, grabbed her hands.

It wasn't violent or restrictive, she just took her hands like someone listening intently might. She felt twitches but Susan didn't fight it. She obviously doesn't want to be hitting herself. It must be some kind of reflex, some form of obsessive compulsive disorder.

That was all the coaching Aimee required. The next time Susan appeared she took her hands and the situation calmed. After that they chatted normally – not about mother-and-daughter things because obviously Susan doesn't know who Aimee is. I've actually been around when Aimee has asked to see Susan. She wouldn't do that if she was scared of her. That comforts me as I feel myself being replaced.

Susan doesn't come out much any more, but I know Aimee misses her. She misses all of the alters who are around a lot and disappear. Hayley and Bonny are the main ones, but there are plenty of others.

Another extreme personality is Salome. She's a Catholic and believes with all her heart that she was put on God's Earth to do His work. She comes out ranting and raving, cursing 'that wicked woman' and bemoaning the unjust fate of 'a good woman – a good woman who died'. Aimee just sits there speechless when she appears because there's not much you can say in the face of religious zealots like that. I know Salome always smiles at Aimee between speeches so I don't worry and at least her appearances are short and sweet – well, short. No one would describe them as sweet, especially Hayley, who seems to be on the receiving end of them.

After years of playing detective Dr Laine has pieced together the story. When our mother was in hospital after her final stroke she suffered a loss of blood and became anaemic. They plugged her into a new supply but it was the wrong blood type and her body rejected it in the most extreme way it could: it died.

Emergency procedures went into overdrive and doctors managed to get her back but she was in a lot of pain as they transferred her to a ward. The consultant realised the end was near and prescribed morphine, the biggest painkiller hospitals have.

Hayley was at Mum's bedside throughout – which is why I missed all of it – watching her scream and writhe in agony. All she could do was watch the clock and wait for the next dose of drugs to come.

When a junior doctor came along he fiddled around with his medication trolley so much that Hayley became nervous.

'She needs her morphine.'

The doctor looked shocked. 'I think Ibuprofen will do it, thank you.'

Hayley flew at him. 'Morphine!' she screamed. 'She needs morphine!'

At that moment there was a switch and Salome came out. She saw her mother lying in bed, ailing. And then she heard the doctor's words: 'I'm not giving her morphine, that would kill her!'

That was enough for Salome. As far as she was concerned, when Mum died on Boxing Day a short while later, it was this other woman's fault. Hayley had poisoned her with morphine. Hayley had killed Salome's mother, a 'good woman'.

Lorraine corroborated everything. She had been at the bedside at the time, too upset to pick up on the different personalities coming into play before her.

After years of hearing about her, I was glad to hear that

Salome was filmed for our *Oprah* show. That was a revelation. It was just as Aimee and Dr Laine had described. A whirlwind of harmless anxiety and then, before you knew it, she'd stormed out the door and switched again.

Switches can be random or they can be defensive – for example, when Ken tries to take the body into the men's toilet – or they can be triggered by other visual stimuli. Salome will always come out in the presence of a church. She can smell them. We visited one on holiday once. No sooner had we stepped through the door than Salome came out. Aimee said it was lovely. There was no shouting, no accusations, just pure, quiet, respectful worship.

Speaking of triggers and, I suppose, of the body protecting us, there is another personality who only comes out in the presence of water. It's only since I began to understand DID that I realised something quite staggering: I've never had a bath.

I am fifty and I have never had a bath!

I've never had a shower, been swimming or dipped my toe in the sea. I've run a bath – I've run hundreds of them – but when I think about it, I've never actually stepped in. I know about bathing and washing and swimming and hygiene and I know I've always intended to bathe and, more importantly, I know I'm always clean! So it's amazing that I've never experienced it and, what's more, the body had managed to block my mind for so long from ever questioning it. But it did. All aqua time belongs to someone who calls herself the Spirit of the Water!

A few years ago, when I was just emerging as the dominant personality, Dr Laine saw how seriously I was taking my responsibilities. I felt very uncomfortable letting Aimee out of my sight. As a consequence, we didn't stray too far from home. By that time, after so many years, Dr Laine was like a therapy grandma as much as my therapist. She said, 'When the other children at school say what they did in the holidays, what does Aimee say?'

Not much, I realised. We never went anywhere.

So Dr Laine decided we would have a break. Initially she was upset on our behalf that while some places would take Aimee for a break or some would take me, nowhere wanted to help us together. She was also worried that in protecting Aimee from being outside in a strange place with 'me' not there, I might just spend the holiday in a hotel room. Ever inventive and supportive, Dr Laine booked a weekend on the south coast for not only me and Aimee, but also herself and her husband.

I don't know what Dr Laine was expecting but I'm sure it wasn't to be running around like old mother hen. The second I saw the sea there was a switch. Out came Spirit of the Water and she just made a beeline for the shore. Shoes off, socks off – thank God she stopped there. As soon as she found her swimming costume, that was it, there was no keeping her out.

The problem was, of course, from Dr Laine's point of view: not all of the personalities can swim. What if one of the children appeared?

I don't think that would happen. The body wouldn't let itself drown. Spirit of the Water wouldn't let that happen. What we couldn't guarantee, however, was that Spirit of the Water would look after Aimee, so poor Dr Laine spent the weekend watching us like a hawk. Afterwards she said she was the one who needed a holiday!

There's always a swimming pool or ocean at the heart of

any break so I can predict that Spirit will put in a few appearances then. I joined a gym recently and while I go along to use the running machine, Spirit likes to take Aimee swimming. One sniff of chlorine and she's off with Aimee in tow.

I don't know how old Spirit is but as soon as she's near water she's like a child. I can always tell when she's had a bath with Aimee because of the mess on the floor. Aimes says she always jumps in, starts splashing and sings, 'I'm Spirit – Spirit of the Water'.

Occasionally it's more than the bathroom that gets a soaking. Dr Laine's surgery is in north London so I decided once to drive there via Regent's Park. By the time I reached Dr Laine's I was dripping wet.

'What on Earth happened to you?'

I switched back at that second, as nonplussed as her. A few minutes later, however, Spirit of the Water came forward. She'd seen the fountain in the park, pulled the car over onto the verge, then dived in. I'm sure she must have had a blast but the thought of all those people seeing my body doing that makes me cringe. I won't be going back there for a while!

I don't know if we'll ever get to the root of Spirit of the Water's story, but she seems playful and cavalier. By contrast, many of the child personalities are anything but carefree, despite their age. It makes me so sad to think of them and their tragic, tormented lives. The worst thing is knowing they will be looking for their Mummy and Daddy. Imagine enduring what they've gone through and not being able to have your parents wrap a comforting arm round your shoulders. I wish there was something we could do for them. I suppose the less they come out the better.

Mum dying is a problem for lots of them, not just Salome. Judy is stuck at fifteen – which the body would have been back in 1976 when Mum was alive and well. So even now, decades later, she's always looking for her mother. She knows she can't have gone far. It's just a case of being patient.

She'll come home soon.

This explains why she's always so rude about me. Judy thinks I'm a terrible mother because as far as she's concerned I'm always abandoning Aimee with her. When you realise Judy would give everything to see her mother again you can see how this must twist the knife.

Another child in pain stands out. For a start, his name is Diabalus – we can make our own assumptions from even that. I remember asking Dr Laine what she knew about him.

'I know he can't speak English.'

'Really? How does he communicate then?'

'Through letters – written in Latin!'

I hadn't seen that coming.

'But I don't know any Latin. I've never had a single lesson.'

'Well, Diabalus has learnt it from somewhere.'

Dr Laine doesn't speak more than basic Latin either but she does have some French and fortunately the young boy spoke that. She seemed rather relieved by that. I, on the other hand, was paralysed with wonder.

How can he learn two other languages without my knowing a single word?

Is it really possible the body attended Latin and French classes without my knowing anything about it?

Stranger things have happened.

*

Coming to terms with the personalities was awkward but fairly straightforward. Empathising with them was a different proposition. It was like being told stories about people I didn't know. Or reading about strangers in the paper. Some of them sounded interesting, some of them seemed like people I'd like to meet. Others less so. Either way, it was all theoretical, conversational and, as hard as I tried to get involved, very little to do with me. I just wasn't connecting as much as I, or Dr Laine, hoped. And then, quite by accident, I discovered a new way to meet them all.

Painting.

CHAPTER TWENTY-ONE

I am not Kim Noble

Perfect, *Bonny thought as she finished wrapping the large box. I can't wait to see her face when she gets this.*

Mothers like nothing more than spoiling their children but on birthdays you can really push the boat out. Aimee had been asking for a pink typewriter for ages and Bonny had always said, 'No, we can't afford it.' Aimee knew they weren't the richest of families but, even so. A lot of her school friends had one. Why did she have to be the odd one out?

Of course, what Aimee didn't know is that Bonny had rushed out immediately and bought it for her daughter's sixth birthday. Just a few days now until the big surprise.

In the end, though, it was Bonny who was surprised.

A metallic clattering noise the following Saturday had been bothering Bonny for the entire time it had taken to prepare dinner. In the end she couldn't bear it any longer.

What on Earth is going on up there? *she wondered, marching up the stairs.*

As she reached Aimee's room the noise grew louder. It sounded like tiny little hammers punching away: thud, thud, thud.

No idea, *Bonny thought, and opened the door.*

Her mouth fell open as she stared at Aimee typing with one-fingered gusto on a shiny pink typewriter.

Bonny couldn't hide her anger. 'Who said you could open that?'

The wind knocked out of her sails, the little girl could barely spit out an answer.

'I-I-I . . . '

'Yes?' Bonny asked sternly. 'I can wait all night.'

'I was out with Ken this afternoon,' Aimee managed, 'and he bought it for me.' She was close to tears. 'Is something wrong?'

Bonny didn't know whether to laugh or cry.

'No, darling, there's nothing wrong. Nothing at all.'

B ecoming the dominant personality was a daunting prospect. Of course, I wanted to spend as much time 'out' as possible but with that came the responsibilities of keeping the body's day-to-day life on track, which in turn would prove we were capable of looking after our daughter. Looking after Aimee was the first thing I thought of when I woke up and usually the last thing at night – assuming I was the one who took the body to bed! Most of the time they were routine upkeep thoughts: must buy this, must do that, must take her there. Every so often, though, the dark cloud hanging over our happiness as a family would return and I would remember:

Aimee only lives here on a 'placement'.

Just writing it now makes my blood boil. Back then, knowing each six-monthly check-up was due made me feel even worse.

It's not in my nature to make a fuss, to bang a drum or feel comfortable being the centre of attention. But if that were the difference between being treated as a foster parent to my own daughter and winning her back, then I would have to bite the bullet. After some research on the internet I made a call to a solicitor and by the end of the day wheels were put in motion. You'd think that would have made me feel better but, try as hard as I could to relax, I felt worse than ever. Again and again the same idea kept floating into my waking thoughts:

What if I lose? What if I've just made it worse?

In the early days Dr Laine was concerned that the pressure of dealing with everything on top of realising I had a daughter to care for might be too much. The last thing she wanted was my retreating – like Kim, Hayley and Bonny – and chaos to descend again, so she scrabbled around for as much support as possible. When the official channels ran dry she looked closer to home.

Debbie McCoy was a trainee art therapist doing a placement at Springfield Hospital. Dr Laine suggested she might like to spend some time with us as a support worker. Debbie would find it useful for her studies and we would benefit from having a friendly ear. I welcomed any help so I agreed – although if I'd known she was an art therapist I might not have been so keen. My experiences at San Martino's and Arbours hadn't exactly lit my fuse.

Debbie started coming over a few days a week and we'd just have tea and chat or watch television. It was nice to have a break from worrying about Aimee on my own. I could relax knowing that if there was a switch and one of the kiddie personalities came out, there was still an adult in the house. These days I'm confident that all the alters have Aimee's best interests at heart but I didn't know that then.

We were sitting in the front room one night and Debbie asked Aimee if she liked painting.

'I'm not very good at it.'

'Of course you are,' Debbie said. 'Everyone can paint.'

I think I must have snorted at that because Debbie looked at me. 'Yes, Patricia, even you can paint.'

You didn't see my efforts at Arbours!

Debbie disappeared upstairs and came down with an old roll of wallpaper we'd finished with and a pot of Aimee's poster paints.

'Come on then, let's see what you can do.'

It was all a bit of fun, splashing colours and shapes on the back of the wallpaper, and Debbie never let on that she was studying art therapy. I didn't really get any pleasure out of my results but it was just nice to be doing something while we chatted away about the usual old nonsense. Best of all was noticing how happy Aimee was for us to be doing something together. There's no replacement for that bond.

I don't think Aimee or I looked likely to win any prizes but we kept it up for a few weeks or so because without the pressure of therapy I realised it really was a bit of fun. There are worse ways to spend an evening than doodling away with a glass of wine in your hand, and maybe the telly on in the background for Aimee while we giggled and gossiped. The only downside was the clearing up every day. At the end of the session we'd wash the brushes and pots up and leave our latest masterpieces on the table to dry.

Coming down the next morning and seeing our work in the cold light of day was always a bit disappointing. I pinned a few of Aimee's up on the wall but mine went straight in the bin. No one needed to see those again.

One day, though, I trotted down ready to chuck mine as

usual and I stopped. There were more pictures than I remembered – and some of them were very good. Distinctive lines, striking colours and very vivid, detailed scenes.

I don't remember Debbie leaving these.

I checked my watch. Had there been a switch? Was it actually evening, not morning? Had Debbie brought these paintings to show us?

No, it's eight o'clock. The sound of Aimee thundering around upstairs as she got ready for school confirmed it.

So when had Debbie brought these? I picked one up and studied the small figures in it.

And why would she bring such disturbing images into my house?

Realising that the other personalities had started to paint was a complete shock. Aimee and I had only picked up the brushes for something sociable to do. Neither of us at that stage showed any aptitude for it – although I was beginning to enjoy the soothing act of actually painting. And yet here were a couple of pictures that were actually very good.

First a personality who can speak Latin and French. Now one who can paint!

Every day with DID there are new and wonderful surprises.

The only problem was the content. I really wanted to show Aimee what had happened but the last thing I wanted her to see was this. I couldn't be sure but it looked to me like a picture of a child being bullied by a tall man. I rolled the picture up and thought, *I'll see what Debbie thinks.*

Over the next few nights several more paintings appeared. There were a few more unpleasant scenes, which I kept from Aimee, but also some nice ones too.

'It looks like there's more than one of them doing it,' Debbie suggested. 'Maybe you should show them to Dr Laine?'

Of course! I rolled them up ready to present them at our next session. Now it was Dr Laine's turn to play detective.

The next morning I made a point of coming down early enough to intercept any paintings I didn't want Aimee to see. I opened the dining room door and couldn't help gasping.

What the hell's happened here?

There was paint all over the table, and on the chairs and on the floor. Everything was speckled in red and black and white. *And, my God, look at the walls!*

Where's that bloody dog? It had to be him. Somehow he'd got the paints open and had a field day chewing them.

'Arthur!'

Then I took a closer look at the table. There, on a strip of wallpaper as usual, was an incredible sort of Jackson Pollock dot print drying. Arthur was a clever dog – but not even he was up to this.

I examined the picture. It was entirely abstract but it wasn't random. Someone had put a lot of thought into it.

Two personalities who can paint, I thought. *Maybe I should get practising. I don't want to be left behind.*

Over the next couple of nights, and days when Aimee was at school, more pictures appeared. Some were disturbing and obviously painted by the first personality. Others were red, white and black abstracts, so I knew where they'd come from. Then another style appeared. These were people, quite intricately shaped, so much so in fact they seemed almost skeletal. This time there was a note next to the work. It was by Bonny.

Incredible, I thought. *Three different people and three starkly individual styles.*

Knowing that Bonny had recently told Dr Laine that her brain was 'scrambled', it was comforting to see she had discovered an outlet. I didn't know what she was trying to say with her figures but I was sure there was a message. That, as I recalled, was the point of art therapy: to express your feelings, memories and fears without words. (Later, Bonny painted one piece which I had no trouble interpreting: 'I'm Only Another Personality'. It tells you how she was feeling when she accepted DID and perhaps began to fade.)

The impetus behind the Pollocks was just as cloudy as Bonny's inspiration. Unfortunately, there was only one possible interpretation of the other paintings – and it was one I didn't want to hear.

Dr Laine was like a Sherlock Holmes of the art world. By a process of showing the paintings to whoever came out at her sessions, she gradually established who was doing what. More importantly, through dialogues about the paintings and their content, she was able to delve further than ever before into a lot of the alters' pasts. Even though many of the artists had been around for a while, and were no strangers to the therapy sessions, Dr Laine was still amazed by the level of new insights the work led her towards. It's one thing hearing someone's stories, experiences and fears, yet quite another to see the result of their imagination exposed on three-by-two-feet canvases. I think even Dr Laine, although no art expert, was surprised at the new revelations. And I, of course, lapped up every fresh morsel of information. It really was a wonderfully exciting time.

Bonny we knew, of course. The abstracts, however, were created by a personality I hadn't heard of before. The problem was, even after a session we were none the wiser. Missy – or 'MJ' as she sometimes refers to herself – is an elective mute. I think she's a younger personality, possibly in her low teens, and she's physically capable of speech but for some reason – whether mischief, illness or fear – she chooses not to use it. Years later I'm still at a loss to explain the thoughts behind her work. What I do know is that since she doesn't want to talk about her inspiration, it's unlikely to be good.

Hearing from Dr Laine what Missy had probably been through, I decided to forgive her the regular mess in our dining room. *But,* I thought, *it can't go on like this. I need to make a plan.*

The artist behind the disturbing images obviously had a message to convey. Dr Laine tracked her down as a twelve-year-old girl who was clearly still traumatised by the things that she had either seen or experienced herself. The paintings – of adults and children engaged in sexually explicit behaviour – told us a lot. Her responses to basic questions told us a lot more:

'What's your name?' Dr Laine had asked.

'Pratt.'

'Pratt?'

'Yes.' She nodded and looked around, terrified.

'Who are the people in the paintings?'

'These things happen.'

'Are you in the paintings?'

'Bad things happen. These things happen. Children should be protected.'

It was heartbreaking stuff to be told. I can't imagine how harrowing it must be to have experienced it. Even the poor girl's name – 'Pratt' – told its story. I can picture a scenario where a normal little girl got so used to being ordered about by some abusive nickname – 'Come here, Pratt', 'Do this, Pratt' – that she grew to believe that was what she was called.

'I can't call her that,' I told Dr Laine, who agreed. In the end we decided on 'Ria'. I don't know where it came from but hopefully it gives her some dignity.

Hearing stories about what had happened to my body was one thing – as I've said, it's comparable to reading about something hideous like the Bulger case or Madeleine McCann's abduction. Your heart bleeds but you don't have that first-person experience. It might have been my body that had been abused but with no personal recollection of that I was always going to be on the outside looking in. That remained the case, obviously, but there's no denying Ria's paintings brought me closer to the epicentre. As the saying goes, every picture paints a thousand words. I defy anyone to look at her work and not bleed inside at the idea of those acts happening to a child. You can't not be moved by them, and of course I was.

But then I had the extra pressure of wondering: *Is the child in those pictures me?*

Ria wasn't telling, however. She didn't come out very often except to paint. Whenever Dr Laine did come across her she would always be told the same things: 'Bad things happen, children get hurt, people are bad.'

I honestly thought that would be as much as we would ever know about Ria. Then the *Oprah* cameras came to town and she was one of the people the producers selected to interview. I don't know if it was the fact it was a different person asking or whether she'd just had enough of biting her tongue, but Ria told us more in that short piece of film than we'd learnt in ten years. It was on camera, for example, that she revealed she was twelve years old – finally we had an age.

And it was on camera that she was asked if she'd ever been abused and she pointed to her painting, put her finger to her lips and said, 'Shh.'

What a breakthrough! It's amazing when the other personalities can shock you.

I wasn't the only one shocked by this bombshell. The body went into protection overdrive and it took me five or six attempts to watch that segment of *Oprah*. The first time I was sitting there with Aimee and the moment Ria came onto the screen, Ria entered the room as well. The same thing happened the second and third times. Eventually I managed to sit through it without switching but I can see why the body wanted to protect us. It just brought our hideous past that one step closer.

While the body has a responsibility towards all of us, as the dominant personality I realised I had responsibilities too. Aimee was my number one priority, obviously. After that, however, I had a duty of care towards the other personalities. Painting had done wonders for Ria, Missy and I think Bonny, so rather than curtail it I needed to take it further. After a few months, I decided to make a bespoke art room. If that's how the personalities wanted to communicate then I would give them the best facilities possible.

And it would also save Missy destroying the dining room with her mess!

I knew it was a good thing for the body when I realised we'd all chipped in. I remember going out to buy an easel in the January sales, but I think it was Bonny who bought the canvases and proper paints. Then it was a group effort after that to prepare the little box room upstairs. We took out everything that didn't need to be there and turned the place into as close to a proper studio as we could. Not only did we have room to paint and to pose and reflect on our work and relax, there was also room to mess around and hang some work. Gone were the days of not being able to eat breakfast because the table was covered in drying masterpieces.

Debbie was impressed. From suggesting a spot of daubing as a way to pass the time as a family, she'd begun to photograph every painting and write notes on how they made her feel. 'You'll be exhibiting in no time,' she said.

I looked at my early attempts at a landscape and couldn't help snigger. 'Not outside this house I won't.'

She was right though. From setting up the art room in January to our first public showing took about two months. I still don't know how we had the nerve to even think about it. I'd like to blame one of the others but I was the one who made the calls looking for exhibition space.

With Debs winding down her visits as her training drew to a close, a family worker called Shirley had been appointed by social services to spend a bit of time with us. I remember seeing an article in the *Croydon Advertiser* about a new vegetarian restaurant, Pepperton's, so I went along with Shirley to try to pitch our show. Even as we stepped in the front door I thought, *What on Earth am I doing here? You've only painted a few pictures of grass and trees.*

But it was the alters I was there for. They had done the work that deserved to be shown.

I'd decided that as no one ever signed their paintings we'd go under the banner 'Kim Noble'. That was the obvious choice. I devised a little hieroglyphic that looks like 'KN' and put that on most of the paintings. Of course, when we turned up at Pepperton's, Shirley instinctively called me 'Patricia' in front of the woman.

Bang went the lovely relationship we'd built up. Suddenly there was this awkward atmosphere as if I was some kind of fraudster. In the end I had to explain how Kim Noble had DID, how I was one of her alters and how many others had contributed the artwork. Saying it aloud rammed it home more than I'd appreciated.

If I'd had to explain that to a stranger on my own behalf I don't think I would have bothered. I'd never uttered those words before in my life. Telling this woman in a restaurant seemed a bizarre way to break my silence. And yet, it was for the good of the body, I could see that. I didn't even think twice: *Anything to help the others.*

It worked. The woman selected a few of our pictures and they went up on the walls. It wasn't exactly Tate Britain but just six months after we'd started slapping paint on the back of wallpaper, a few of us were being seen by the general public.

It didn't always work out. Dr Laine's husband, Andrew, took our portfolio into a London gallery and, while admiring, the verdict was: 'Tell Kim to come back when her style has settled'! The Fairfield Hall in Croydon also paid us compliments but couldn't show our work because it lacked a community angle.

Okay, I thought, *we've tried the free route. It's time to put our money where our mouth is.*

The Burgh House in Hampstead, London, had an impressive space and a good reputation for attracting visitors. After a tour of the gallery space I knew it was worth a gamble. *This is a venue worth paying for.* From messing around on our dining room table to paying to stage our first proper solo show had taken less than a year – and I couldn't have been more thrilled.

The prospect of seeing our early work collected and mounted properly in Hampstead created such a frisson of excitement around the house. Even though I was the one making the arrangements and counting down the days in the diary, I'm sure the other personalities felt it too. I couldn't imagine the body letting their work be exhibited like this without letting them know. Pepperton's had been one thing but this, I felt, would be the real deal.

I was right. I'd seen my alters' work lying around the house and a few of them I'd even admired on a restaurant wall. But nothing prepared me for the sight of everyone's art mounted and properly presented at the Burgh House. It truly took my breath away. For the first time in my life I felt genuine pride. Even seeing my own landscape up there alongside the figures of Bonny, Missy's abstracts and Ria's scenes of degradation wasn't as embarrassing as I'd feared. And, I realised, as I took in the different styles on show, it was our first public announcement that Kim Noble had DID. Until that moment I hadn't appreciated how heavily the pressure weighed on our shoulders.

It was a very emotional time. I was wandering around, really studying the paintings with fresh eyes, learning new things about each artist. I felt a real closeness to them that I'd never really appreciated looking at them individually at home. Not having any training, our work comes from the heart, not the head, and standing there in a gallery for the first time, I realised that part of every personality was up there on canvas.

I truly got the sense that, *Here we all are together in one room.*

This was not only the nearest I will get to ever meeting them, but it was the nearest thing to integration we will get. That feeling never goes away. That's why I still love exhibitions today.

If my emotional response had taken me by surprise, the press's interest in the exhibition really knocked me for six.

As quickly as we'd gone from amateur to semi-professional artist, we'd rocketed from private DID sufferers to appearing in the culture section of broadsheet newspapers and on websites accessible the world over. Not everyone got every detail right but I was amazed at the level of attention.

I don't know if it's a facet of my general dissociation, but I wasn't at all fazed by the publicity. I'm a shy person normally but speaking about my painting doesn't bother me in the slightest. Having people know about my personal circumstances isn't a problem either and I never once felt hounded. I suppose it helped that people only referred to Kim Noble. Whatever they say, whatever they write, I am not Kim Noble.

Dr Laine was blown away by this unexpected development in our lives, and once Debbie had returned to Durham to pursue her career she found us another art therapist from Springfield – Ami. This time we did actually work through the therapy side for a while, but mainly it was great to have another pair of eyes cast over our efforts. Despite my natural reticence I think Ami must have seen or heard something she liked because one day she said, 'How would you feel running a group with me at Springfield?'

Ami had completed a placement at Springfield Hospital while doing her training and she was now a qualified working art therapist. We spoke about the wonderful space and the possibility of running a social art group where people with mental health problems, physical disabilities and learning difficulties could all meet to chat, drink tea and paint. We both agreed that a mixed group could be so beneficial.

I worked at Springfield for more than two years and, as their first artist in residence, also got to display plenty of our pictures. If I saw a spare square of space in a corridor I'd be straight over to the hospital manager offering to fill it. As a result I entertained for the first time the idea of actually being an artist.

At the early exhibitions I would have to say my pictures, along with Missy's, proved the most in demand. At Springfield, however, a surprising candidate for the most popular artist was Dawn. As, one by one, other alters had joined our art group and new and varied works appeared on an almost daily basis, I was most pleased to see Dawn had found her way to the paint room. I've never felt so sorry for anyone as I do her. I think her paintings show her confusion: she specialises in word pictures – shapes and colours with poems and messages laced around the picture. I hope it's a calming outlet for her.

Dawn's connection to Aimee – or Skye – is obvious.

Another personality called Suzy seems to have as much of a fixation on motherhood as Dawn but I don't know why – and I'm glad I don't. Suzy is always interesting. For several years all she would paint was a mother with a baby. Week after week, canvas after canvas, all she would produce was the same image over and over. At one point we had fifteen of them filling up the room. It was actually a very powerful sight even if no one knew why she did it. Then one day I noticed the easel was covered by a gold curtain.

What on Earth's this? I wondered as I gingerly lifted the drape. That's when I realised it was by Suzy. Yet I almost had to do a double-take because there was the mother, exactly the same as usual, but where was the baby? It was missing. At first I thought she hadn't finished but considering the elaborate way she'd dressed the painting that was unlikely.

No, I thought, *whatever problem Suzy had I think has been worked through.*

If just one alter was finding solace in her work that was amazing. Suzy still paints but ever since then she has only dabbled in celebrity portraits. She's our very own Andy Warhol – celebrities, footballers, the more famous the better. Simon Cowell, Oprah, Marilyn Monroe. The only exception to my knowledge was a portrait of Aimee when she was young.

I'm sad that Aimee never took to painting but the art room has become a really important part in all our lives. I feel it's my responsibility to give the other personalities an environment where they can come out and express themselves so whenever I haven't got anything else to do I'll wander upstairs and just sit at the easel. Rarely these days do I actually paint myself but I just like to give one of the others the opportunity to pop out and work on something. If Aimee's in the house she usually comes to sit with me because she loves hanging out with the others, especially the younger ones.

Judy has always got on well with Aimee – despite her reservations about me and her abandonment issues – and now they're nearly the same age I think the bond's even closer. After our appearance on *Oprah*, a Japanese TV company filmed us at the house. It was a very professional operation with lots of hidden cameras around the lounge. I knew about them, obviously, but the idea was that anyone switching wouldn't and so would just act naturally. I was about to find out how it felt to be an animal in a David Attenborough film.

Dr Laine was sometimes there to support the personalities who came out. With lunch approaching, though, I knew we didn't need to do much before Judy showed up for her meal. My last words to Aimee before the switch were, 'Remember you're being filmed. Best behaviour at the dinner table!'

I may as well have been speaking another language. Judy arrived and within two minutes they were trying to name as many words for a boy's willy as possible! And all of it's captured on tape for all of Japan to see.

Judy's paintings are really interesting and she knows it. I occasionally leave notes out for the others and she is the only one who responds rudely. I know she really resents always having to share her exhibitions with this person called Kim Noble who she's never even met. She's said that to plenty of people. Of course, she said the same sort of thing to our publishers about this book. 'Why are you writing about Patricia? You should write about me – I'm much more interesting!'

The arrogance of youth.

(She doesn't like me at all actually because she thinks I'm always dumping my daughter on her to look after while I disappear to a pub or the shops. It's a complicated relationship.)

Judy tends to operate on a large scale so her canvases are bigger than anyone else's. Ask her why and you get something stupid like, 'Because I'm bigger than everyone else.' Still, if that's what she thinks. Her style is strong colours, a good eye, and subjects ranging from chessboards to self-portraits. She's annoyingly good at it, I have to admit. In fact, the Saatchi Gallery wrote to us once saying they were fans of our work – and Judy's in particular. And of course she has such a lovely time chatting with Aimee while she does it.

Aimee's favourite in the art room, though, has to be Missy. Even though she's mute there's nothing quiet about her sense of fun. If I thought she was messy when we painted downstairs, I hadn't seen anything yet. She is very energetic with her work and it doesn't seem to bother her if all the paint lands on the canvas or not. Aimee loves watching and helping her. They both stand there in bare feet, sliding around and having a ball. I always know when Missy has been out because I'm covered in red, white and black. I don't mind – Aimee gets on with her so well.

Another messy one, for different reasons, is Ken. He's the last of us – so far – to have taken it up. I don't know what makes them start. Dr Laine always recommends people try it as a way of expression so I suppose after five or six years of being around the smell of paint, curiosity got the better of him. In a way I'm glad he didn't start earlier because I don't think the house would stand it. His first attempt was a train –

he loves painting them for some reason – but it didn't go well. In a fit of temper he picked up the canvas and lobbed it at the wall. Because he'd been pasting the paint on so thickly – which could explain his problem with the picture – the canvas just stuck to the wall rather than fell down. When he pulled it off, Ken discovered he really loved the texture of the mirrored image on the wall – and so that's how he always does it now. He paints onto a canvas, slaps it onto the wall and then when he pulls it off – hey presto! – he has his painting. I think it's a really interesting idea but it's ruining the wall. All the plaster's coming off where layer after layer of paint is making it heavier.

And he's running out of space!

I'm the one with the roller who has to keep painting over everything to try to get it smooth again. If it was left to Ken we'd have half-inch-deep spikes and bobbles all round the room. *The curse of being the dominant personality . . .*

The biggest thrill from our painting was the emergence of several personalities I'd never heard of before – which meant they hadn't played very significant parts in the body's life to date or, more fascinatingly, they were strangers even to Dr Laine and all the other therapists. It's incredible to think that, purely by chance, they reacted to the acrylic and easel and decided to step out for possibly the very first time.

Perhaps if we'd taken up a different hobby – basket-weaving, yoga or car mechanics – other personalities would have emerged.

I noticed quite early on that of all the paintings worked on during the night, one style kept recurring. Most personalities kept daylight hours and occasionally stayed up late, but this particular style – using just white paint on thick, black backgrounds – only seemed to be active in the dead of night. Once I recognised the pattern I took a few examples to Dr Laine, who was none the wiser. We were clearly dealing with a nocturnal creature, so there was no reason why he or she would have appeared during our daytime therapy sessions. To this day, however, we still have no idea who it is, whether it's a boy, a girl, man or woman. I didn't want the personality's anonymity to hold him/her back from being seen as an artist, however, so when we show the work at exhibitions we just refer to the artist as 'Anon'. I'm happy with that, although Dr Laine disagrees. We've discussed assigning a more personal name but I won't do that. In the case of 'Pratt' I think we're helping her. But generally, as someone who grew up with the whole world calling me the wrong name, I wouldn't wish that on anyone except as a last resort.

At least with the artist called Karen I know her name, although at first I just recognised we had someone else on our hands with their own way of doing things. Her pictures are also abstract but the thing that sets her apart is she paints with a toothbrush. It's very well thought out, not at all random. Her most successful picture was a wonderful sprayed circle with a name hidden in the centre. It's very striking and sadly, to date, just about the only thing I know about her.

Key is another interesting one, although unfortunately, her work suggests she's also suffered abuse. Her usual theme is the tree of life, but she alternates between detailed scenes of sexual acts on children and bright, coloured patterns incorporating the teachings of the Kabbalah. I have no idea where she gets this information. I don't know anything about that religion and I don't have a clue where the body would have learnt about it. If I could speak to her, that's the question I would ask.

Generally speaking, most of the personalities who paint do so fairly regularly. The exception is Mimi. In all the time we've had the art room she's only finished three paintings: one is of Tower Bridge, and there are two country scenes. She also started doing Battersea Power Station and the Houses of Parliament but who knows when they will be finished? Perhaps she doesn't get the same benefit as the rest of us. What's just as confusing is her name. We call her Mimi because when Aimee asked her name that's what she replied. Only afterwards did Aimee wonder, 'Was she saying, Me, Me?' And now Aimee insists it's too late to ask again. 'Mum, how would you feel if someone you'd known for five years asked you your name?'

I'm probably the worst person to ask that question but I get her point.

The content of a lot of the personalities' paintings makes me sad, especially when there are children involved. Only one of them seems to make me angry, though – and that's Abi (her artwork is on the front cover). It's quite weird disliking someone who shares your body but it's exactly because she shares my body – with men! – that I can't warm to her. As far as her work goes, she paints wonderfully spartan pictures of handsome men. I think they're amazing, aesthetically, and I like to have them up in the house. Having said that, I think there's such a lonely quality in her art that makes me think all is not well. There's such a lot of empty space surrounding the figure in the foreground it makes me think she feels cut off from things and this is her way of reaching out.

So I should feel sorry for her – except I know her other way of reaching out is to advertise for male companions online, which sickens me, to be honest. The idea of Abi chasing men with my body while our daughter is so young is completely out of order – although if they're as handsome as the ones she draws then maybe it's not so bad!

I'm not the only one who admires Abi's work. I'd say she was probably the most in demand of all the personalities.

Our confidence as 'Kim Noble – artist' increased when Henry Boxer accepted our work for his online gallery. For the first time we had a permanent – albeit virtual – display space. Obviously Henry has his favourites but he cares about 'outsider' art, as we're called, and introduced us to James Brett, who included our work in his Museum of Everything.

Like Abi's, Ria's work has brought a lot of attention, too. Galleries are always keen to display her prominently. I think public spaces have more of a remit to shock. Very few individuals have ever bought one of hers, however. Can you imagine having those painful images on your sitting room wall? Having said that, some anonymous interest was expressed in Ria's paintings after one of hers had been chosen as the art critics' favourite on Saatchi-online. We also got a lot of positive feedback from his office about Judy's work.

Of course, it wasn't Charles Saatchi himself but the fact that it might have been makes me pinch myself. Not so many years ago I couldn't paint and now I've had more than forty solo and group exhibitions. Exciting times. Yet you only have to go back a little further and I couldn't even say I had a life: everything was a mess, too chaotic to breathe. Thanks to my painting I've come out of my shell and entered the world head on, rather than skirting around the edges. From not understanding DID for most of my own life, then hiding away when I did, I now find myself promoting our lives on chat shows, in interviews and now in a book. I even have a website! I never saw that coming.

But then most of what's happened to me I didn't see coming. The only difference now is I'm the one in control.

Action!

I never imagined, as I cried desperately to be released from my cell at Warlingham Park, that one day I'd be flown over to Chicago as the guest of the world's biggest TV star. If you'd told me then that Oprah Winfrey would be interested in me, I'd have found it as unbelievable as all the lies people were spreading about my trying to commit suicide or having an eating disorder.

Ironically, of course, without one I wouldn't have had the other.

Having an insight into Oprah's world for just a few weeks was quite mind-blowing. After years of struggling to get by on very little income – not helped by different personalities spending separately, I realised – and a lifetime of fighting to be heard, not only was I being given a platform on the largest possible stage, but I was being spoiled a little as well. Not much, not for very long, but it was nice while it lasted.

Before Aimee and I flew over to Chicago, a lovely producer called Kirsten came to London to meet us. She then returned with a production crew and spent five days filming in our house, at Dr Laine's, out and about, just capturing our normal daily lives. She even smuggled a hand-held video camera into TGI Friday's when we went there for Aimee's thirteenth birthday.

I knew *Oprah* was big news but even I was impressed by the lengths Kirsten went to get her shots. She decided it would look good if all the personalities' artworks were displayed together, with me standing, being interviewed, in the middle. It was a nice day so she led us into the garden.

'Perfect,' she said.

'How are you going to hang the pictures, though?' I asked, thinking we could put one or two on the shed wall.

'We need easels,' Kirsten replied matter-of-factly. A second later she was on the phone. Hardly any time at all had gone by when a car arrived with as many easels as we needed. Absolutely amazing. I've waited longer than that for takeaways.

Clearly money was no object, as I was to discover further. With the paintings arranged like my own private exhibition – they really looked beautiful, I think, as you can see on the programme – Kirsten interviewed me. Every so often we'd have a pause when the soundman wearing large earphones detected an aeroplane or a car in the distance. Once the disturbance had passed he'd give a signal and off we'd go again. *Action!*

Our road's pretty quiet, so there weren't many cars interrupting us. But when a pneumatic drill started from the roadworks round the corner, I thought, *That's the end of this idea. We'll have to continue indoors.*

Once again I doubted the power of television. Kirsten went over to one of the crew and handed him a handful of notes.

'Have a word with those guys,' she said. 'Suggest it's time for a tea-break – preferably a long one.'

I couldn't believe it. Ten minutes later we had blissful

silence – for about half an hour. Then, Croydon being Croydon and builders being builders, I think word had got round. Before the afternoon was up she'd paid off about three different road crews who funnily enough all seemed to be in the area for the day.

With that level of attention to detail in London I was ready for a few surprises by the time we reached Chicago. I wasn't disappointed. A sleek chauffeur-driven car took us from the airport to our lovely hotel and then Aimee was given $200 to go and buy a new outfit. Stupidly I'd already told them I had brought mine so I was kicking myself afterwards. Then once the show was over we were given expensive 'Oprah' goody-bags. Aimee's had a cute little teddy bear in it, which we thought was nice.

As for the show itself, it was over in a flash – and for once I couldn't even blame switching. Even though we recorded lots more than was shown I still came away thinking, *I wish I'd said that, I wish I'd told her this.* The bits that stand out for me, though, are about Aimee. Watching her with the other personalities was so moving and then when Oprah brought her onto the set to be interviewed next to me I couldn't have been prouder.

I don't know if it was an American thing or whether it was Oprah herself driving it, but every time they showed a clip of Aimee with the personalities Oprah announced that it was my and Dr Laine's decision to allow Aimee to know everything. I wondered if the producers were telling me off, really, or just covering themselves in case viewers were horrified by the sight of Aimee crying with Dawn and Bonny. I would defend that decision to the death. I want Aimee to know these personalities. Whether I like it or not, they're as much part of her life as I am. What's more, she wants to know them as well. She's always asking to speak to different ones and she can't spend enough time in our art room because there's always someone working away in there.

I didn't mind Oprah's little caveat, although I was disappointed when a couple of viewers wrote to say Aimee seemed lost and abandoned when she was crying on stage. They didn't see me lean over to cuddle her because those moments were edited out for time reasons.

What really concerned me, however, was when another guest on the show, the adult daughter of a woman with DID who'd died recently, was asked if she had any advice for Aimee. She had three words: 'Support your mother.'

Aimee and I were sitting in the audience by this stage. If we hadn't been I'd have leapt up to answer that. I've got support workers and therapists to support me. Aimee's my daughter, not my carer. She deserves the childhood this body was so brutally denied. It's my job to love and raise her to the best of my abilities, not to depend on her. She's a child, for goodness' sake!

It was so frustrating not being able to reply. What's more, sitting in the audience, the emotional magnitude of what I'd seen on film really hit me and I started to cry. Tears were streaming down my face and the last thing I wanted was to be seen crying when the rest of the audience was laughing at Oprah's jokes. So I said to Aimee, 'I need to get out of here. If it doesn't finish soon I'll have to walk.' A moment later, Oprah walked to the other side of the stage and a crew member appeared at my elbow and led us out. I thought, *Wow, they think of everything here.*

I forgot we were still wearing microphones!

Someone in the director's booth had heard every word.

If anything, having DID only makes us more determined to give Aimee the best life possible. She's not just the number one priority in my life. All the personalities love her – especially Bonny and Hayley obviously – which is why birthdays and Christmases are so much fun. It's not unusual for Aimee to get cards and presents from a dozen of us, depending on who's around at the time. I do sometimes leave a note in the art room reminding people that the birthday is coming up, but they all shop for gifts themselves. I can't complain, even when I see my money disappearing without my doing anything. After all, it's Kim Noble's name on the credit cards and cheque books, not mine. They've as much right as anyone to spend it.

The biggest compliment anyone can pay Aimee – or me – is that she seems like a normal kid – because she is! She likes too much TV, she leaves her homework much too late, she wants more pets in the house than I do – in other words she's exactly the same as all her friends.

Ten, twenty, even thirty years ago my greatest ambition was to remember today more clearly than I remembered the previous one. Memory was always at the heart of my problems. I felt if I could recall exactly what had happened or what I'd done, then the myriad medics and interfering do-gooders wouldn't have had a leg to stand on. They could bully me all they liked with their claims that I'd done this or said that and I would have been able to stand up and say, 'No. This is what happened.' I tried to do that anyway, of course, but there were always such gaps in recollection that even though I knew I was innocent I couldn't prove it. I couldn't usually even come up with a plausible alibi.

Three decades later I can't believe how much my life has changed. I haven't seen the inside of a hospital since God knows when and I'm not on any medication at all. To think how differently things could have turned out if Hayley hadn't fought the schizophrenia diagnosis and not gone to a mental health tribunal. From what other people have told me, I'd probably still be a ward of court now. Once you're on the slippery slope it's hard to change direction.

But the psychotic shuffle wasn't for me – or us. All the personalities were united on this, I think. We each, in our way, railed against the enforced medication. We schemed and plotted and lied and we refused to take the pills.

Hayley, again, has to take credit for the way she triumphed over the forces conspiring against her. She was the one subjected to the horrific acid and arson attacks. She saved us all. But the rest of us can take some reward. For every personality inclined to fall by the wayside or give in, there are many more who will come out fighting. I'm proud to feel that I am one of those.

Coming to terms with DID has obviously been the single largest moment of my life. As I've said, in many ways it would be more plausible to be informed I was from the planet Krypton or I was actually a character in a movie, like Jim Carrey in *The Truman Show*. But I hope I've repaid the body's faith in me. I was always the personality who came out on social occasions, at parties, lunch hours, pubs or on dates. I was the one with the glass of white wine and the witty remark. Even after years of subjugation and experimentation at the hands of the medical profession I never stopped smiling. I'm not exactly a tub-thumper like Hayley but I'm no quitter. Knock me down and I will get up – stronger and still smiling.

These are the qualities the body identified when it chose me as a dominant personality, the character traits that allowed me to establish and promote Kim Noble as an artist, to raise a young daughter despite towering opposition, and to even write this book. They're the qualities that I hope anyone reading this who suffers from DID or knows someone with multiple personalities will take on board as well. If I can get this far in life, if I can keep so many plates spinning without the whole crockery set smashing down, then anyone can. DID shouldn't have to be the end of one life. It should be the beginning of many.

They're also the qualities I hope to pass onto our daughter.

Having said how strong I've needed to be, there is one thing that scares me.

When Kim, Hayley and Bonny were our body's dominant personalities, I only came out for an hour or two per day, if that. One by one those women faded into the background, however, until I took over the mantle of main alter. There are no rules where DID is concerned. What if that happened to me? What if I just began to fade away again?

I've already been dominant for longer than the last two so in a sense the writing is on the wall. On the other hand, I haven't had to endure the trials they were subjected to. If anything, by introducing painting into our lives, I've actively helped to steady the ship. According to Dr Laine, our lives have never been less chaotic. The painting seems to have provided an alternative outlet for some of those with suicidal thoughts and in other cases has just made the rest of us strong enough to resist. And Aimee, Dr Laine says, couldn't be in better hands. After all, she managed to be voted Head Girl at her school.

That's my true reason for not wanting to fade away, of course. What mother could ever countenance being separated from her daughter? I may not have given birth to her but there is no one and nothing more important in my life than Aimee.

The truth is, I have been a bit part player in Kim Noble's life for most of my existence. If I'm honest, I never noticed, so in theory it wouldn't be so bad to return to that.

And yet I didn't have Aimee then. Mentally I was stuck at twenty-one years old for so long I was oblivious to anyone else ageing. Now I know about DID, however, I wouldn't be able to walk in and out of Aimee's life without being acutely aware of every passing day, every minute I've missed.

And who would replace me? I can't think of a single personality who I would trust. It's nothing personal, because obviously I've never met any of the others, but I do have the classic over-protective parent feeling that no one is going to be good enough for my little girl! From what I've heard there isn't another one in the same mould as me, Bonny and Hayley. What if Abi became my replacement? Would she be prepared to alter her lifestyle? Or Dawn – could she ever accept Aimee as her own flesh and blood?

And what about Aimee herself? Of course I'd be mortified to slide out of her life but I'd be just as worried about the effect on her. When Bonny left she was heartbroken. It took months of concerted effort between me and Dr Laine to win her trust, to convince her that I could be a mother to her. I would truly hate to know she was going through that ordeal again. Bonny and Aimee still see each other from time to time but the reunions are tinged with sadness. There's always so much to catch up on that they don't get a moment to just enjoy being together.

I couldn't bear that to be me. Every time I saw her little face I'd feel guilty that I'd left.

It's one thing talking a good fight. A few years ago I had the chance to do something about it.

Ever since I became the dominant alter, the care order imposed on Aimee at birth has been hanging over my head. I'm not a litigious person like Hayley, I don't thrive on confrontations like Bonny, but as every year passed and we were subjected to another patronising, intimidating placement meeting every six months, I could see why Bonny got so angry.

I am Aimee's mother. I'm not some foster carer. Look at her – you can't even be contemplating taking her away.

Month after month went by, with solicitations made by each side. Our solicitor said this, social services came back with that. As far as I could see it was a game of legal table tennis with no sign of anyone dropping the ball, so eventually a court date was set. The car journey there was the most nervous of my life. It felt like the worst hangover ever. I couldn't bear to think of the consequences of failing. Hayley and Bonny had achieved so much for the body – I didn't want to be the one to let the side down.

I also knew that the pressure of fighting authority for so long had taken its toll on both of them. It was a very real fear that the stress of taking the council on again could have the same result for me. I could disappear for good, someone else could take over, and I would never see my daughter again.

The idea petrified me. I'd already been the dominant personality for as long as Bonny and Hayley and I didn't know if there was a maximum time for running the body. But if I was going to fade into the background again like them, I needed to make sure Aimee's future was secure first.

I could drag the story out, tell you every detail of the court case and all the arguments for and against. But I won't. I will just say that in December 2008 the care order on Aimee Melissa Noble was finally lifted.

She was mine – *ours* – for good, forever.

After everything our body had been subjected to by abusers, doctors and red tape, we'd kept on fighting. And now we'd won.

Useful Resources

Mind
The leading mental health charity for England and Wales.
15–19 Broadway, Stratford, London E15 4BQ
Tel: 0208 519 2122
www.mind.org.uk

The Survivors Trust
A national organisation for over 120 specialist voluntary sector agencies providing a range of counselling, therapeutic and support services for survivors of rape and sexual abuse.
Unit 2, Eastlands Court Business Centre, St Peter's Road, Rugby CV21 3QP
Tel: 01788 550554
www.thesurvivorstrust.org

Clinic for Dissociative Studies
The clinic provides specialist expertise in the care and treatment of people with dissociative disorders.
Tel: 0207 794 1655
Email: vsinason@aol.com
www.clinicds.com

Mosac
Offers practical and emotional support to non-abusing parents, carers and families of sexually abused children.
141 Greenwich High Road, London SE10 8JA
National free helpline: 0800 980 1958
Tel: 0208 293 9990
Email: enquiries@mosac.org.uk
www.mosac.org.uk

CIS'ters (Childhood Incest Survivors)
PO Box 119, Eastleigh, Hampshire SO50 9ZF
Tel: 02380 338080
Email: admin@cisters.org.uk

The National Association for People Abused in Childhood (NAPAC)
NAPAC, PO Box 63632, London SW9 1BF
Free support line: 0800 085 3330
www.napac.org.uk

First Person Plural
A national survivor-led charity working exclusively for and on behalf of people affected by DID.
PO Box 2537, Wolverhampton WV4 4ZL
Email: fpp@firstpersonplural.org.uk
www.firstpersonplural.org.uk

PODS (Partners of Dissociative Survivors)
PODS raises awareness and provides education and information for people who suffer from a dissociative disorder.
PO Box 633, Huntingdon, Cambridgeshire PE29 9GJ
Tel: 01480 878409
Email: info@pods-online.org.uk
www.pods-online.org.uk

TAG (Trauma and Abuse Group)
TAG provides support, information and training for counsellors, therapists, professional workers, carers and anyone involved in working with individuals who have suffered trauma and abuse.
The Willows Centre, 11 Prospect Place, Swindon SN1 3LQ
www.tag-uk.net

RAINS (Ritual Abuse Information Network & Support)
PO Box 458, Godalming, Surrey GU7 2YT
Tel: 01483 898600

Izzy's Promise
A charity based in Dundee offering free and confidential support to sufferers of ritual and organised abuse.
1 Victoria Road, Dundee DD1 1EL
Tel: 01382 206222
Email: lormac1053@aol.com
www.izzyspromise.org.uk
See also the **Ritual Abuse Network**: www.rans.org.uk

The Oxford Stress and Trauma Centre
47 High Street, Witney, Oxford OX28 6JA
Tel: 01993 77 99 94
www.oxdev.co.uk

Edinburgh Traumatic Stress Centre (Rivers Centre for Traumatic Stress)
Royal Edinburgh Hospital, Morningside, Edinburgh EH10 5HF
Tel: 0131 537 6874
www.riverscentre.org.uk

Europe

ESTD (European Society for Trauma and Dissociation)
1ste Hogeweg 16-a, 3701 HK Zeist, The Netherlands
Tel: 0031 30 6977841
Email: info@estd.org
www.estd.org

Australia

The Australasian Society for Traumatic Stress Studies (ASTSS)
ASTSS, PO Box 6227, Halifax Street, 5000 Adelaide, Australia
Tel: 41 173 936 013
www.astss.org.au

Lifeline Australia
Provides services in suicide prevention, crisis support and mental health
support.
PO Box 173, Deakin ACT 2600
Tel: 13 11 14
www.lifeline.org.au

SANE Australia
A national charity working for a better life for people affected by mental ill-
ness.
PO Box 226, South Melbourne, Victoria 3205
Helpline: 1800 18 SANE (7263)
Email: info@sane.org
www.sane.org

North America and Canada

Mosaic Minds
Provides information and support for those affected by DID.
Mosaic Minds, Inc, PO Box 24, Marysville, WA 98270
www.mosaicminds.org

Sidran Institute
A non-profit organisation helping people to understand, recover from and treat traumatic stress, dissociative disorders and other issues.
200 East Joppa Road, Suite 207, Baltimore, MD 21286-3107
Email: info@sidran.org
www.sidran.org

The American Professional Society on the Abuse of Children (APSAC)
A national organisation supporting professionals who work with children and families affected by child maltreatment and violence.
APSAC Headquarters, 350 Poplar Avenue, Elmhurst, IL 60126
Tel: 630 941 1235
Toll Free: 1 877 402 7722
Email: apsac@apsac.org
www.apsac.org

American Psychiatric Association
1000 Wilson Boulevard, Suite 1825, Arlington, VA 22209
Toll Free: 1 888 35 PSYCH or 1 888 35 77924
From outside the US and Canada call: 1 703 907 7300
Email: apa@psych.org
www.psych.org

American Psychological Association
750 First Street, NE, Washington, DC 20002-4242
Tel: (800) 374 2721 or (202) 336 5500
www.apa.org

Institute on Violence, Abuse and Trauma (IVAT)
(Including the Family Violence & Sexual Assault Institute)
10065 Old Grove Road, San Diego, CA 92131
Tel: (858) 527 1860 ex 4160
www.fvsai.org

New England Society for the Treatment of Trauma and Dissociation (NESTTD)
NESTTD, PO Box 242, Southborough, MA 01772
Tel: 508 598 5553
Email: info@nesttd-online.org
www.nesttd-online.org

The Trauma Center at Justice Resource Institute
1269 Beacon Street, Brookline, MA 02446
Tel: (617) 232 1303
www.traumacenter.org

The National Child Traumatic Stress Network (NCTSN)
NCCTS, University of California, Los Angeles, 11150 W. Olympic Boulevard,
Suite 650, Los Angeles, CA 90064
Tel: (310) 235 2633
www.nctsnet.org

Canadian Psychological Association
Traumatic Stress Section (CPA TSS), Douglas Mental Health University
Institute, 6875 Boulevard LaSalle, Perry, Montreal, Quebec H4H 1R3
Tel: +1 514 761 6131 ext 2375
Email: alain.brunet@mcgill.ca
www.cpa.ca

South Africa

The Trauma Centre for Survivors of Violence and Torture
Cowley House, 126 Chapel Street, Woodstock 7925, Cape Town, South Africa
Tel: (021) 465 7373
www.trauma.org.za

International and other territories

ISSTD (International Society for the Study of Trauma and Dissociation)
8400 Westpark Drive, Second Floor, McLean VA 22102
Email: info@isst-d.org
www.isst-d.org

Argentine Society for Psychotrauma
Campichuelo 215 (C1405BOA), Ciudad de Buenos Aires, Argentina
www.psicotrauma.org.ar

Asian Society for Traumatic Stress Studies Limited
Room 402, Chuang's Tower, 30–32 Connaught Road Central, Hong Kong
Email: info@asianstss.org
www.asianstss.org

Japanese Society for Traumatic Stress Studies (JSTSS)
Hyogo Institute for Traumatic Stress, 132 Wakihamakaigan-dori,
Chuo-ku, Kobe, Japan, 651-0073
Tel: +81-78-200-3010
Email: kato@j-hits.org
www.jstss.org

The Artwork in *All of Me*

Preliminary pages

'Frieze People By Night' by Bonny
Canvas size: 80cm x 30cm
'Frieze People By Night' features Bonny's customary stick figures. To me they look like two groups squaring up to each other but it could also be an al fresco moonlit party in the shadow of city skyscrapers.

Plate section

Page 1
'Pratt' by Ria Pratt
Canvas size: 102cm x 76cm
The producers from *Oprah* asked if the personalities could paint some self-portraits for the show. I left a note in the art room and eight personalities responded. Ria is the child personality who calls herself 'Pratt' and who seems to still be suffering the effects of her abuse. This painting of a child on a table includes mirror writing: 'help' and 'Pratt was here' are written in backwards lettering on the walls. The painting also features the familiar teddy bear that appears in many of her paintings.

Page 2/top
'Ken' by Ken
Canvas size: 50cm x 40cm
Ken was the most recent personality to take up painting. His first attempt in 2008 was a painting of a train. When it didn't turn out as he hoped, he slapped the painting against the wall. Peeling it off, he realised he liked the texture and the way the colours mixed, so to this day that is how he paints – much to my annoyance because the plaster is coming off the wall! So whenever he goes in the art room he puts paint on canvas, splats it on the wall, then spins it round and adds detail afterwards. You can see the swirls in this self-portrait, and where Ken has added the features later. Ken ties his hair back in a ponytail. I can't see that it's my face at all.

Page 2/bottom
'The Art of Starvation' by Judy
Canvas size: 92cm x 72cm
The skinny girl in the room sees a fatter girl in the mirror but it's not a self-portrait. Judy has told Dr Laine that the subject is a girl she met in hospital who suffers from anorexia. Judy refuses to accept she's a sufferer too, but she always paints on the largest canvases to reflect her size. She usually applies thick paint with a pallet knife.

Page 3/top
'Lost in Play' by Ken
Canvas size: 62cm x 46cm
After slapping the painting on the wall, Ken turns his canvas round and then highlights whatever shapes he discerns. In this one he saw a girl with a red balloon and so that's what he painted.

Page 3/bottom
'Thinking Man' by Abi
Canvas size: 102cm x 77cm
This is a lonely figure from Abi. As I said on *Oprah*, if they're the men she's spending time with then I won't complain!

Page 4
'The Naming' by Dawn
Canvas size: 102cm x 77cm
Dawn uses a sponge to apply the paint and often likes to add a verse or poem. In this painting there are three sections containing a poem called 'It is the Time of Naming'.

Page 5/top
'Reaching Out' by Bonny
Canvas size: 101cm x 50cm
Bonny always used to paint stick figures or robotic shapes but one day she told Aimee she was worried people thought she couldn't draw 'real' people. So this was her attempt. It's inspired by our fight with Social Services, in particular how our baby was taken at birth and handed to foster parents. The woman – who is Bonny – is reaching out but her baby is just out of range. So near, and yet so far. I know the woman is her because the people at Pepperton UK, where we first exhibited, said the hand is definitely mine. Apparently it's very distinctive.

Page 5/bottom
'Aims' by Suzy
Canvas size: 50cm x 40cm
This is a portrait of Aimee when she was younger, copied from a photograph in which Aimee was modelling for a children's magazine. Suzy had a bit of trouble painting the bend of her arm but Aimee really likes the painting. She loves being in the art room with any of the personalities and when one of them paints her or gives her a painting I think she feels closer to them. This was Suzy's first painting after her nine 'Mother & Baby' works. These featured an infant and parent in different poses. I remember when I saw her first painting, a picture I named 'Pure'. I thought it was finished but the next day I was shocked to discover she'd scribbled all over everything apart from the baby. To me this spoke of a chaotic mother desperately trying to cope with her 'pure' child. Suzy scribbles on all her paintings now with a permanent marker pen, even this one, so I'm used to it now. But I like finding her pictures before she 'finishes' them with the pen.

Page 6
'Golden Kabbalah' by Key
Canvas size: 30cm x 23cm
Key either paints the Tree of Life from the Kabbalah religion or scenes of abuse. The latter are very much like Ria's in content but are definitely Key's in style. For example, one painting features a stick figure in a cage. Her Tree of Life paintings usually have 'mirror writing' like Ria's, although this one has words facing the correct way. Sometimes she appears to be translating passages by putting words next to certain signs or colours.

Page 7/top
'Longing Rose' by Judy
Canvas size: 122cm x 92cm
This is the second painting in a series of three. It's called 'Longing Rose'. The first painting in the series is just called 'Rose' and the third is called 'Crying Rose'. As I interpret them, it's the three stages of sexual awakening: waiting, then longing and then finally, of course, with the rose's petals strewn on the floor, disappointment! This sequence is unusual because the character has facial details. The majority of Judy's work features striking black-and-white and faceless subjects. She once painted a school class photo, realistic in every detail, except not one of the children had a mouth, nose or eyes.

Page 7/middle
'Mystery of the Prayer' by Anon
Canvas size: 102cm x 76cm

There is a personality who only paints in the early hours of the morning so Aimee and Dr Laine have never met her. I didn't want her work to be unrecognised so I call her 'Anon'. She pours the paint onto the canvas and uses the pallet knife sparingly, leaving the paint fresh and untouched.

Page 7/bottom
'Hangman' by MJ
Canvas size: 80cm x 60cm

MJ or Missy will only paint with three colours: red, black and white. She creates with much energy, her canvas on the floor and paint flying around the room. Aimee loves watching her and I always know when MJ has been out because I'm covered in paint. This particular work was completed over a number of weeks and it appears to be a game of hangman between MJ and another personality. Each time I saw it there was a new letter. I think the answer was 'dog' or 'god'. We've got space in the art room for about five pictures on the go at once. Most of us hang canvases on hooks on the wall. Any overspill I line up in the hall and the personalities find what they want and continue working on them.

Page 8/top
'Oh!' by Suzy
Canvas size: 31cm x 25cm

When I left the note requesting self-portraits for Oprah, Suzy decided to paint Oprah instead. As usual, she's taken the magic marker to the figure. All the pictures used on the show were shipped a few weeks in advance but at the last minute I decided I would take this one as a gift for Oprah. When we reached the studios, however, I saw a sign saying: 'Please do not bring presents for Oprah'. I think it was aimed at the audience members but I felt uncomfortable handing over the picture after that so I put it back in my case. Aimee wanted to take something for the school that Oprah sponsors in Africa so she gave Kirsten, the producer, one of Abi's paintings.

Page 8/bottom
'Silent Blue' by Patricia
Canvas size: 91cm x 51cm

I don't like my paintings at all but they're quite popular with collectors. Gallery owners tend to like the more arresting or controversial images but when people are looking for something for their dining room it's often my landscapes they go for. I really enjoy painting but the end results of my own efforts bore me. If I'm honest, I usually only go into the art room in the hope that another personality will come out and create something wonderful. I always feel better when there's painting happening in the house. Even if it's not me doing it, I can feel the creativity in the air and I look forward to seeing the results.

Note: the paintings are all signed by me, Patricia, using the body's name 'Kim'. Most of the other personalities are not interested in exhibiting or selling their works although they don't mind if I organise things for them. The only one who has a problem with our progress so far is Judy, who hates being part of a group show. Her ambition is to have her own solo exhibition under her own name.

About the Author

Kim Noble is an artist, a mother to her teenage daughter and has Dissociative Identity Disorder (DID), the new term for Multiple Personality Disorder. Without any formal art training, thirteen of her personalities are artists and have exhibited nationally and internationally in solo and group exhibitions. She was the first artist in residence at Springfield University Hospital, where she also co-ran a group for health service users. In 2010 she was a guest on *The Oprah Winfrey Show* and has taken part in conferences, radio and TV documentaries. She lives in London, England with her daughter, two dogs and a rescue cat. For more information, visit www.kimnoble.com.

Jeff Hudson has written or ghostwritten more than twenty books, including *Sunday Times* bestsellers, and his work has been translated into a dozen languages. He lives in London.